The
FIRSTS

The Inside Story
of the Women
Reshaping Congress

Jennifer Steinhauer

ALGONQUIN BOOKS OF CHAPEL HILL   2020

Published by
ALGONQUIN BOOKS OF CHAPEL HILL
Post Office Box 2225
Chapel Hill, North Carolina 27515-2225

a division of
WORKMAN PUBLISHING
225 Varick Street
New York, New York 10014

Cataloging-in-Publication Data for this title is
available from the Library of Congress.

ISBN 978-1-61620-999-5

10 9 8 7 6 5 4 3 2 1
First Edition

To all the women who have dared to run for Congress,
especially those who were told they could not.

Contents

The FIRSTS

INTRODUCTION

The New Arrivals

Yeah, we have to fix this shit.
—Rep. Katie Porter (D-CA)

ON MOST DAYS of the year, tourists stream through the National Statuary Hall, a resplendent room in the center of the US Capitol in Washington, DC. Here, prominent American men, from Sam Houston to Thomas Edison, are celebrated with giant effigies, surrounded by colossal marble columns and ornate drapes. On the first Thursday of 2019, however, the august chamber felt like the bustling arrivals terminal at John F. Kennedy International Airport.

New members of Congress, sworn in just an hour earlier, mingled with their excited families as they waited to have their photos taken in a chaotic mass of ill-formed lines controlled by barking security officers who could not yet recognize a single one of them. The most diverse Congress in history was on full display. Ilhan Omar of Minnesota, her head covered in a festive orange scarf, clutched a string of pale prayer beads in one hand, her son Adnan's hand wrapped in the other. An entire family dressed in traditional Laguna Pueblo garb traipsed through toward the Capitol Rotunda, trying to keep up with Deb Haaland of New Mexico. Abigail Spanberger of Virginia, a former CIA operative, stood with her three daughters, who were dressed in identical blue-and-gold-flecked fancy frocks, the same ones the girls wore the night their mother defeated a Republican Tea Party incumbent after a brutal race. Small children in velvet dresses with itchy crinolines, overly large suits, or African-print pants clung to parents. Exhausted, at least one curled up on the floor by a statue of Brigham Young.

Rashida Tlaib of Michigan, in a cranberry-colored thobe, the native dress of Palestine, pushed a wheelchair carrying her mother, who fretted in Arabic about the jacket she had left back in Tlaib's new office. "It's an office, Mom. Nothing is going to happen to it!" Tlaib said. As they made their way through the Capitol, Iowa's senators, Republicans Chuck Grassley and Joni Ernst, swept by. "Who is that?" Tlaib's mother asked. Her daughter, a brand-new representative, shrugged. She had no idea.

Just shy of a century after women were granted the right to vote, the 116th Congress boasts the greatest number of female members ever: 106 women in the House of Representatives and 25 in the Senate, a milestone at once momentous and paltry. Democrats were ebullient, having retaken the House after eight years in the minority, picking up forty new seats, a bit more than 60 percent of them filled by women. In all, thirty-five new women joined Congress in 2019—including two who won in special elections—and all but one was a Democrat. Beyond gender, 22 percent of the House and Senate in 2019 were members of racial or ethnic minorities, a percentage that has steadily increased over the last decade. The new House class tilted younger and less wealthy, too.

This younger, more diverse, and more female legislative branch would become immediately consequential. The members would alter the way that representatives and senators communicate with each other and the outside world, and how policy debates would be framed. So long a hermitage from the social and economic upheavals in American life, Congress would soon become their fulcrum, with racial, ethnic, class, and generational conflicts a central narrative. Deep divisions over the direction and future of the Democratic Party would surface between the new generation of progressives, eager to push the party to the left, and centrists, who thought moderation was the key not only to the party's survival, but also to getting rid of Republican president Donald Trump.

Two women in particular, Rep. Alexandria Ocasio-Cortez (D-NY), at twenty-nine the youngest woman ever to serve, and Rep. Ilhan Omar (D-MN), one of the first Muslim women ever elected, would in short order dominate the national political discourse, unheard of for freshman lawmakers in general and women in particular, who historically had not arrived in Washington, DC, armed with self-assurance, outspoken views, and millions of followers. The new women would upend conventional political and legislative conversations and challenge notions of comity in a body where duplicity and spuriousness had long been concealed by quaint rules governing acceptable speech. They would face off with their colleagues and their leader, Rep. Nancy Pelosi (D-CA), the first woman to be Speaker of the House and one of only seven Speakers to hold the gavel in nonconsecutive terms. Within months of taking their seats, the freshmen would spar directly with the president himself, who would attempt to use the women as tools to demonize the newly empowered Democrats as politically dangerous and to starkly cleave the nation over questions of race and belonging. In short, the story of "the Firsts," while still being written, would mark a historical turning point both for Congress and for American women.

This day of elation for Democrats also represented a tumultuous new beginning for many men in Congress, who had just spent the last year in a state of thinly disguised terror as House women led a movement to change the process for handling sexual harassment claims on Capitol Hill. On the one hand, some of the more liberal men were careful to wax on about how thrilled they were to have these exciting new women in Congress. But several months later, even they would let it be known to House leadership that they were sick of hearing about them. "The men wanted us to know they were still in charge," one senior female Democrat, unamused, told me some months later.

And before this historic day was over, the freshmen had made it clear they were a new voice in town. Rep. Rashida Tlaib (D-MI) startled her colleagues—and stepped on Pelosi's message of a restrained and temperate new House—by announcing to supporters that she was going to "impeach the motherfucker," foreshadowing the protracted debate among Democrats over how to handle President Trump, which would eventually result in an impeachment showdown.

The new members arriving on Capitol Hill in January of 2019 found themselves in the oddest of work spaces. On most Wednesdays when Congress is in session, tourists parade through the Rotunda, their necks craned toward its spectacularly domed ceiling. Groups who have convened for lobbying "fly-in days" cram the hallways and cafeterias of House and Senate office buildings— one day, it's the vision-impaired, tapping canes along the floor; another, it is medical students in white jackets, mainlining Dunkin'

Donuts. Sometimes, it's presidents of children's museums; another time, it's dairy lobbyists toting ice cream. I recently saw a group in medieval garb; I have yet to unpack that one. Occasionally, a dog will scamper down a hallway, escaping its human, perhaps a member (or more likely an aide) preparing to take it for a walk.

Some elevators house emergency black rotary-dial phones from the *Mad Men* era. Mail slots exist in no small number. There are secret passageways and spots of lore, including a set of marble stairs in the House wing of the Capitol still stained with the blood of congressman-turned-lobbyist William Taulbee of Kentucky, who was fatally shot in 1890 by Charles Kincaid, a newspaper reporter who had implicated Taulbee in an extra-marital affair. Along myriad bleak cement corridors are cafeteria kitchens, offices that fulfill requests for American flags, and nondescript doors that look like they conceal custodial closets but actually lead to hearing rooms, perhaps containing the maple desk of a long-dead famous lawmaker, or hideaways where members can take meetings near the floor of the House. It is a place at once regal and utterly prosaic, with government-issued office chairs and scores of sets of mahogany furniture, too.

On any given moment, my colleagues and I, the bearers of the coveted plastic press pass that gives us access to the majority of the Capitol, might smack into a craftsperson about to fix a priceless painting, or a culinary worker fixing lunch for a sultan or the chair of the Senate Appropriations Committee. A member may say, "Hi, I'm Elaine," but we understand to still address her as "Congresswoman," and someday, perhaps, "Madam Chair."

The vast majority of the new women were just starting to navigate these twisted passages (Tlaib, seeing me in a basement hallway, once looked at me with bewilderment and shyly asked for directions to a House Oversight Committee hearing); the daily use of bizarre procedural language ("Pursuant to clause 12(a) of rule I, the Chair declares the House in recess until 2 p.m. today"); and the endless string of buzzing sounds heard through the Capitol (two buzzes means it is now time for a fifteen-minute vote by electronic device; four buzzes, adjournment of the House). These freshmen seemed in a state of perpetual if mild disorientation.

Many found that congressional conventions were more traditional than practical. Rep. Katie Porter (D-CA), a law professor from Orange County, California, recalled being baffled by the process of voting for the party's leaders by filling out a ballot on a piece of paper procured on one side of a large room, then trudging across the crowded floor, squeezing like a subway commuter past her new colleagues, and casting it in a box on the other side. She and a fellow female freshman whom she had just met rolled their eyes at the antiquated spectacle. "Yeah," Porter said. "We have to fix this shit."

Of course, the class of 2019 was not the first to storm Washington seeking broad institutional change after a period of political trauma. The House class of 1974, elected right after the Watergate scandal, also came in with youth, idealism, and an appetite for disruption. Those ninety-three freshmen "represented a new breed of politician," wrote former senior congressional staff member John A. Lawrence in his book, *The Class of '74*, "born of an age of political turbulence, hardened by political struggles, willing—even eager—to challenge authority, and devoted to pursuing new policy objectives." But that class was almost exclusively white and male.

In the 2018 midterms, most of the new Democrats campaigned and won fueled by the power of an incandescent collective rage that had been ignited by the election of Trump and fanned by the policies of a Republican-controlled Congress that year. In the 2017 report *The Trump Effect*, political science scholars Jennifer L. Lawless and Richard L. Fox found that about one quarter of the female Democrats who became interested in running for office that year started thinking about it only after Trump was elected. "It's hard to overstate Democratic women's dismay with the president," they wrote. "When asked whether they'd rather have a colonoscopy or a private lunch with Trump, more than half of female Democrats chose the colonoscopy. But that's not all. More than a quarter of Democratic women would rather spend a night in jail than at the Trump White House. Republicans' reactions are far less negative, but notice that almost 20 percent of Republican women said that seeing Trump on the news makes them sick, too."

Donald Trump had, after all, sought victory in part through division, and in the 2018 midterms, Americans clapped back. "It's not about diversity; it's about the fact that finally we are starting to become more representative. There's a difference," Mae Jemison, the first female African American astronaut, said at a Martin Luther King Day breakfast in Saint Paul, as Omar, once a Somali refugee, looked on. "This representation is not a nicety; it's a necessity."

This biggest class of women in history contained all sorts of firsts: the first two Muslim women; the two first Native American women; the first female members of Congress from their state or district, or the first black or Latina from their state or district, or the youngest, or a combination of those. They came with disparate résumés—community organizers, air force pilots, CIA officers, entrepreneurs, a once-homeless National Teacher of the Year award recipient, and state and municipal lawmakers, along with that now-famous former bartender known as AOC, so inspiring to young girls across the United States that at the swearing-in, I watched a few Republican members abashedly accompany their kids across the House floor to meet her. Some freshmen brought a millennial perspective and irreverent style. Others were middle-aged, with impressive, even monumental, accomplishments from their pre-congressional lives. The oldest freshman, Rep. Donna Shalala (D-FL), had been a cabinet secretary and the president of a university.

All of their campaigns were rooted in authentic messages delivered by candidates who, a decade ago, might have tried to hide what they now put on full display: Deb Haaland talked struggles with alcoholism. Rep. Angie Craig (D-MN) discussed growing up in a trailer park, and did not hide her wife and four kids, even in her conservative district. Katie Porter talked openly about having experienced domestic abuse, and her fear of losing her children. The women with national security backgrounds volleyed between showcasing their tough sides, an outgrowth of intense military training and wartime deployments, and their roles as Girl Scout troop leaders.

At least one senior male Democratic official was overwhelmed by the significance of the moment and the cultural shift in his own political lifetime. As a young aide in the early 1970s, he told me, he was standing in the cloakroom off the House floor—a space where members go to relax, chat, and file bills—when he witnessed an older congressman lying on a couch, relaxing between votes. Rep. Pat Schroeder (D-CO), then a new congresswoman, walked in. "Are you looking for a seat?" the congressman said, pointing to his wrinkled face. "How about here?"

That kind of egregious behavior may largely no longer exist, but its ghosts are plenty close by. In my roughly decade on and off Capitol Hill as a reporter for the *New York Times*, I have listened as women shared stories of elderly male senators flirting with them, about male members of the Senate who questioned why a female fellow member was using the Senate elevator, and in the case of former senator Kelly Ayotte (R-NH), about the sergeant at arms who asked her to leave her own desk on the first day she entered the Senate chamber, because the chamber was "for senators only." I heard from one senator that Senator John McCain (R-AZ) hurled so many insults at her (while ignoring her male counterpart who had cosponsored the legislation that had so infuriated the often-crabby senator) that she had to call her mother to regroup. Senator Kirsten Gillibrand (D-NY) recounted in her own book the time she was told not to lose too much weight by a certain senator from Hawaii, because, he said, "I like my girls chubby." A few weeks into her term, Kyrsten Sinema, a freshman Democratic senator from Arizona decked out in a hot-pink dress and metallic spike heels, was stopped by Capitol police, who asked her if she had any ID. "She's a senator," barked her male aide. Others recounted a story to the press about a male colleague who made a sexual innuendo about one-minute floor speeches that stunned the colleagues who surrounded her, just three months after an orientation session on office sexual-harassment liability.

Summer camp, middle school, or a new job: everyone needs a posse. It's no different in Congress. Many of the women of the 116th Congress quickly fell into distinct cliques—the most famous of which is "the Squad," made up of Alexandria Ocasio-Cortez, Rashida Tlaib, Ilhan Omar, and Ayanna Pressley—and those friendships would soon prove to be their salvation as they made the challenging transition into public life, one many of these trailblazers were not quite ready to bear.

This book is their story as I followed them during most of their first year: I watched them on and around the House floor, where they argued about bills, gossiped about their families, and occasionally straightened each other's flyaway hairs or errant lapels in between votes. I sat through long committee hearings, during which they would sometimes land a forceful punch against an administration official or bank executive. I visited with them back home, meeting their kids, listening to their phone calls with constituents, and trailing along for what seemed like endless tours of medical centers. I sat with them in their offices at the end of long days as the sun slid behind the Washington Monument and they mulled a policy move or discussed a colleague who had disappointed them. I noticed their forgotten dry-cleaning receipts and lipstick emergencies and tiny tattoos (congresswomen—they're just like us!), along with their frantic staff trying to keep up as they rattled off orders (So maybe not exactly like us.).

The questions facing these women were not so unlike those faced by Rep. Jeannette Rankin (R-MT), the first woman elected to Congress, or Rep. Shirley Chisholm (D-NY), the first black woman in Congress, or any other woman who has ever run for Congress to alter the status quo: Would they change Washington, or would Washington—with its power struggles, and Sunday talk shows, and $250-a-head fundraisers with lemon-drop cocktails at Charlie Palmer's, overpriced housing, and petty disputes over who stands where at a press conference—change them? Would the window of good intentions remain open before the realities of American politics shut it for the next election?

Perhaps more profound: What would the long-term impact of 2018 be? Did the election of a gay Native American woman in Kansas, and a black woman in a nearly all-white suburb of Chicago, and a Hispanic woman in a heavily Republican border region of New Mexico represent a real shift in US politics? Or was this just a short-lived reaction to President Trump? Would issues like health care and pay equity give new coherence and meaning to our body politic, transcending boundaries of race, gender, and sexual identity forever? Or would this group end up as brazen and out for themselves as anyone? Could they shift a culture in which members find no shortage of terrain on which to strut and clash with others—over whose name is at the top of a letter to a cabinet official, who gets credit for saving an air base or getting a childcare bill passed, or who gets called to the White House for a meeting, even for a browbeating? Members from the same delegation and party have been known to not speak for weeks as the result of such zero-stakes squabbles. Would the new women, largely dedicated to a social and political theory that relies on uplifting other women, break through?

The life of reporters who work the Capitol entails many, many steps each day as we race from the Senate to the House in search of lawmakers and hearings on the Hill. Still, during long days of traversing the Capitol, I often stop to stare at the portraits of the few women hanging there, trying to imagine the click of the heels of these exalted lawmakers on the tile floors beneath me. When no one is looking, I sometimes give them a tiny prayerful namaste bow. Who in this class of women would become the legislative and cultural descendants of those very first female lawmakers, I wondered. Who would have staying power, and who would be gone in two years?

Longevity in the era of twenty-four-hour news and nonstop social media feeds has taken on new meaning. Indeed, before the year was even over, one high-profile female freshman would resign amid a scandal that would underscore the naivete of many of the new members, who believed that their sheer will and unusual biographies would be an equal match for the unforgiving nature of Washington and the desires of its denizens to ruin others. Many of them would learn the hard way that a new generation's campaign tools—Twitter, texting, and photo documentation of life—could be weaponized against them in the most conventional of ways. Even the most promising of newcomers would find themselves at times in a job they were not quite prepared for in full.

On the afternoon of Trump's first State of the Union address to the new Congress in February, a large group of women in white clothing gathered on a circular staircase for a portrait in celebration of the one hundredth anniversary of women's right to vote. "One more, one more!" yelled a congresswoman as harried colleagues in white vests, gowns, and business suits rushed in from meetings to join the festive scene.

Just before this gathering, a smaller group of women, most of them senior House members who had spent years vying for their power, held a press conference to celebrate female achievement over the last century. Rep. Ayanna Pressley (D-MA), one of only two freshmen invited to join, came to the mic in her long, stylish snow-colored coat, her lips bright red, her voice more powerful than the previous speakers. Already a force in the class of 2019, she nodded to the past, while very much trying to author the future. "We have the conviction," she boomed. "We have the political courage." And, she said, "We have each other."

ONE

French Heels, Kidney Punches, and the Dead Husbands' Club

> *Which senator's wife is that?*
> —Unnamed Capitol Hill reporter

EVEN BEFORE KYRSTEN Sinema, the first female senator from Arizona, was sworn in, Senator Amy Klobuchar of Minnesota felt she needed to deal with her new colleague's shoulders.

Women had recently rebelled against the prohibition of bare arms on the House floor, which prevented female members from wearing sleeveless dresses even in the sweltering heat of a Washington, DC, summer. Former House Speaker Paul Ryan (R-WI) finally lifted the ban in 2017. On the Senate side of the Rotunda, however, strict dress codes remained intact: no shorts or skirts above the knee; jackets and ties for men; and for women, while the no-pants rule had long ago been shed, they still had to keep their shoulders covered. Sinema, a triathlete who favored sleeveless shifts on the campaign, needed to be allowed to wear what she wanted in Washington, Klobuchar reasoned, and as the most senior senator on the Senate Rules Committee, which oversees the rules for the Senate floor, it would be up to her to appeal to the largely male leadership of the Senate to make it happen.

"This is now professional attire, and this is a modern discussion," she explained to the committee that January. Another senator asked why she couldn't just don a sweater, but Klobuchar framed the ban as impinging on all women's rights to dress as they liked. Some of the male senators seemed uncomfortable with the conversation; one placed a folder over his face, and another grumbled, "The world is crumbling around us, and we are talking about sleeveless dresses!"

Klobuchar, whose will can be formidable, prevailed. Sinema showed up for her swearing-in wearing stilettos, a bejeweled tank top, and a formfitting skirt splattered with a giant pink rose, but she donned a gray fur stole on the floor, perhaps out of respect for Klobuchar, who had quietly counseled her to ease into the sleeveless look. Bounding through the Capitol with her Marilyn Monroe–shaded hair, which had replaced her sensible campaign bob, the openly bisexual Sinema, with her hand on the Constitution, took the ceremonial oath, administered, with some visible discomfort, by conservative Republican vice president Mike Pence. (Officially, senators are permitted now to "self-enforce" their own dress code, while staff members must follow the dress code rules, according to a spokesman for the majority leader's office.)

Although it may seem trivial, the restrictions around what women wear on the Hill—and the fact that they have been enforced by what are effectively morality officers—have rankled women almost since they arrived in Congress. From cluck-clucking about lace and pastel-colored dresses early on to the fight to wear pants, to the argument for exposed arms, women have often pushed for more fashion autonomy. Men are also required to dress for business, and former House Speaker John Boehner (R-OH), whose affinity for a hotel-room iron was rivaled only by his love for a nine iron, was known to issue occasional starchy reproaches, using his "I will turn this car around!" voice to chastise members for wearing jeans or improper footwear on the floor. After then-Speaker Paul Ryan capitulated on the matter of sleeves, House women still maintained a fairly conservative manner of dress, although they often acknowledge political and other causes through "color days," which would be familiar to anyone who participated in spirit weeks in high school.

Now, the diversity of the freshman class has ushered in a new era of style. Deb Haaland, one of the two first Native American women in Congress, elected in 2018, mixes turquoise and silver with classic suits. Ilhan Omar, whose first impact on Congress was to change the rules around religious headwear, brings an endless array of chic headscarves. Alexandria Ocasio-Cortez alternates between her signature red lipstick and oversized pink suit or simple black pants, when on the Hill, and her social-media look of owl-eye glasses adorning a makeup-free face, giving her the vague air of a teenager about to curl up with *Go Ask Alice*. Rep. Sharice Davids (D-KS) keeps a fetching collection of lapel pins in her office, which she rotates through; the Frida Kahlo one is especially impressive. Several women choose to wear their member pins on necklace chains, rather than pierce their clothes with their round little badges of power, and hand their necklaces off to the staff during TV standup hits so they will not get tangled in the mics.

Sinema, whose spokeswoman has explained that her politically careful boss "does not want to be known as the first female anything, only for what she does for the people of Arizona," would continue to bust sartorial boundaries as soon as she joined the Senate. As a result, one reporter confessed to me that during the first week of the new Senate he asked colleagues, "Which senator's wife is that?"

The right of women on the Hill to dress as they wish and to gain access to basic amenities like convenient bathrooms and the use of the members' gym and swimming pools, as well as to more significant achievements like substantive committee assignments and, ultimately, a shot at the Speaker's gavel, was the result of painstaking battles fought for centuries. Indeed, these battles began even before all American women had the right to vote.

Jeannette Rankin became the first female member of Congress in 1917, three years before the ratification of the Nineteenth Amendment. A suffragist leader from Montana—just one of less than a dozen states where women had already won the vote—Rankin fought a grassroots campaign that would fore-shadow those of the current era: unsupported by institutional forces, fueled by female voters, and centered on women's, children's, and workers' rights as well as international pacifism. The national media, which had largely ignored or mocked her campaign, reacted to her victory with near obsession, chronicling both her policy positions and her cooking skills.

In 2018, Ocasio-Cortez shredded cheese for an Instant Pot recipe during an Instagram livestream; a century before, the *Baltimore Sun*, in the first paragraph of an article detailing Rankin's historic move into Congress, noted that she, "aside from achieving a political victory, holds the honor of making the best lemon pie in Montana."

And then, of course, there is clothing! While (mostly male) members of the media would fixate on Ocasio-Cortez's outfits, so, too, did the *Washington Post* with Rankin, as in this headline: CONGRESSWOMAN RANKIN REAL GIRL; LIKES NICE GOWNS AND TIDY HAIR. According to the historian of the House of Representatives, Matthew Wasniewski, "People were desperate to know, 'Did she wear a hat? Did she wear French heels?'" Yes to the French heels.

Over the years, as female senators and representatives have gained in number, they have often focused on legislation intended to attain greater economic and political security for women and families. Rankin designed that template early on. One of her first acts was to call for and become appointed to a committee to study a constitutional amendment on women's suffrage, and she soon became its ranking member, unheard of for a freshman. She opened the first House floor debate on suffrage in congressional history, against the backdrop of World War I. "How shall we answer their challenge, gentlemen?" she asked, addressing critics who thought suffrage ought to remain a state issue, according to the *Congressional Record*. "How shall we explain to them the meaning of democracy if the same Congress that voted for war to make the world safe for democracy refuses to give this small measure of democracy to the women of our country?" (The House passed the measure on that day, January 10, 1918, but it died in the Senate.)

Like the women of the 116th Congress, Rankin challenged foreign policy norms. A dedicated pacifist, she voted with other skeptical members against entering the war in 1917. But during a second stint in the House, in 1941, she was the only member to cast a vote against a US declaration of war against Japan after the attack on Pearl Harbor, becoming the only member of Congress to vote against participation in both world wars. "As a woman I can't go to war, and I refuse to send anyone else," she said, before taking refuge in a phone booth to hide from the press and enraged fellow members.

The late John Dingell (D-MI), who became the longest-serving member of the House and whose wife, Debbie, now serves in his seat, was a House page when he witnessed this moment. "Well, she sputtered. It was kind of an incoherent speech, and they just weren't going to hear her," he told Wasniewski during an oral history interview in 2012. According to congressional records, the powerful Speaker of the House at the time, Sam Rayburn (D-TX), refused to recognize her at all.

Thus ended Rankin's electoral career; knowing the vast majority of Montanans did not support her, she did not bother to run for reelection. She spent the rest of her life as a globe-trotting peace activist and, according to several accounts, never regretted her votes. "Never for one second," she said, "could I face the idea that I would send young men to be killed for no other reason than to save my seat in Congress."

The congresswomen who came right after Rankin were a homogeneous bunch—wealthy, white, well educated, Protestant— and products of the Progressive Era. The majority had a pre-existing familial connection to Congress, largely as widows who won their husbands' seats after they died; of the twenty women who entered Congress between 1917 and 1934, eight were widowed into office and four had other family links that helped propel them to Washington. It is worth noting that one of them eventually succeeded her bootlegging jailed spouse, because America! Even those, like Rankin, who did not fill their husbands' seats were beneficiaries of men's wealth or political connections, without which women could not climb what was already a politically arduous hill. Rep. Mary Norton, who represented New Jersey for thirteen terms in the early twentieth century, was a protégé of a local Democratic political boss who wanted to gain some credibility with the newly enfranchised women in his home state, and an interesting pick, given that she was a proud nonsuffragist herself. But she had been leader of a nursery school—perhaps perfect experience for a career in politics—and her prodigious fundraising skills got her noticed by local politicians, who would help pave her path through the party system.

Norton, too, was focused on bills that would benefit families; most notably, she pushed the Fair Labor Standards Act of 1938 to the House floor for a vote, providing for a forty-hour workweek, outlawing child labor, and setting a federal minimum wage (then, twenty-five cents an hour). It was the last and only significant New Deal reform to pass in President Franklin Roosevelt's second term.

Norton is also famous for a retort she once made. To this day, women and men are acknowledged when they come to the floor for debate as "the gentleman from Georgia," and "the gentlewoman from Oregon." When recognized during a debate on the floor as a "gentlelady," Norton said: "I am no lady, I'm a member of Congress, and I'll proceed on that basis."

During the 1920s and 1930s, more and more women began to pepper the House and make their mark, though never in great enough numbers to form a real coalition. Some of them may have been mere seat fillers for dead husbands, but they nevertheless came armed with political acumen, having been informal advisors to their husbands' campaigns or, in some instances, actual campaign or congressional aides. Many also had relevant professional experience, and they made significant contributions, especially when viewed in the context of contemporary women. At the same time, their gender continued to impair their progress; often assigned to second-tier committees, they struggled to gain seniority and grab gavels on the key policy-making panels.

While this cohort helped the next generation of women lay tentacles into this Byzantine operation, one dominated by seniority, patronage, and patriarchy in its purest expression, the most significant era for women in Congress before the current one came two generations later, as part of the overall tumult in the 1960s–1970s. Like now, the '60s and '70s ushered in some high-profile women who generally fit two modes: agitators and incrementalists.

Rep. Patsy Takemoto Mink started as an incrementalist when she became the first nonwhite woman in Congress in 1965, relying on a grassroots campaign of volunteers and door knocking. In her home state of Hawaii, Mink was judged for her "deviation from the expected middle-class female norms," her daughter, Wendy Mink, told me. "The undertone of the comments was, 'Shouldn't she be a good mother taking care of her child before running for office?'" When Patsy Mink arrived in DC, she relied on a deep knowledge of education issues, initially, to ward off more general sexism. "Until her authoritative knowledge of an issue was established, there was a way that male colleagues would just sort of tolerate her interventions," Wendy Mink said. "Securing legitimacy was an important thing."

Women began to clash most strongly with men on the Hill when they identified and took ownership of legislative issues that the men had declined previously even to consider, such as an Equal Rights Amendment to the Constitution (never to be ratified), or the exclusion of women from opportunities such as vocational education. This type of battle defined Mink's legacy, and left her deepest scars. In 1972, Congress passed the Title IX law, prohibiting sex discrimination in educational programs and activities that received federal aid. As the law rolled out, it became increasingly controversial; male lawmakers began to fear that women's sports programs would get financial favor over men's. Mink became the guardian of Title IX. "I recall the almost monthly relentless attacks on the definition on Title Nine that various male members of the House and Senate kept trying to raise," Wendy Mink recalled. "My mother kept having to mobilize and beat those initiatives down."

Patsy Mink, who was once rejected from multiple medical schools because she was a woman, also later helped pass the Women's Educational Equity Act in 1974, which took on discrimination in educational programs, with a goal of equity for girls and women, especially in the areas of math and science. (It also gave money to lobby for the removal of the stereotypes of male doctors and female homemakers from textbooks.) Some of the women of the 116th Congress have picked up Mink's mantle decades later in their fight on behalf of equity for LGBTQ students and athletes. Most Americans may never have heard of Mink, but we can burn a candle of thanks in her name for the path she paved a generation ago for the glorious 2019 US women's soccer team—though even now its players are fighting for equal pay.

In the '70s, the high priestess of agitators was Shirley Chisholm, the first black congresswoman, whose photo now hangs in the offices of many of the women of the 116th Congress. A community activist and respected educator, Chisholm won her seat representing Brooklyn in 1968, following a campaign that centered squarely on gender. Her primary opponent, a civil rights leader, ran unabashedly on the suggestion that a man would be better suited to represent the area, with a campaign slogan stating that "a man's voice" was needed in Washington. Her campaign motto was "Unbought and unbossed," which would later be engraved on her vault in Forest Lawn cemetery in Buffalo, the city she eventually moved to in her retirement.

Like most of the women who were victorious in 2018, Chisholm gave her shoes a workout, campaigning door-to-door to grab every vote; also like today's class of female lawmakers, she was a master at building political coalitions, bringing together young voters and multiracial constituencies to circumvent the male-dominated political machine. "When she gets to Congress," Barbara Winslow, a professor emeritus at Brooklyn College and founder of the Shirley Chisholm Project, explained to me, "she is a celebrity so like AOC you can't believe it. They were both snazzy dressers who liked to dance and both have rapier wits."

With a desire to expand her reach and influence as a political outsider, Chisholm ran for president in 1972, which alienated many of the black men in the House who felt she was overstepping. "Her huge defeat demoralized her," Winslow said, but it also made her shift from political activism to more savvy legislating. A cofounder of both the Congressional Black Caucus and the Congressional Women's Caucus, she had a unique perspective on what we now call "intersectionality." "To date, neither the black movement nor women's liberation succinctly addresses itself to the dilemma confronting the black who is female," Chisholm said during a 1974 speech at the University of Missouri. "And as a consequence of ignoring or being unable to handle the problems facing black women, black women themselves are now becoming socially and politically active."

But men, she believed, had held back her political career the most. "When I ran for the Congress, when I ran for president, I met more discrimination as a woman than for being black. Men are men," she told a reporter on her way out of office. After she left, in 1983, "Shirley Chisholm had just been erased," Winslow said. "No one had heard of her in her old neighborhood. She was a working-class woman of color out of the public eye."

In the years leading up to the fiftieth anniversary of her ascent to the House, however, scholars and Chisholm fans revived her place in the political canon. Some of the new women referred to her during their campaigns and on their victory nights, as she was, all told, the mother of resistance politics. Rep. Lauren Underwood (D-IL), the first black woman to be elected in her district, referred to herself as "unbought and unbossed" in her victory speech. In Chisholm's honor, House Democrats even enshrined a contemporary collage, made by staff, in their caucus room, featuring several photos of her and the image of a chair in reference to her famous line "If they don't give you a seat at the table, bring a folding chair."

Chisholm paved an indelible path, and that road bent back toward her legacy in 2018. "I feel a soul tie to Shirley Chisholm," Ayanna Pressley, the first black woman from Massachusetts to win a seat and the current tenant of Chisholm's old office, told me. "Not only was she a 'first,' she was disruptive, she was brave, and she a was trailblazer. Her commitment to fighting injustice and lifting up the voices of the left out and left behind is an inspiration, and an example I hope to follow. The vibe of her office fills me with the courage to boldly lead, boldly legislate, and to never forget those who sent me here."

Surprisingly, Chisholm and the other women of the 1970s faced perhaps a far more insidious resistance to their presence on the Hill than their forebears. For the most part, the first generation of women in Congress had been not only of a certain social class, they also tended to be familiar to other members from their years as congressional wives and informal advisors, and were seen in some ways more as extensions of late husbands' values and agendas than as their own people with political agency. But, as Debbie Walsh, director of the Center for American Women and Politics, put it, "They were not running in the midst of a feminist movement."

In the '70s, on the other hand, the chin-out feminism of members like Bella Abzug and Pat Schroeder seemed to rankle the men of the House, and they made sure to let the women know every chance they had.

Abzug (D-NY) embodied both the feminist and antiwar movements in one colorful, outspoken congresswoman. Noting once that "women have been trained to talk softly and carry a lipstick," Abzug was a lawyer who didn't run for office until she was fifty years old. Her gender became central to her campaign, perhaps more than any female candidate who preceded her. Her campaign slogan was "This woman's place is in the House . . . the House of Representatives." She showed up in Washington with a wide-brimmed hat (which she began wearing as a young lawyer because she believed, for some odd reason, that wearing a hat was the only way a man would take a woman seriously) and battled unsuccessfully for the right to wear it on the House floor. Besides her patently feminist campaign, Abzug's platform centered on opposition to the Vietnam War, financial and legal enfranchisement of poor and working-class New Yorkers, government accountability, and needling her party's establishment, with which she often battled over committee assignments, legislative agendas, and whether or not positions were sufficiently liberal.

As a member of Congress, Abzug, who was monitored by the CIA for more than twenty years, turned her distrust into significant legislation. She coauthored the Freedom of Information Act and the Right to Privacy Act, but is best known for authoring the "Sunshine Law," which required governing bodies to meet publicly, perhaps the most enduring government accountability move of that era. Government accountability would remain a major topic of interest to female lawmakers in the decades to follow.

While Chisholm is a current heroine, Abzug is rarely spoken of, even though her battles presaged many of the battles of the current class of women. Despite her accomplishments, her insolent New York edge, her political-purity litmus tests for colleagues, and her general aggressiveness often alienated the very people she was seeking to entice. According to a *New York Times* account, she even once punched one of her own campaign workers in the kidney. "Democratic women who wanted Republican women to participate in their bills were very wary of her," Wasniewski told me. "It wasn't until she left the House that many of the women who helped organize the Women's Caucus in 1977 felt there was bipartisan momentum for it."

Although there had been working mothers in Congress before Pat Schroeder of Colorado, she (enthusiastically cheered on by her husband and with her kids in tow) ran for the House in 1972 in a relatively conservative congressional district. She, too, ran on a platform of ending the war and empowering women, and she, too, ran a grassroots campaign focused on the social issues of the era and those close to her Denver constituents. Because she had trouble raising money, her main campaign materials were cheap black-and-white commercials and posters depicting her opposition to the Olympics in Colorado and the war in Vietnam (that one featured gravestones and a bird flying out over the top) and a poster supporting migrant workers. She became the first woman from her state elected to Congress, and held her seat for eleven subsequent terms.

Judging by her numerous accounts, Schroeder seemed to suffer more rank sexism than perhaps any of her progenitors. There was that story about the male member of Congress who offered her his face as her seat in the cloakroom. And while her most often reported slight was delivered by a colleague in an elevator, who told her, "This is about Chivas Regal, thousand-dollar bills, Lear jets, and beautiful women. Why are you here?" Schroeder endured insults and affronts throughout her long career. Men and women both, including Abzug, would question how the mother of young kids could possibly do the job, and that thought also occurred to Schroeder from time to time, particularly when her children's pet rabbit once escaped on a plane home from Washington in search of an airline-issue salad.

Schroeder's experiences were instructive particularly when compared with the last great member of the dead husbands' club, Lindy Boggs (D-LA), who won the seat after her husband, House majority leader Hale Boggs, was lost when his plane disappeared during a campaign trip to Alaska in 1972. Boggs, the first woman from Louisiana elected (as opposed to appointed) to the House, represented a bridge of sorts between the two generations. Over her nine terms, she used the relationships she formed during her husband's many years in Congress to gain plum committee assignments and legislative help. She played a key role in the creation of the House Select Committee on Children, Youth, and Families and the Congressional Women's Caucus, and claimed that she had never experienced discrimination as a woman in the House.

When Schroeder, on the other hand, managed to win a seat on the prestigious House Armed Services Committee, the chair, Rep. Edward Hébert, a Dixiecrat from Louisiana, was so offended by the appointment that he forced Schroeder and Rep. Ron Dellums (D-CA), an African American member from Oakland, to literally share a chair during a committee organizational meeting. (In a 2012 interview, Dellums recalled: "You know, even though we wanted to scream, we said, 'No.' We just let our silence and our behavior handle it. And they didn't know what to do, because we didn't scream. So the next time, the two seats were there. We made our point, and we moved on.") Hébert didn't treat every congresswoman like that. "Lindy Boggs comes in as a widow a couple of months later, and he tells the press Lindy is going to be a great member of the House," Wasniewski recalled. Indeed, according to House records, Hébert once blurted, "She's the only widow I know who is really qualified— damn qualified—to take over" her dead husband's spot.

Lindy Boggs concerned herself less with the Equal Rights Amendment or fighting sex discrimination and more with fixing the financial systems that kept women from getting loans, owning homes, or amassing credit and wealth. Her style was on full display when the House Banking and Currency Committee wrote the Equal Credit Opportunity Act of 1974. That bill included a clause barring "discrimination on the basis of race and age" and "status as veterans" in obtaining credit. Boggs wanted "sex" and "marital status" added to the list, so she quietly wrote the words into the bill by hand, then walked to the photocopying machine and doled out the copies of the edited bill to fellow members of the committee with a honey-dripped remark: "Knowing the members composing this committee as well as I do, I'm sure it was just an oversight that we didn't have 'sex' or 'marital status' included. I've taken care of that, and I trust it meets with the committee's approval." Today, Boggs is one of only two women (the other is former representative Gabrielle Giffords) to have a room in the Capitol named in her honor, and congresswomen flock to it like a holy site when they first arrive on the Hill.

Before 2018, the next significant wave of women to enter Congress occurred in 1992 in the wake of the Supreme Court confirmation hearings for Clarence Thomas; twenty-four new women were elected to the House, many more than in any preceding decade, bringing the total to forty-seven, and women took an additional three seats in the Senate, joining incumbents Nancy Kassebaum (R-KS), Barbara Mikulski (D-MD), and Dianne Feinstein (D-CA), who had won a special election. Rep. Kay Bailey Hutchison (R-TX) won a special election in June of the following year.

In many ways, 1992 shared some of the same dynamics as 2018—minority women gained in number both at the federal level and in statehouses, and the rights of women in the workplace was a central theme. But numerical gains did not equal power; in Congress, seniority has historically been destiny.

Women have increasingly gained prominence through leading committees and simply hanging on, which is often the greatest career asset in Washington.

Longevity multiplies the novelty factor; the 116th Congress has both. "I was in Pelosi's office talking about the budget the other day, and I looked up and it was Pelosi, [Rep. Nita] Lowey, [Rep. Lucille] Roybal-Allard, and me," Rep. Rosa DeLauro (D-CT), who was first elected in 1990, told me. "I thought, 'Wow, this is all women making major decisions about strategy on how to move us forward.'" Women with a combined eleven decades in Congress.

Of course, getting to Congress has been only part of the battle. Day-to-day life on the Hill has historically posed a challenge and the material culture there, particularly its amenities, has long served as a metaphor for the marginalization of women. For decades, the House gym, built in the 1920s to improve the health of the often-corpulent and largely inactive members, was festooned with a sign that read MEMBERS ONLY, but it effectively meant "men only." When that gym was remodeled into a state-of-the-art fitness facility in the 1960s, complete with a pool, a tiny "Ladies Health Facility" was added to the Rayburn House Office Building, featuring a Ping-Pong table, exercise "machines" that looked like they had come straight from a midcentury fat camp, and bonnet hair dryers. One afternoon in 1967, Rep. Catherine May (R-WA), Rep. Charlotte Reid (R-IL), and Rep. Patsy Mink wandered over to the House gym and proclaimed their desire to take a calisthenics class. The women, who were looking more to make a statement than to get in a workout, were denied entry to the gym; they promptly took a photo of the MEMBERS ONLY sign as an official register of complaint and slipped off.

Their outrage was not so much about a lack of aerobics as a lack of access. Like the golf course, the gym is where friendships were formed and deals were cut, and women were left out of the action. Their gym gambit did not get traction right off the bat; when asked by reporters about this in 1979, Herb Botts, who managed the basement facility, said: "When the building was planned, they didn't envision twenty women members. The ladies understand."

So women got access to the men's pool during specified hours but not the men's gym proper; they were stuck with their own inadequate facility until 1985. In an interview with the House historian's office, Rep. Nancy Johnson (R-CT), who served from 1983 to 2007, recalled the Great Gym Rebellion, when a group of congresswomen from both parties made the second attempt to make the men's gym officially coed. "[Senator] Barbara Boxer came to me, and she said, 'The [women's] gym equipment is terrible,'" Johnson recalled. "And I said, 'Well, I've never been there.' So, we went over and looked. And it was those old-fashioned rowing machines—wooden rowing machines—and wooden bars on the wall." Noting that no one wanted to use *that* stuff, Johnson said, "She and I, and we got a couple of other Democrats and a couple of other Republicans, and we took the congressman from Springfield, who was chairman of the gym resources or whatever they called them. And he was quite elderly. And we toured him around, and we said, 'Now, we want machines like you have,' because they had all these exercise machines. So, we were talking about what we wanted and what we had, and so on and so forth. And the bell rings to go to vote. The second bell rings, so then we really do have to go. And so we go to vote, and then, on the floor, Barbara and

I come up to him and say, 'Well, what do you think?' 'Well,' he said, 'I don't know why you want machines. You know, those machines only build muscles.'"

Even in 2008, female senators were not permitted at all in the Senate pool, an artifact of the proclivity of certain male senators (reportedly Democrats Ted Kennedy of Massachusetts and Chris Dodd of Connecticut) for sometimes swimming in the nude. The MEN ONLY sign at the pool was finally replaced after some una-mused female senators complained with a placard warning sena-tors to swim clothed, even as—remember—bare arms remained officially prohibited on the House and Senate floors.

Only after Republicans took over the House in 2011 did women finally get a bathroom off the House floor (men had had one since the chamber first opened in 1857). A few years later, female senators got the restroom near the Senate floor expanded, with additional stalls and some storage space after years of cramming into a tiny one. In recognition of the increased num-ber of parents in Congress, many members-only restrooms now have changing tables and there are places around the Capitol to express milk. In the 116th Congress, the chair of the Committee on House Administration, Rep. Zoe Lofgren (D-CA), had tam-pons added to the women's bathroom off the House floor, and allowed members to use their official budgets for the first time ever to pay for menstrual products for their offices.

Along with this evolution of physical and external change, the culture around how members talk about policy has shifted dra-matically. "The very first bill we were debating when I came here was a Ted Kennedy bill about the family medical leave policy," recalled Senator Patty Murray (D-WA), who was among the tiny wave of new female senators elected in 1992. "I went out to speak on the floor. I talked about a friend of mine who I had known whose fifteen-year-old son was diagnosed with leukemia, who worked for a major company in my state, and who was literally told, 'If you take time off to be with him, we can't guarantee your job will be here.' And she just went through this horrible stress of, you know, will I lose my job? And I actually had a male senator, come to me afterwards and say, 'We don't tell personal stories on the floor.' But now it's standard. You listen to the debate now. And it's much more human and real, and it makes people understand why we're doing things we're doing. I mean, when I got here, the standard thing was graphs and charts and, you know, economic analysis—and fine. But policy is important to people. And if they don't get the connection between what we're talking about and what's happening in their life, it's very hard to get things passed." (That same male senator later thanked her, she said, for helping him to rethink how to talk about policy in public.)

No discussion of the role of women—and the evolving power dynamics—in Congress would be complete, of course, without considering Nancy Pelosi, perhaps the House's most durable member. She has survived contests of wills for power and legislation, been written off by many after the disastrous-for-Democrats 2010 election, fended off numerous challenges to her leadership in the minority, where she often outwitted a splintered Republican majority, and finally rose again to manage the historic class of 2019.

The daughter of a politically powerful former congressman and mayor of Baltimore, Pelosi learned at her parents' elbows how to raise money, call in favors, pressure supporters to step it up at election time, and, perhaps most important of all, how to count votes. After marrying her husband, Paul, a wealthy real estate investor, in 1963 and moving to San Francisco, Pelosi raised five children, but she remained involved in politics, holding fundraisers—for which she cooked and her children served—in her elegant home while still driving carpool and sewing her kids' clothes. She kept close ties to party leaders in Maryland and her new state of California, where she eventually became chair of the state Democratic Party. Her attempts to rise to chair of the Democratic National Committee were thwarted at least in part by sexism; a labor leader siding with another candidate called her "an airhead." Upon withdrawing, Pelosi said: "It is clear to me [that] many of you did not think the right message would go out if a woman was elected chairman of this party."

In 1983, when Rep. Phil Burton (D-CA) died, his wife, Sala, won an election to complete his term. But in 1987, she became ill with cancer and suggested from her deathbed that Pelosi take her place in the district that encompassed much of San Francisco. Pelosi had the financial advantage over her many opponents in a nasty primary fight, as well as the grassroots volunteers networking learned in Baltimore, and it all added up to a win by fewer than four thousand votes, delivered in part by Republican voters and a defeat for her more liberal challenger; she outran the Republican in a runoff by more than 60 percent. (Therein lies the first myth of Pelosi: she has never been the most liberal person in the United States or even San Francisco.) Her proclivity for outorganizing and outhustling everyone around her was on display as well, underscoring the value of one of her favorite aphorisms, "Proper preparation prevents poor performance."

Pelosi picked a hometown issue early on, announcing in her first House floor speech in 1987 that she had come to Congress to fight AIDS, and she went on to increase funding for AIDS research and secure the ability for the NAMES Project AIDS Memorial Quilt to be displayed on the National Mall. In 2013, when Lindy Boggs died, Pelosi went to the floor to honor her mentor. "When we would have our heated discussions on the floor," Pelosi recalled, "she would call us back and say: 'Darling, Hale used to always say: 'Don't fight every fight as if it's your last fight. We are all friends. We are a resource to each other to do good things for our country.' No wonder a room was named for her."

The trailblazers of the 116th Congress recognize the debt they owe to the women who came before them: Boggs and Pelosi, yes, but especially Shirley Chisholm. The first—and for a long time only—piece of art in Ilhan Omar's office was a rendering of Chisholm. Rep. Katie Hill (D-CA), a millennial lawmaker from Southern California, had been assigned Chisholm's office in the lottery used to determine freshman offices, but she turned it over to Ayanna Pressley, knowing its significance to her. Along with her official congressional swearing-in, Bella Abzug took a "people's oath" on the House steps, administered by Chisholm, signifying her fealty to the people who elected her. Decades later, Pressley and Rashida Tlaib took a similar oath in their home cities. Abzug, like Tlaib, was among the first freshmen to call for the impeachment of a president (in Abzug's case, Richard Nixon; in Tlaib's case, Donald Trump). Abzug and Chisholm also cowrote the Child Development Act. Alexandria Ocasio-Cortez's and other new members' blistering cross-examinations of officials over drug pricing, child separation policies, police misconduct, and corporate malfeasance would not have been possible without the unbought and unbossed women of the 1970s.

But quite soon after the January 2019 swearing-in, gender unity was overshadowed by political conflicts that mirror the broader internal battle facing the Democratic Party. A new group of women was eager to push forward a politically progressive policy agenda focused on health care, wages, and climate change, often framed through the lens of multiracial liberalism that the group believes defines the next generation of the party. The lawmakers' policy ideas, and often their perspectives as young members who won by appealing to new voters, have at times put them at odds with Pelosi and the older, whiter party leadership of the House, and they have often chafed at being made to feel like a thorn in the side of their fellow House Democrats.

Indeed, once the members of the 116th Congress were seated, there was almost instant conflict between members who expected their exciting but still junior colleagues to sit down and listen, and the large, opinionated, diverse, and self-confident group of new members whose campaigns, life stories, and paths to power diverged dramatically from those of their predecessors.

Here, the new class of women, the largest ever in the history of Congress, would have a chance to demonstrate to what degree, if at all, a growing gender parity would impact the institution and policy. Pat Schroeder, now seventy-nine, lives in Florida and remains active in politics. She recently told me that while she agrees that the dead husbands' club is defunct, she does not think congressional women have yet achieved safety in numbers. "I was so excited to see the new women who have been in military service and intelligence service and all sorts of careers that women really were not into back then," she said. "But for all the great job they are doing, I think, 'Oh my God, it's 2019, and we are not even a full twenty-five percent of the House.' You need critical mass in an institution to change it. The question is always, What is a critical mass? I don't think anyone thinks it's twenty-three percent."

TWO

They Did It Their Way

Women like me aren't supposed to run for office.
—Rep. Alexandria Ocasio-Cortez (D-NY)

"NO ONE LOOKED at me and said, 'Girl, it's you,'" said Lauren Underwood as she shuffled a pile of envelopes on the otherwise bare desk in her new congressional office. At thirty-two, she had become the youngest person, first female, and first person of color to win her seat in the suburbs of Chicago, and the youngest black woman ever in the House.

No one but Underwood even seemed to understand that she could pull it off. Like scores of women who turned anger and frustration into a decision to run for Congress in 2018, she was appalled by President Donald Trump; also like many other women in 2018, she was a first-time candidate in a Republican district, leveraging the alchemy of Trump fatigue (particularly among suburban women), a growing fear among voters that health insurance protections were under attack by Republicans, and an appealing comfort in her own skin.

From Lauren Underwood in Illinois to Sharice Davids, the first openly LGBTQ person to win a congressional race in Kansas and one of the first two Native American women ever to serve in the House, to Ayanna Pressley and Alexandria Ocasio-Cortez, who had both defeated powerful Democratic incumbents on the East Coast, the formula was much the same: break it. These women remained their authentic political selves throughout their campaign, and, thanks to this cohort, Pelosi regained the gavel.

In many cases, female voters in Republican-majority districts were at odds with their husbands, a conflict sometimes manifested by dueling yard signs for congressional candidates. Other times, voters' efforts were more stealth—some women in central Michigan, for example, would tell their husbands they were going to book club when they were actually attending a volunteer session for Democratic candidate Elissa Slotkin, a former CIA officer who went on to beat a Republican there. Underwood, Slotkin, and others in districts with more Republican than Democratic voters had an especially arduous mission: they needed simultaneously to energize a Democratic base to get through a primary and ensure turnout in the general election, while also appealing to Republican women. Once on Capitol Hill, they would need to continue this balancing act.

For all women who choose to run for office, there can be additional obstacles, sometimes through betting against themselves. They may feel discouraged from running, even though statistically they win about as often as men (unless they are Republican women in primaries). According to a 2013 study by professors Jennifer Lawless and Richard Fox, men are 15 percent more likely to be recruited to run for office than women.

And women rarely come up with the idea on their own; someone usually has to recruit them. Sometimes, their hesitation stems from hating to ask people for money, which is a central feature of modern campaigns. Just as often, however, they consider themselves unqualified.

This concern is one that women already in office seek to tamp down. Former senator Heidi Heitkamp (D-ND), who, like many female senators, spent a fair amount of her time trying to convince women to run for office, told me she repeatedly heard them worry about their qualifications, something that seems rarely to distress men. "I used to tell them, 'Have you seen the North Dakota legislature?'" she joked. Even among those queried in "feeder" professions, such as the law, only 57 percent of women said they thought they were qualified or very qualified to run for office, Lawless and Fox found, compared to 73 percent of the male respondents.

For the women who prevailed in 2018, self-determination was part of their secret sauce. Of the roughly twenty women I followed closely, the vast majority had made their own decision to run, motivated in large part either by the Trump presidency or the Republican congressional agenda. They sounded a lot like people who chose to go into public service after 9/11, believing they were called to duty as part of a larger national emergency response.

"This is exactly what I signed up for," Rep. Mikie Sherrill (D-NJ) told me. A former US Navy helicopter pilot and federal prosecutor now representing a swath of northern New Jersey, Sherrill sometimes cites Trump's attacks on Senator John McCain, even after McCain's death, and on the Khan family, whose twenty-seven-year-old son, a US Army captain, died in a car bombing in 2004 in Iraq, as among her motivations to run. Rep. Elissa Slotkin (D-MI), who has said that being in New York City on 9/11 is what compelled her to pursue a job at the CIA, wanted to continue the mission in Congress.

The candidates also worked to make themselves unusually accessible to those they were trying to woo, especially folks who had been ignored by Democrats in past years. Slotkin began her campaign in Michigan, which became one of the most expensive in House history, with a listening tour dubbed Snowboots on the Ground, in which she painstakingly knocked on door after door throughout the district, a technique many women embraced. Women of color like Lauren Underwood, Ilhan Omar, Sharice Davids, Jahana Hayes, and Ayanna Pressley, all of whom won majority-white districts, knew they needed to make deep one-on-one connections in order to be accepted by people who did not look like them.

Most importantly, candidates believed that if they were relatable, consistent in their message no matter the neighborhood they campaigned in, and cheerfully themselves, voters would get on board. Black, Muslim, young, and gay candidates did not try to subdue those identities. They casually embraced them, with the expectation that constituents would find themselves in general agreement with their policy positions. Angie Craig, who in 2016 narrowly lost her first House race in the suburbs of Minneapolis, let herself talk about her wife and their kids the second time around in an easy, matter-of-fact way. "I will just bring it up naturally. Like when talking about education costs, I say, 'My wife and I have four sons, and college isn't for all of them.' I saw you can be a lesbian, and it made no difference at all in the campaign here." She also ditched the business suit that so many women feel they need to don on campaigns, trading it in to match the more casual look of her district. Honesty, charm, and self-confidence all went a long way.

Lauren Underwood and I first met in her new congressional office in the Longworth House Office Building, which she had decorated with color photos of her district and a few books, including *How to Be Successful Without Hurting Men's Feelings*. A trained nurse with a congenital heart condition who had worked in the Obama administration on health-care policy, she felt singularly motivated to run when Republicans began to pursue legislation that would remove protections for patients with preexisting medical problems.

At the Women's March in 2017, she learned that Democrats had set their sights on the four-term incumbent, Rep. Randy Hultgren, who held a seat that had historically been almost exclusively Republican. It was once the redoubt of former Speaker of the House Dennis Hastert, who was hugely popular before he was exposed as a child molester after his retirement from politics. While solidly Republican, the district, like other suburban strongholds, was flashing warning signs in the era of Trump. Then–Republican presidential candidate Mitt Romney had won it by 10 percentage points in 2012. Trump won it by only 4, and didn't cross the 50 percent threshold. "I thought, 'Great, I will support whoever runs,'" Underwood told me. Then she got to thinking: "whoever" in her district could be her.

Underwood grew up in Naperville, Illinois. Her father was a corporate controller. Her mom was a buyer in manufacturing. The Underwoods were one of the few black families in a district where blacks make up less than 5 percent of the population. "I never had a black teacher," she said, and she had almost no black coaches. A product of a close family and a community where she always felt embraced, she believed she understood precisely what the district—a mix of rural swaths of pastures and grain stores and Chicago suburbs full of half-empty strip malls—needed. "I went to lunch with my friend Sarah Feldmann at this barbecue place and said, 'I am thinking of running for Congress.' So Sarah pulls out a notebook and starts writing. She was totally down to help. I was underestimated by everyone, but we knew the Fourteenth was winnable."

She was not exactly welcomed by the party, given that six other Democrats were ready to go—and then she won the primary with more than 57 percent of the vote; her closest competitor took a mere 13 percent. Even so, she entered the general election as an underdog.

Underwood insisted on making her own decisions. She wanted to manage her own money, for instance, and chose a post office box to receive donations, carrying around the tiny key herself, rather than funneling funds through the Democratic Congressional Campaign Committee (DCCC), and she often avoided costly consultants. "This was the most data-uninformed thing I have ever done," she shared with me over a late-night meeting in her office during the government shutdown, when she and her skeleton staff were stuffing their own envelopes. "I didn't have the staff they advised. I did not allocate money for that. I did my own thing."

After her decisive primary victory, Underwood knew that health care was going to be the central policy issue in the general election. She also knew she could outwork Hultgren. "I found that there was so much value in just showing up," she said. "We would go and stand in people's living rooms. People would host us for house parties. They were not even supporters. They just wanted to hear. We would be in cul-de-sacs, standing in soybean fields, where no Democrat had been in years." The conventional wisdom of the consultant class, she was told, was that candidates like her ought to focus on traditionally Democratic areas and ignore the rest. "But we went everywhere," she said. "We invested in all corners of the district, and as a result we won every county."

Her message was relentless but did not focus on Trump: Republicans, she said, over and over and over, were trying to take away coverage of preexisting conditions. "The president was not so unpopular," she said, and she sensed that an anti-Trump message would not "be a bridge opportunity to connect with people across the district."

As the race tightened, former vice president Joe Biden stumped for Underwood, and former president Barack Obama endorsed her at a Democratic rally in Chicago. Her defeat of Hultgren by 14,871 votes was among the most surprising of the night: 5 percentage points was not simply an upset for that district; it was a rout. In her victory speech, Underwood, dressed in a conservative navy grosgrain suit and her "power pumps," said cheerfully: "I aim to be the very best congresswoman this area has ever seen. And honestly it won't be that difficult, because I'll be the first congresswoman to represent this district!" She exited the stage at the Kane County Fairgrounds to the Alicia Keys song "Girl on Fire." (Pelosi would use the same song, months later, as her walk-off song for a speech to rally Democrats in New Jersey shortly after announcing the impeachment investigation.)

Underwood's roommate in Washington would be a friend she made along the trail, another promising millennial freshman,

Katie Hill, who had turned her idealism—and practical skills—as an advocate for the homeless into a winning campaign. Her district, California's Twenty-Fifth, includes the dusty, working-class cities of Lancaster and Palmdale, stretches of high-desert brown hills and tired strip malls, and hospitals lacking sufficient mental-health care, but also includes priced-out Angelenos, the wealthy largely Republican subdivisions of Santa Clarita, and rural areas populated by Latino workers. It is heavy with police officers and veterans, and home to the Reagan Library in Simi Valley.

Hill understood intuitively that Republicans in her district were distinct from those whose voices were loudest in Washington—disproportionately southern, socially conservative, suspicious of government. Those in her district support gun rights but also gun safety, low taxes but the preservation of government-supported health care, defense spending but climate-change consciousness, too. Like Underwood, Hill's first task was to vanquish better-known primary contenders. At the California Democratic convention, she moved successfully to block her main challenger, a onetime corporate lawyer named Bryan Caforio, from getting the endorsement of the state party, in large part by pushing a poll that showed her the most likely Democrat to unseat the incumbent, Rep. Steve Knight (R-CA), a US Army veteran and former LAPD cop. Walking out after this incremental victory, Hill reflected on her final challenge to Caforio: "We're gonna fucking crush him." (She ended up winning by 2 percentage points, but who's counting?)

Next target, the seemingly entrenched Knight. Word quickly spread around the bluer enclaves of Southern California: a talented, politically amalgamated, dog-loving, goat-owning, rock-climbing, real-talking millennial woman had just won a

Democratic primary battle in a Republican district at the north end of Los Angeles County. She quickly raked in big bucks from celebrities like Jimmy Kimmel, whose infant son's heart condition drew him to the health-care issue, as well as wealthy LA women who were eager to see this young woman rise.

In a Vice documentary—ever-Vice-ly titled "Who the Hell Is Katie Hill?"—Hill's campaign office resembles the basement apartment of a college kid, with piles of paper and a half dozen wine bottles stashed at the top of an open closet. She watches coverage on a large-screen television propped up by empty printer boxes. The documentary captures a typical race for a first-time candidate: all dialing for dollars and stops for all of twelve votes at a pizza party. At one point, Hill's mother is forced to schedule breakfast with her through a campaign staff worker. The ability to raise money, the holy grail of House campaigns in which the fundraising never stops, is best depicted in a scene from her campaign manager/finance director's house/campaign headquarters as Hill and her staff call potential donor after potential donor as a fundraising deadline approaches. "We are all doing like booty calls," she laments, adding that her sister "is texting all her ex-hookups." Looking at a clock as the deadline looms, Hill says, "You have twenty-eight minutes! That's probably longer than most of the times you slept with them!" Her staff erupts in a reminder of the running video camera: "Katie!"

More money poured in, and Hill spent it almost precisely disproportionately to how she was advised. While most consultants pushed her toward television ads, she spent more on digital ones. "I invested a lot more in field than you normally do," she told me, convinced that her path to victory would be paved through young people and others who don't watch television but do share stuff they see on social media. Some financial supporters were turned off by the approach and held back money. "The normal DC crowd looks at your expenditures, and there is skepticism," she said. "They wanted to see higher numbers of cash on hand to spend on TV in the end. But I spent as we raised on digital because I was an unknown person, and I believed we needed to spend. People say to win you need to get low-propensity Democratic voters or you have to convince independents and moderate Republicans to vote for you. We thought we could do both. Also, I raised all my money at the end of the quarter. I feel like we conditioned our donors to have a sense of urgency."

The success of these efforts was largely invisible to the traditional race watchers. Katie Hill, like many female contenders that year, was often dismissed by reporters for spending time at small events with new and, often, younger voters and volunteers who energized the campaigns, or she was written off as no match for her male Republican opponent. "On a recent Friday afternoon, she was in Lancaster at a sparsely attended meeting of a high school political club, some of whose members were not old enough to cast a ballot," sniffed one reporter writing up her race. "Hill, for her part, is full of optimism," he went on to say. "'We're seeing the energy everywhere,' she said. Outside the Lancaster high school event, however, it was hard to ignore the desert silence, the empty parking lot, and the line of Knight campaign posters hanging defiantly on a fence across the street." (Note to future campaign reporters: Yard signs. Are. Not. Votes.)

The reporter failed to see that the zeitgeist was shifting, and that the polls—as they did during the 2016 presidential campaign—often failed to capture the shift. On Halloween, dressed in a zombie costume with full makeup, Hill stood with some staff in a Chili's in Stevenson Ranch as they all stared at a *New York Times* poll on someone's phone. The news was bad: she looked 4 points down, spelling an almost-certain defeat. Then a waitress came over and told Hill that her little sister loved her. "I said, 'See, we are going to win by ten.' My staff said, 'Katie, we are down by four points. That's within the margin of error. There is nothing that says we are going to win by ten.' But I said all along the turnout is going to be like nothing we have ever seen before. I felt completely sure that there was enthusiasm and that people who never felt like someone got them and gave them a voice were gonna show up."

When all was said and done, Hill annihilated Knight by more than twenty-one thousand votes. Or close to 10 points.

For young nonwhite progressives looking to get into public office, the most natural path is to challenge a more senior member in the primaries—also known as "primarying" them. Most of the time, this strategy fails. Incumbency is a powerful thing, and the Democratic machine that helps House candidates loathes insurgents; DCCC officials firmly believe that members of its party should target only Republicans. In fact, they sometimes actively seek to quash primary challengers by basically blacklisting them from consultants and other firms that work with candidates.

But there are others in the party, many of whom work on campaigns, who believe the only way to increase the number of women in the House is by picking off men in safe seats. This was the theory of the case for Ayanna Pressley in Massachusetts's Seventh District. The Pressley model represents one of many central conflicts roiling House Democrats: Do they protect their own, or do they let all comers, which almost inevitably means more women, bring the fight? The child of a single mother and a father who was in and out of prison, Pressley had attended Boston University in the 1990s but dropped out to help support her mother, a community activist. She eventually landed jobs with both Rep. Joseph P. Kennedy II and Senator John Kerry, and in 2009 she became the first woman of color to win a Boston City Council seat.

In 2018, there was not a lot of political light between Pressley and the Democratic incumbent, Rep. Michael Capuano, a popular progressive who had held the seat for almost two decades. Her task was to convince core suburban voters that it was simply time to mix things up in their increasingly diverse, economically mixed area, where, like in many liberal enclaves, they had become deeply frustrated with what they perceived as Washington Democrats' reluctance to steamroll Trump. Her slogan: "Change can't wait."

Voters in the district, which includes most of the city of Boston but also struggling areas like Pressley's hometown of Dorchester, with large Haitian, Latino, Chinese, and African communities, felt voiceless, and so she made heavy use of both shoe leather and social media, hammering home the notion of racial and economic justice. "We had two hundred fifty incarcerated black men organize families on the outside to get to the polls," Pressley said during an interview with me in DC. "I had been engaging them not for the purpose of their vote but the purpose of their voice." Like Katie Hill, she bypassed television ads, save for a few that ran on Telemundo and Univision, featuring community activists.

Unlike other challengers that year, Pressley was not an unknown, having served on the city council for years. Her self-assurance—she walks through a room and seems to dare someone to talk to her—height, booming oratory, and compelling life story seemed to be appealing to a wide range of voters. "I am an outsider insider," she explained to me. "I am not new. I spent sixteen years as an aide here, but I think of myself as an outsider because of what I carry in these spaces. What is the point of being a black woman who has the experiences I have and not bringing that to the table?" (In the 2019 off-year elections, seven of the Boston council's thirteen seats were won by Asian Americans, blacks, or Latinos, a path Pressley helped pave.)

Shortly after the election, I was chatting with a couple near the cheese plate after a Friday night service in a synagogue in Brookline, an upper-middle-class area of Boston and the birthplace of President John F. Kennedy. The couple had supported Capuano for years but had voted for Pressley, whose message "The people closest to the pain should be closest to the power" had beguiled them. "We just thought she was so exciting," the wife said.

Pressley's transparency and outreach paid off across class, age, and racial lines, which distinguishes her achievement from that of Ocasio-Cortez, to whom she is often compared but whose victory was delivered largely by young, white new voters in her district. "I was at a bar fairly late at night in downtown Boston with a girlfriend," Amy Pritchard, a consultant to Pressley's campaign, told me. "There was a group of firemen, a mixed group of young and old, and somehow her name came up. Two of the guys were big Trump guys, old-school, like every Boston movie you have ever seen. This one guy said, 'Fuckin' Ayanna is the most fuckin' ballsy woman I have known.' I realized in that moment that if older white guys were going to be for her in a city that is this racially charged, that was something I don't know would be captured in a poll."

Pressley took home 58.6 percent of the vote, crushing Capuano, who barely carried his hometown of Somerville. "It's not just good enough to see the Democrats back in power, but it matters who those Democrats are," Pressley said in her primary victory speech in an uncharacteristically soft voice, likely made so by aggressive last-minute campaigning. "Change can't wait."

When she arrived in Washington, DC, her first speech on the House floor would be to denounce Donald Trump—"the occupant of the White House" as she has insisted on calling him—over the ongoing government shutdown. "You devalue the life of the immigrant, the worker, and the survivor. I see right through you, and so do the American people," she said, and was mildly rebuked by the Speaker pro tempore, who admonished her in the typically fussy prose of *Robert's Rules of Order*, originally published in 1876 but still in use in Congress, to "refrain from engaging in personalities toward the president," a violation of the House's prohibition for casting personal aspersions.

Who cared? Not Pressley.

That day, hardly anyone was in the press gallery that overlooks the floor, and I watched from my own almost-empty row, but in the era of shared video, this didn't matter. The speech was viewed thousands of times. *Essence* magazine wrote it up.

This was the life of these brand-new freshmen, a group that in any other Congress would have been largely ignored by everyone outside their hometown papers and trade reporters following how the new members were voting in reference to the specific bills they were interested in. But the new freshmen barely seemed to realize their own anomaly.

The story of Rep. Jahana Hayes is also unusual. She was not one of the women watching her Republican congressman on TV that year, getting angry and gathering her friends around a table to figure out how to raise money and spark an insurgent campaign. She was asked to run for an open seat in Connecticut's Fifth Congressional District, and she said no. Senator Chris Murphy, a liberal gun-control activist, had held the seat, followed by another Democrat, Rep. Elizabeth Esty, who declined to run for reelection in 2018 after reports surfaced that she had protected a former chief of staff for months after discovering allegations that he had harassed and threatened a female coworker. While parts of the district are known for country clubs and second homes to rich New Yorkers, other areas have long suffered from gun violence and educational and other inequities that have left generations of residents living in the shadows of the state's elite colleges and universities and its bucolic waterfront towns. Murphy wanted to see the seat reflect the diversity of the district, which includes affluent towns like Kent as well as Wolcott, a blue-collar outpost where Hayes lives and where Trump had won big, and Waterbury, the embattled city where Hayes grew up—the largest city in the district.

For several years, Murphy had been following Hayes's career with interest. A onetime high school dropout, she had been named the National Teacher of the Year in 2016, and video of her enthusiastic clapping at the award ceremony with then-president Barack Obama had become its own meme. "You just need to settle down," the president joked as Hayes jumped up and down with joy. Murphy, seeing Hayes for the first time in person at the White House, watched with amusement but also awe. "I represented Waterbury for decades, and I had heard about this teacher," he told me. "I had a group of students who would come do big community-service projects. I remembered the stories I had heard about her. But I was just blown away by how powerful she was in person and onstage."

Hayes, who was raised by a drug-addicted mother who often found herself homeless, had given birth at seventeen and dropped out of school before pulling herself back, going to college, and earning a master's and two other advanced degrees. Murphy called her up and pushed her to run. Hayes was against the idea. She liked her job and was busy with the youngest of her four children. Raising money sounded awful, and she had no idea how to do it.

Murphy and his staff kept leaning on her, even though Mary Glassman, a long-time local politician who had twice run unsuccessfully for lieutenant governor, seemed to be embraced by the fairly solid Democratic district. Murphy was ready to have someone mount a challenge against a politician with ties to the state's Democratic apparatus. "I found it maddening in Connecticut how few young African Americans and Latinos are able to break into the political process even at the local and state level," he said. "I don't think you can talk about the importance of diversity in elected office if you are not willing to do something about it. It was time for our party to think about diversity at the highest levels."

It was the job Hayes was reluctant to leave that ultimately convinced her to run what would become a truncated campaign. Her particular brand of teaching relied on encouraging students to get involved in projects for Habitat for Humanity, Relay for Life, the American Cancer Society, and local community groups. And beyond encouraging a service orientation generally, Hayes had formed a club to get kids from compromised economic circumstances to do projects that would help them see that they too had the power to change other people's lives. For spring break one year, she took seventeen students from Waterbury to rebuild Habitat houses in California, which had been devastated by fires. Hammer in hand, Hayes had an epiphany: How could she tell kids, none of whom had parents who owned their own homes, to step up in spite of their circumstances if she would not step up herself? "When I saw these kids, I was like, "You don't get to do nothing," she later said in a speech. "So literally with a press release to my local newspaper, I declared that I was running for Congress."

She started her campaign just twelve days before Connecticut's Democratic convention. She had no experience. She had no money. She had no political favors to call in and no party ties, other than Murphy, a key ally who would find himself more than matched by the unblinking supporters of her opponent, including many far-left groups whose leaders struggled to explain why they were backing a previously failed middle-aged white candidate over an African American insurgent.

At the convention, Hayes won enough votes to qualify for the primary, but she did not get her party's endorsement. "I think for everybody it was so deflating," Murphy recalled. "She had it in her hands, and then it was taken away from her. Most of me expected she was going to hang it up and live to fight another day." Undaunted, Hayes pressed on. "The next day she called me to tell me she was going to go forward with the primary," Murphy said. "I will always remember this. She said, 'I don't know that I can do this, but what I do know is that I will never know if I don't try.'"

It was then that Hayes scored an underfunded and infrastructure-poor contemporary candidate's perfect kill: the viral campaign video. In it, Hayes embraced her own story, detailing her teen pregnancy and life with her grandmother while her mother battled addiction. "People are strong, but they aren't supposed to run for Congress," she said. "If Congress starts to look like us, no one can stop us."

Suddenly, new voters in Connecticut's Fifth District were fired up. Here came Students for Jahana. (She had a youthful campaign, she admitted, because it was all she could afford, and then was taken in by their enthusiasm.) Diverse crowds showed up to hear her speak. "Jahana just connected with people," Laura Maloney, Senator Chris Murphy's then–deputy communications director, told me, after having observed much of the campaign. "They liked her story. They wanted to listen to her. She screamed authenticity." Almost instantly, the video, produced for less than $20,000, yielded $300,000 in donations.

Hayes's efforts in her hometown turned out voters, too. "But the bigger story was new voters," Murphy said. "I went to my polling place at seven p.m. that night in Cheshire, where I live. Cheshire is ninety percent white and high-income. A worker I have seen for years was standing outside my polling place. He told me, 'Chris, I have been standing outside this polling place every election for twenty years, and I don't recognize anyone coming here today. These are not normal primary voters. Something is going on.'"

In a stunning turn of events, Hayes prevailed. She then took her strategy to her general-election fight with Manny Santos, a former mayor of Meriden and a veteran.

In 2016, Stacey Abrams, then the minority leader of the Georgia General Assembly, told me that Democrats needed to stop trying to convert Republicans and start mining their own party for voters who were simply not making it to the polls.

"This is a party that is comprised of what is being referred to as the new American majority," she said. "Those are progressive whites, people of color, and millennials. We have to focus our politics on turning out those voters."

This is just what Hayes did, repeatedly making the point that Congress needs to look more like the population that it's representing and focusing on such progressive measures as making college affordable, Medicare for all, and creating a pathway to citizenship for undocumented immigrants.

Like other women who ran that year, Hayes brushed off advice from Murphy and other Democrats. "I had people tell me, 'You have to quit your job,'" she said, noting that this was not going to be possible. She and her husband, a police officer, could not afford it, and she was not going to abandon her pupils. "So I worked during the day and did calls at night," she said. "It was the most foreign thing for people."

The habit has followed her into Congress, where she refuses to leave her committee hearings to go make calls to donors. "We have to force people to think differently," she told me. ("Call time" is the scourge of any member of the House, and the need for it begins literally the day after one is sworn in. The shortness of House terms—two years versus six in the Senate—and the endless troughs of cash that now flow through US politics make begging for more money a second full-time job for members. One particularly endangered incumbent, I was told, had not been to a committee hearing in months because he had spent his entire time at the DCCC, calling donors to help him get reelected.)

While the Connecticut district Hayes was seeking to win leaned Democratic, there were no guarantees. Some working-class areas had gone for Trump, and her opponent had pressed his support for the president. Joe Biden, campaigning in the state, gave Hayes a plug. Rep. Hakeem Jeffries (D-NY), who is on the short list of potential House Speakers post-Pelosi, joined her at a rally. National press chronicled Hayes's journey. Her opponent—who clung to Trump throughout the campaign—was outmatched. Hayes became the first African American woman from her state to win a seat.

But before Pressley and Hayes and a slew of other new victors, there was AOC, the OG of insurgent vanquishers. On a typically temperate night in Los Angeles in late June of 2018, I was standing in a green room at UCLA, arranging my colleague *New York Times* correspondent Maggie Haberman's hair. She was staring at her iPhone as she munched indifferently on a carrot from the catered vegetable tray. We were doing last-minute prep for a panel I had arranged with three other *Times* colleagues, Adam Nagourney, Nate Cohn, and Alex Burns, to talk about the upcoming midterm elections. It was around 10 p.m. back on the East Coast, and shocking news had just come across the transom. A young unknown bartender from the Bronx had just obliterated ten-term incumbent Joe Crowley in the Democratic primary in New York.

Trouble on the horizon for Crowley had been on few people's radar but his own, and he had tried to downplay it during his campaign to keep from tainting his future shot at a higher leadership spot among House Democrats. His challenger had failed to capture widespread media attention during her campaign, the result of her poor polling and intense competition for stories about challengers that year, and the *Times* would later be criticized for ignoring her.

So, to refresh, a then-twenty-eight-year-old self-identified democratic socialist had picked off one of the most powerful and senior Democrats in Congress, just as the party was poised to retake the House. My colleagues and I all cheerfully agreed we had some hot news to discuss on our panel.

By the next night, when we took our show to San Francisco, every Democrat in the United States knew the upsetter's name: Alexandria Ocasio-Cortez, soon to be simply AOC.

Ocasio-Cortez began her campaign an unknown idealist. Like Jahana Hayes, like Katie Hill, her breakout moment came via video, this one showing AOC riding the New York subway, her signature red lipstick a shock of chromaticity against the dreary backdrop of aging subway cars and the foreboding edifices of an unaffordable city streaming by. In lieu of the cheery "Let's work together, everybody" dispatches that used to be the stuff of campaign videos, Ocasio-Cortez instead offered a blunt narrative of her experience as a working-class minority, who, like the rest of her age cohort, grew up in an era of economic insecurity, encroaching late-stage capitalism, and a seemingly endless war. "Women like me aren't supposed to run for office," she says in the ad. "I was born in a place where your zip code determines your destiny." At one point, she struggles with her postcommute high heel, a sly nod to both working commuter ladies and her own undeniably stylish appearance. "Going into politics wasn't in the plan," she goes on, adding, "Who has New York been changing for?" Her final shot: "It's time we acknowledge that not all Democrats are the same." She had written the script herself, her staff said, and had picked some of the locations to shoot.

The video, which has now been viewed more than five million times, would be typical of the rest of Ocasio-Cortez's campaign and her first months in Congress, when social media would be her primary mode of talking to voters, reporters, colleagues, Republican hecklers, and her growing base of fans across the country who liked both her bold progressive policy ideas about climate change and the economy, and her straightforward delivery of that message, often offered with a side of pop culture. Like President Trump, AOC is unafraid to be unfiltered and even at times factually imprecise, minus the crass personal insults and typos. While previous female candidates tended to don power suits and trot out their health-care PowerPoints at political club meetings, she opted for posts on Twitter and Instagram, showing her shyness about campaign door knocking, her mascara application, and her drink mixing while throwing in casual but cogent chatter about prescription drugs costs and demands for a higher minimum wage.

"People look at her going to work in that video and they see themselves," Rep. Peter Welch, a progressive Democrat from Vermont, told me. "If I were to make a video that says, 'This is me, relate to me,' it wouldn't work and I wouldn't be comfortable with it." (He is bald, septuagenarian, and white.) "But she says things clearly," he went on. "She says there is a fiction up in government that we can't do hard things."

Ocasio-Cortez's biography was unusual for someone challenging a senior incumbent in Congress. Born into a working-class Puerto Rican family in the Bronx, she moved to nearby Yorktown in 1992 for access to its better schools. Known then as Sandy, she was studious and, by her own description, nerdy, though of the teenage rom-com variety, a pulchritudinous geek who came in second in the microbiology category of the Intel International Science and Engineering Fair, with a research project on the effect of antioxidants on the lifespan of the nematode *C. elegans*. After high school, she attended Boston University, majoring in economics and international relations. She also ran the university's Alianza Latina, a club focused on issues like student debt and economic inequality. Although after her election to Congress, AOC's Instagram discovery tour of the dank passageways of the Hill and the funny swag bag that all new members get were massive hits that seemed to come out of nowhere, the terrain was not actually so unfamiliar to her. During college, she had interned for Senator Ted Kennedy, working on his immigration portfolio.

Her father's death from lung cancer in 2008, during the depths of the national recession, was, she has often noted, a transformative event in her life, deeply paining her and sending her family into economic insecurity (he owned a small company and had not left his financial house in order), from which it would never fully emerge. After graduation, she returned to New York and started a small publishing venture through a local startup network, Sunshine Bronx Business Incubator, which charged some $195 per month for shared work space and business advice. "What Brook Avenue Press seeks to do is help develop and identify stories and literature in urban areas," the then-twenty-two-year-old said of her startup, which produced positive children's books set in the Bronx. "Rather than think of it as somewhere to run from, the Bronx is somewhere to invest," she told the *New York Daily News* the following year.

The entrepreneurial stage of her life—during which she advocated for tax breaks for small businesses—is not one that Ocasio-Cortez often touts, preferring to focus on her work as a community organizer, but it did win her honors from the

National Hispanic Institute, which named her its "social entrepreneur in residence."

From there, her work life became intensely millennial and
modern, and increasingly progressive, as she moved among a
flurry of community-organizing jobs for nonprofit groups, while
also helping her mother clean houses and taking on bartending
gigs to support her and her brother and to fend off foreclosure
of their Bronx home. She alternated between an Obamacare
health plan, with a huge deductible, and no insurance at all, and
was saddled with $25,000 of student loan debt.

Shortly after Trump's victory in 2016, Ocasio-Cortez took
two steps that would help define her political career. She and
some friends piled into a car to drive to North Dakota, where
she spent several weeks with indigenous activists fighting the
construction of an oil pipeline near the Standing Rock Indian
Reservation. "I felt so galvanized spiritually and morally by that
experience," she told me. "I felt ready to dedicate my whole self
to work on social change." She also labored as a field organizer
for Senator Bernie Sanders during his 2016 presidential campaign, and became steeped in the language of Medicare for All,
free college, a $15-per-hour minimum wage, and breaking up big
banks. This platform would prove instrumental in her own congressional campaign two years later, in which she advocated for
specific policy positions, unlike her opponent, the Democratic
incumbent, who ran largely on his anti-Trump credibility.

Three staff members from the Sanders campaign—Saikat
Chakrabarti, a Harvard grad who had worked on Wall Street
and in tech startups; Corbin Trent, a food truck operator from
Tennessee; and Alexandra Rojas, a community-college student
from California at the time—started a political action committee

called Brand New Congress in April 2016. "The original idea was to recruit four hundred people to run for Congress, all running together in a giant national campaign and with a single plan for economic rejuvenation and justice," Chakrabarti told me. "We were looking for people who really led, whether that was in the workplace or in their community, and who had had chances to sell out but didn't do it."

The notion was to try to harness the Bernie energy and recruit congressional candidates from both parties who could reflect the views of the working class. "When you saw Sanders run, there was this moment where we could radically shift what the dynamics of the conversation could look like," Rojas told me. "My generation will be less well off than my parents. I am seeing radical changes in our climate. I am seeing my rent skyrocketing. My experience is a lived one. I did not get to go to college and get a fancy Wall Street job, but there is an intuitive understanding that America can be so much more. We believe our country can rise to the occasion."

BNC solicits recommendations from the public. "We're looking for leaders who put people and policies before party loyalty—every time," its website says. Ocasio-Cortez's younger brother, Gabriel, sent in her name. "He let me know when he did it," AOC confirmed. "But I didn't think much about it. I thought, 'I am a waitress.'"

The PAC received about eleven thousand nominations and dispatched a team of volunteers to research different districts in search of local community leaders: maybe a county teacher of the year who had bucked the system, or a water-plant worker who had blown the whistle on contamination. Team members would then call them up and ask if they would run. Of the fifteen candidates they recruited this way, AOC—the only one who would win—was of instant and special interest, said Rojas. "She was this superclear, incredibly talented communicator on issues we really cared about."

Ocasio-Cortez was suddenly a candidate for New York's Fourteenth Congressional District, which includes the eastern part of the Bronx and portions of north-central Queens. "We are in a movement moment," Rojas said, "which is why people like AOC, who look like us and are one of us, can succeed."

While BNC's political theory was meant to apply specifically to working-class, largely nonwhite candidates and voters, it would prove to have broader appeal—among young voters across the demographic spectrum who were feeling priced out of life, and voters with more privilege who themselves were on the rising edge of gentrification in formerly poor and working-class hubs. Similarly, the younger candidates were more inclined than the moderates who preceded them even ten years earlier to embrace some more progressive positions as a treatment plan for generational inequality.

Katie Hill put it pretty simply. "You have a younger generation that has come into power. That is why you are seeing this stuff," she told me over a glass of wine in a Capitol Hill happy-hour chardonnay mill one summer night. "Overwhelmingly, most of us don't have political backgrounds. We were mobilized because we realized things are fucked-up."

Eventually, the three founders of Brand New Congress went off to form Justice Democrats, with no more pretense at bipartisanship. Instead, steeped in Sanders-heavy policy platforms, the new PAC focused on getting progressive Democrats to take on incumbents across the country and, ultimately, to transform the

party into something that would be, in some sense, the political analog of the modern Republican Party, which had been
transformed by the Tea Party movement that began during
the Obama administration and was fully realized by Donald
Trump—more partisan, more confrontational, and uninterested
in compromise, preferring instead to lean into the policy positions of its base.

In AOC, the group found its perfect candidate. Ocasio-Cortez
quit her bartending gig at Flats Fix in February 2018 to run. "It
was a leap of faith," she said as she gazed at a television behind
us in a hallway where daytime talking heads were debating the
rights of sex workers in her city. "I felt ready for this. It felt like,
'Why not?'"

Her campaign was certainly scrappy and shoestring: she
refused corporate money and shunned groups like EMILY's
List, which, one of its staff members told me, "she wrote off
as an old-white-lady organization." But it was not without an
institutional framework. Justice Democrats provided a policy
vision and unusually talented and well-connected volunteers
and staff members who had cut their teeth on a federal campaign. Chakrabarti moved back to New York to become Ocasio-
Cortez's co–campaign manager, working with her on media
training and brushing up her policy positions. (He went on to
become her chief of staff, until his resignation in August 2019.)

Corbin Trent said Chakrabarti called him in February of 2018
and begged him for help. "He said they saw something special
there, but I would have to come to New York," Trent told me. He
abandoned his food-truck business and left his wife and two little
kids back in Tennessee to run communications, and moved in
with Chakrabarti in the West Village, where he slept on the couch.

("If you're going to sleep on a couch," he said, "the West Village is the place to do it.") Trent was responsible for securing a lot of the press hits and endorsements that built up AOC's momentum, including an endorsement from Rep. Ro Khanna (D-CA), a liberal congressman who had already put his name behind her opponent, and later, a glowing profile in *Vogue* and with the *Intercept*. Meanwhile, Alexandra Rojas harnessed her considerable organizing know-how from her Sanders days to run the campaign's phone banking and its all-important text-messaging effort.

A group of fundraising volunteers from across the country eventually descended on Queens and the Bronx like stealth army ants, focused on victory, all while Congressman Crowley repeatedly insisted to senior Democrats and campaign officials that there was nothing to see. He even skipped a planned debate, sending a well-meaning but feckless surrogate in his stead, misjudging Ocasio-Cortez's threat to his incumbency despite the impressive number of signatures she received to get on the ballot.

While her campaign materials were put together on a small budget, they were polished and chic, and she drew from the city's creative community for a digitally native campaign. One of her earliest supporters was Jake DeGroot, a lighting designer and activist who signed on to her campaign as digital-organizing director. AOC's poster, inspired by the Cesar Chavez–era United Farm Workers of the 1960s, framed Ocasio-Cortez as a tough but glamorous working-class underdog. Only on the last day of the race did Democratic establishment officials in Washington begin to sound alarms. Too late: the massive turnout operation that materialized on primary day was for the challenger, not for Crowley.

"We had volunteers in every single polling location in the district," Rojas recalled. "There were people from Iowa, people from Australia and California, who flew in to help us get out the vote. At three p.m., I was like, 'There are so many people here!'"

Trent had been less sanguine. Again, as in so many races that depended on voters who often don't come out for primaries, polls had undercounted who was going to show up. An internal poll taken by the AOC campaign a little over a month before primary day showed Ocasio-Cortez down 35 percentage points. "We had no idea whatsoever that we were going to win, and anyone who says they did is totally full of shit," Trent said, because for Justice Democrats, losing was a way of life. "We had spent the last two years of our fucking lives facing loss after loss after loss."

His wife and children had joined him in a pool hall to watch returns. But as he waited for inevitable defeat, the numbers came pouring in, all of them good. Ocasio-Cortez had not just won, but won decisively. "For like twenty minutes, it was the most amazing feeling I have ever had," Trent said. "It's a great moment for a field operator, because their work is done. But I was the comms guy, so my job had just begun." The press was so unprepared for AOC's victory, he said, that reporters did live shots from Mitt Romney's headquarters in Utah, where he had just won his Senate primary.

The calls never stopped. "This is everything we had hoped for," Rojas told me. "But I don't think anyone could have expected the earthquake we saw with her race." Her victory that June night sealed Ocasio-Cortez's seat in Congress; a Republican challenger had zero shot in a heavily Democratic district in New York City. For her defeated opponent's part, although he had just been more or less nationally humiliated, Crowley seemed to take the loss with cheer. After thanking his supporters at his (non)reelection party, he picked up a guitar and announced,

"This is for Alexandria Ocasio-Cortez," and launched into a not-all-that-bad rendition of "Born to Run."

But in July, there began a short interregnum of unpleasantness. Revealing both her future Twitter trigger finger against opponents and her underrated political instincts, Ocasio-Cortez accused her defeated opponent of trying to stay in the race by refusing to remove his name from the Working Families Party line on the ballot for the general election. ".@repjoecrowley stated on live TV that he would absolutely support my candidacy," she tweeted. "Instead, he's stood me up for all 3 scheduled concession calls. Now, he's mounting a 3rd party challenge against me and the Democratic Party."

Crowley attributed the lack of call to her staff failing to follow up (believable to anyone who has tried to reach them) and said he had no intention of challenging her. But no matter what had led up to it, her tweet was a shrewd way for Ocasio-Cortez to gin up her base of small donors. And the conflict, a notably elbows-out move for a victor in a noncompetitive race, eventually melted like so much soft serve on a hot summer Bronx sidewalk as Crowley advanced to the work of cannabis lobbying back in the swamp he had just been expelled from.

Ocasio-Cortez's outsized presence in the 116th Congress would soon force the party to confront its future writ large. Would the party focus on pulling in independent and disenchanted Republican voters with incremental policy propositions and traditional campaign mores? Or would it jettison that plan by focusing on younger and more liberal voters, and the vast array of other Americans who had previously been turned off by politics, with policy notions rooted in more socialist terrain? Could congressional Democrats pick and choose between these menus without the progressive left threatening them with primary fights or the conservative wing dragging down their ambitions? Speaker Pelosi repeatedly attempted to tamp down the narrative of this tension, but that would soon prove impossible.

During orientation week, as the incoming freshmen milled about the Capitol, I saw Ocasio-Cortez slipping by a group of reporters to canter up a flight of stairs. "Congresswoman-elect? Congresswoman-elect!" I called to her while speeding to catch up. She did not turn around. I was surprised and a tad confused.

I soon realized she had no idea I was talking to her, likely because no one had yet called her by that title.

When I finally caught up to her on the stairs, she turned around—perhaps wary of my stalker-like presence—and she finally stopped and smiled politely. Her eyes widened as I asked her what her favorite moment had been so far. "I was in a room with John Lewis and Maxine Waters today," she said, slightly out of breath. "It dawned on me then. They're real. They are human, and I am in the same room with them. It adds a dimensionality I could have never imagined." Then she turned on her high heel and was gone.

THREE

Now What?

If I waited my turn, I wouldn't be here.
—Rep. Jahana Hayes (D-CT)

AFTER GRUELING CAMPAIGNS, victory speeches in low-end hotel ballrooms, and a flurry of local news appearances, the triumphant class of incoming freshmen was ready to stride into Washington and do something big. In their collective imagination, they would sit in their offices writing robust bills to roll back years of Republican tax cuts, torch some Trump administration officials in oversight hearings, and hash out public policy over Chinese food with their new colleagues. They would form alliances with some key Republicans! They would visit the Kennedy Center! They'd guarantee health care for all!

What they found, however, was a sprawling Capitol complex of office buildings and basement byways they could barely navigate, a dizzying freshman orientation dominated by elections for leadership positions they had never even heard of, and the federal government in the middle of what would become the longest shutdown in US history. Republicans, when the freshman

Democrats even saw them, had largely no interest in working with them. And dinner? That would likely be hummus and baby carrots at one of scores of receptions they were required to go to, at places like Sonoma, a wine bar near the Capitol, with groups eager to curry favor with the new lawmakers. "You know what it's like on the first day of high school when you show up and you don't know what's going on but everyone pretends they do?" new congresswoman Sharice Davids said to me. "That is what it was like."

Angie Craig arrived at the Capitol for the new-members reception, giddy with her good fortune, her wife, Cheryl Greene, in tow. But unbeknownst to them, their taxi dropped them on the Senate side of the campus, far from the House. Craig cheerfully asked a Capitol Police officer where she could find the welcome party. She was directed to the Lyndon B. Johnson Room, where a reception was well underway amid the glorious marble walls and period window cornices. She and Greene sashayed in, only to smack directly into Senate Majority Leader Mitch McConnell (R-KY). Oops. This was a reception for Senate members and their spouses. "I had to pretend I was there to see Amy," she said, referring to Amy Klobuchar, from her home state of Minnesota. "I walked over and whispered to her," and the senator discreetly directed her to the other side of the building.

There is no instruction manual for being a member of Congress. The rules are, basically, there are no rules. Are you going to spend your money on as many full-paid staff members as possible or pay more money to fewer? Will you read every press release before it goes out, delegate that task completely, or do something somewhere in between? How many televisions should you have in your office, and what station will they be on? How many weekly meetings will you have, and who will attend them?

"We're basically a small business," Donna Shalala, at seventy-eight the oldest woman ever to be elected to the House, told me. She held several executive-levels jobs before making the somewhat curious decision to run for office. "We control our own salaries and set our own standards. We don't even have human resources. Members of Congress want to be able to hire and fire at will. And they do."

Most new members seem to be surprised by this, as if the secrets of the job will somehow be revealed in the intervening weeks between their election and starting the job. Nope. "Orientation was pretty content-free," Rep. Chrissy Houlahan (D-PA) told me. She is the first woman ever to be elected from her district, which she describes as "a complicated and eclectic purple place, which makes it critical to the national map."

"It is literally where the red meets the blue in Pennsylvania," she said. "In the east, there are affluent suburbs along the collar of Philadelphia. As you go westward, it transitions to rolling farmland, home to the mushroom capital of the world, and many dairy farmers." She traversed the halls of Congress with her face pinched in what appears to be moderate terror. "They told us, 'Here is your health insurance, here is how you get paid.' Well, I could have figured that part out. I could have used more information about how you actually are a congressperson. How do you vote? How do you do a committee?"

Chrissy Houlahan—a US Air Force veteran with a Stanford engineering degree, who worked for several startups before becoming a teacher in North Philadelphia—is an example of the type of highly accomplished woman who won in 2018. She was inspired to run, she said, after Donald Trump won the presidency, because she feared for her father, a Holocaust survivor, and her lesbian daughter.

She soon began to wonder, however, as many of her colleagues did, whether she could accomplish more in her old job than she could being one of 535 members of a fairly dysfunctional institution. "I do feel so isolated as a member of Congress sitting in an office," she said, glancing around at her government-issue furniture in a room bathed in wan winter light. "I am used to startups, and working on top of everybody." But Houlahan recalled that just before she got to Washington, a wealthy donor in her nineties had taken her to the snazzy Pyramid Club in Philadelphia, with a plea to help build a more female Congress. "She said, 'You have to promise me you won't leave until there are more of you.'" Houlahan paused. "I am hopeful that I don't become jaded. I want to remember what a privilege it is to be here."

The animating force for the incoming freshman class, though its members did not know it yet, would be the battle to define the future of the party, embodied, eventually, in the 2020 race for the White House. That struggle began with a fight over the political future of Nancy Pelosi. Pelosi was, of course, the first female Speaker, who has lived for years under perpetual layers of myths and stereotypes, from the left and right, concerning her personal politics and leadership style. The truth about Pelosi is that in spite of the rhetoric, she is politically practical, to the extent that some of the constituents of her San Francisco district occasionally take to protesting outside her office as if she were conservative politician Sarah Palin. She is also an excellent bludgeon against her Republican colleagues, as many long gone from the Hill admit with grudging respect.

On one thing most can agree: Pelosi's ability to manage her fellow Democrats has had few modern rivals. Although dismissed by many on the left as too cautious and overly wedded to the institutional traditions of Washington, it was Pelosi who almost singlehandedly maneuvered among them to bring the Affordable Care Act to life in 2010, rather than the small-ball bill to increase health care for children that Rahm Emanuel, Obama's skittish White House chief of staff, had wanted. Pelosi also delivered President George W. Bush his Wall Street bailout in 2008, showing not only her ideological dexterity but her iron-fisted control of the Speaker's gavel.

Her dexterity (it should be noted that this is a woman who occasionally eats her beloved Dove ice-cream bars with a knife and fork) is matched only by her remarkable skills of self-preservation, even after years of calls from some corners of her own party that she go away. In 2018, Pelosi was seen by many Democrats as a political liability who needed to be replaced. Scores of freshmen had suggested during their campaigns that they would vote against her for Speaker, denouncing her as basically an anachronistic incrementalist who had been insufficiently resistant to the Trump administration.

Pelosi showed up in January 2019 seemingly many votes shy of the job. Most of those who opposed her—both old and new members—hailed from Republican-heavy districts where Pelosi was unpopular. Others, like Rashida Tlaib, who told a *New York Times* reporter, "Trump got elected on her watch," were agitating for generational change.

One ally, Rep. Gerald Connolly (D-VA), frostily and publicly chastised his colleagues for launching a leadership challenge after a record-breaking year for female Democrats, crediting

Pelosi with their victories. "The first thing we do is we thank
that architect who happens to be the only woman speaker in the
history of this body?" he said. "We don't even give her a gold
watch, just 'thank you for your service and get out'?"

Pelosi, unlike her two Republican successors, John Boehner
and Paul Ryan, understood how to bend members' wills to her
needs, through a complex web of cajoling, making offers that
could not be refused, and sheer charm, and by pushing her hundreds of allies to do her bidding. Jon Soltz, the cofounder and
chair of VoteVets.org, a liberal organization, got a call from
Pelosi around this time. She had worked hard with veterans'
groups to get veterans and other service members elected, and
was not keen on any of them signing a letter written by Rep. Seth
Moulton (D-MA), also a veteran, pledging to vote against her.
She hosted a breakfast for incoming freshman veterans, where
she gently made the point that she had spent a lot of money
on their races and that they had helped take back the House.
"Pelosi and her allies probably spent thirty million dollars on
veterans," Soltz said. "It wasn't a secret that I told people, 'Hey
it's best to take a knee right now before you get into a situation
with Nancy Pelosi that you can't win.'"

Also unlike Ryan and Boehner, who did not have the
patience or wherewithal for such intense member management,
Pelosi met individually with every single freshman as well as
potential senior opponents, reading their needs, making promises, and cutting deals. There were big jobs on committees to
dole out, and issues that matter most for members to champion; she defused one member's opposition by promising to
push for his bill that would allow people to buy into Medicare
well before retirement age. She also agreed to not serve a day

past four years if elected Speaker one last time. It wasn't that generous an offer—after all, she would be eighty-two by the time of her promised exit—but it bound the other members of her largely aged leadership team to her two-term limit, a gesture greatly appreciated by Democrats thirsting for a changing of the guard.

When carrots were not useful, there were sticks, some of them the size of a redwood branch, often delivered in a way that reflected Pelosi's hardscrabble Baltimore political roots more than her genteel San Francisco neighborhood and demure day suits. When Rep. Marcia Fudge (D-OH) mulled a challenge to Pelosi for the gavel, reports suddenly materialized noting that in 2015 Fudge had sent a letter of support for a former Ohio judge, Lance Mason, after he admitted to beating his wife in 2014. (By the time the letter was reported—which Pelosi's office repeatedly said it had nothing to do with—he had been convicted of his wife's murder.) Pelosi also announced that as Speaker, she would appoint Fudge the new chair of the reinstated Subcommittee on Elections, which oversees voting rights issues, minutes before Fudge announced she would no longer seek to challenge her.

Votes were accruing, but freshmen were needed. Rep. Veronica Escobar (D-TX) and I were having a cup of coffee near the Capitol the day before she was sworn in, and her mood was nothing short of ebullient. The government was shut down and the party was in a tangle over its leadership slate, but Escobar had won the seat just vacated by soon-to-be Democratic presidential candidate Beto O'Rourke, and she imagined a quilt of favorable circumstances spread out before her. As one of the first two Hispanic women from Texas ever to serve in the House, Escobar saw herself as a potentially important new voice at the border, and specifically in El Paso, where Trump had been threatening to build a wall.

Endlessly effervescent (the only time I saw her grimace in those early days was during a Judiciary Committee hearing when a Republican member from Florida accused immigrants of being criminals) and startlingly optimistic, Escobar reflected on the last big class of freshmen to roll into town, eighty-seven Republicans in 2011. "I think we have the opportunity to do some of the same things," she said. "But they were a wrecking ball. It's a lot easier to tear something down than build something. I think we have to rebuild democracy. It's been eroded."

Her cell phone rang, and it was Pelosi, whom Escobar had decided to support in her bid for Speaker, even as some freshmen continued to suggest they would look elsewhere for leadership. "Leader, how are you?" Escobar said, clearly thrilled. Pelosi asked if she would be one of three freshman women to give speeches supporting her nomination for Speaker of the House. "That would be the honor of a lifetime!" Escobar told her.

The next morning, I caught up with Escobar after her nominating speech before a giant crowd of her colleagues in a large hearing room on the Hill. "I started crying," she admitted as she leaned near a bust of Nicholas Longworth, a onetime Speaker of the House. "I never get nervous before speeches, but these are people I respect and admire. It was intimidating. My heart was pounding. I feel grateful that she has identified me as an ally."

All told, a mere fifteen of the scores of Democrats who had suggested they were gunning for fresh leadership actually voted against Pelosi. Tlaib? She voted for Pelosi (for the "future of our children," she said). Ditto for Ocasio-Cortez, who had also once suggested she would not automatically be giving Pelosi the nod.

So much for the insurrection, especially from the progressive left; indeed, they became the cornerstone of her Speaker reelection. Still, it had been a difficult few weeks for Pelosi, and it was hard not to feel that the fight had diminished her. She had won, but only through what had amounted to high-stakes groveling, often before people a third her age.

The rest of the country had marveled at her December 2018 takedown of Trump in the Oval Office live on television before strutting out into the street in her burnt-orange Max Mara coat. Early in the new Congress, as Pelosi appeared to unmoor the pugilistic president again, many would come to view their choice as profound and prescient, further emphasized when she held out for the right moment to begin impeachment processes against him. But Pelosi and her team had to understand the price tag on her power. The next generation had its foot firmly in the door.

Speaker of the House is a job that most Americans vaguely understand, but there are other leadership positions throughout Congress, and the majority of freshmen are not aware of the bevy of these positions they will be voting on, nor are they always familiar with the colleagues they will be asked to vote for, or against. There is the whip, who counts the votes and pressures members to fulfill the Speaker's wishes, and the caucus chair, who tries to communicate the party's message to other members and the press, as well as various other leadership and political positions. "That was unexpected for me," Rashida Tlaib told me a week after orientation. "You're thinking about hitting the ground running, and instead there are these layers and elections and processes. I didn't expect that much competition even for freshman class president. It was never-ending and overwhelming to keep track of who was running."

Tlaib, the oldest of fourteen children of Palestinian immigrants, was a longtime community activist and onetime state legislator from Detroit, perhaps best known for having been escorted, yelling, from the Cobo Center by security for heckling Donald Trump during a speech in August 2016, when he was his party's presidential nominee. She continued to lead rallies right after being elected, still in the trenches of street political warfare. "Rashida has a totally different political background from most people here," Rep. Debbie Dingell told me. The senior member from Tlaib's home state has known the freshman for twenty-five years. "She has the courage to jump over a fence to say what she is thinking."

Mercurial and prone to tears, especially during emotional speeches about her family, Tlaib would float down the hall to vote one day, smiling and laughing, and scowl at all comers the next. While an early and persistent proponent of impeachment, she spent most of her first days in Congress focused on local issues, like Michigan's high car-insurance costs, and making big changes to her district offices to provide more services to her largely poor constituents. During the orientation sessions with freshmen, Tlaib was expecting long discussions about ethical landmines and cybersecurity concerns. Instead, she told me, "I could not believe that the number one question that came from the audience members was about sexual harassment." Only when it was explained that each office would be responsible for any misconduct there did many members seem to wake up, she said. "The accountability shit is when the hands went up."

Having defeated better-known, better-funded incumbents, many of the freshman women felt a deep confidence when they arrived to govern. But once in Washington, primed to change it, they found Washington eager to intercede. Exhausted by the campaign, Lauren Underwood had hoped to take some time off and regroup with her family. Her first taste of DC came from party leaders: No way, they said. There was orientation, management seminars, staff to hire, an apartment to find. There would be no rest.

Underwood was instantly bathed in a state of grievance. "I did not fully appreciate the dysfunction in our own caucus," she said. "It permeates the place. We freshmen were unilaterally boxed out of all the key committee assignments. Health care was the single issue in my race—well, that and the chaos—but then we get to freshman orientation and *no one mentioned health care*!" Recovering from a cold, I began to cough incessantly, but Underwood, undaunted and voice rising, went on. "I thought, 'Let's review why we won,'" she said. "Was it to enjoy the benefits of being in the majority? I thought there would be at least a conversation."

There was more. Offices were underfunded. Underwood felt pressures to pay interns, a noble goal, she conceded, but one that would cost her precious resources. She felt scrutinized for not having more black staff members. She saw her colleagues in mixed districts like hers "already running again," by taking conservative positions that undermined the Democrats' agenda, but she also saw those in safe districts needlessly fretting about their place in the pecking order on the Hill. "There is such a top-down approach," she said. "As freshmen, our strength is in our numbers. A lot of our people are straight-up stars at home, and yet they are so worried about their reelection. I had a very long policy wish list when I got here, including equal pay, health care, reducing gun violence in a meaningful way."

Like freshmen of both parties who arrive with dreams of legislating aboard a speedboat, she found she had arrived to meet a glacier instead. A senior aide to Democratic leaders told me that Underwood was simply impatient. Too many freshmen had arrived, the aide said, not understanding, for instance, the painstaking way that bills go from notions to carefully vetted pieces of legislation, and from subcommittee to committee to the House floor.

When I suggested this to Underwood, she raised a bullshit-detecting eye at the diagnosis, noting that many bills had been precooked by the leaders before the new Congress even commenced and were handed out one by one to some of the freshmen to "own" for quick victories up front to boast about back home. "We could have gone so much bigger," she said. "It was really a missed opportunity."

At times, Underwood can seem a bit like a serious student who refuses to go to football games or parties, preferring extra-credit homework and the Sunday crossword puzzle while swathed in a flannel bedtime ensemble. She declined to join the ideological caucuses, such as the Progressive Caucus (most progressive liberals) or the New Democrat Coalition (most moderates), where members tend to find cosponsors for their bills, discuss policy agendas, and make buddies. "It probably hurts me," she said. "But I don't fit neatly in any of those boxes. I don't want to be defined by those. As a result, I sort of have my toe in all these different areas: making sure our economy grows, farmers are taken care of, not screwed by the president in trade wars."

Her conservative dresses and perpetual smile often seem to be barely masking underlying irritation—with colleagues, hearing witnesses, sometimes maybe with journalists like me. Unlike the majority of other House members, she also does not fill her nights with receptions, which are networking opportunities or a chance to do something fun, like eat cheese at the French embassy. "I would say my approach is that we were given two years to do something impactful," she said. "I worry about our ability to do that. I don't know if we were given the complete set of tools. Or maybe I haven't found a way to maximize the tools to be successful."

Six weeks into the new Congress, Underwood held a town hall meeting in Sycamore, Illinois, ninety miles from the Iowa border. About 150 people had gathered in the high school auditorium there, and the new congresswoman sat in a classroom powdering her face, touching up her lipstick, and adjusting her own microphone. "We had a lot of antiabortion protesters yesterday," she told me then, hoping that tonight's meeting would draw a less conservative cohort. She knew she was under constant and clear fire. Only a few months into her term, she had three Republican opponents for 2020. She smoothed her sparkling jacket. Show time.

To every question posed—concerning gender pay disparity, the conflicts in Afghanistan, Syria, and Yemen, the Trump administration's family separation policies at the US-Mexico border (hugely unpopular in this family-oriented semirural community), opioids, climate change—she would answer, "Thank you for your question," then offer a careful and informed response. Her parents, who have attended the majority of her town hall meetings, drove her home.

Like all the black Democrats who won majority-white districts in 2018, Underwood seamlessly glides between the white working-, middle-, and upper-class spheres of her district and the power corridors of Washington, while remaining emphatically tied to black American culture and concerns. She stays in close contact with Alpha Kappa Alpha, her historically black sorority, and made the formation of a working group on black maternal health a top priority; an African American college friend of hers had died from complications related to childbirth. "I was standing at the press conference trying not to cry," the generally poker-faced congresswoman said, describing the news conference to announce the new Black Maternal Health Caucus. She added: "We did this because women are dying every day, and I am the first and only young black woman who has ever been here. It actually has negative political ramifications in my district. I accept that, and I will take that risk."

Underwood would quickly evolve into one of the most legislatively productive members of the freshman women, flying forty thousand feet above the enduring controversies and keeping her pen to pad, at times taxing her staff. Horrified by conditions at the border, she had her subordinates clear her calendar so she could draft legislation herself, which they were skeptical could be accomplished, to address sanitary conditions for children. Her legislation to protect children and domestic-abuse victims and her various health-care provisions and measures to help farmers were largely successful, impressing House leaders. They eyed her as a clearly rising star, if she could manage to stay in office.

The new majority in many ways reflects the political and cultural passage of time over the near decade since the party last controlled the House. Ten years earlier, there was a sizable contingent of Democrats opposed to abortion; now their numbers have been thinned to almost nothing as abortion rights has become a litmus test for both parties. Not long ago, support for gay marriage was an outlying position. Now, Democrats of every religious and geographic background advocate for gay rights. While views on gun rights still span an ideological arc, few are the Democrats who do not support more stringent background checks for gun buyers and new rules to allow law enforcement to confiscate weapons from those deemed a threat to themselves and others.

The incoming group was, however, heterogeneous when it came to matters of national security, foreign policy, immigration, and fiscal matters, and were generally divided on the best way forward on health care. But many Democrats who had just won Republican districts were terrified of voting against measures, even those offered by Republicans, that they thought might make their more conservative voters back home turn against them. This reluctance created an immediate and consequential wedge among the freshmen.

"What's been a big surprise and disappointment is how much fear people are operating with here," Katie Hill told me early on in a hallway between meetings, her blond bangs hanging in her eyes. "I'm not here to win reelection. I am here to do what I said I am going to do, and I am trying to set an example with taking risks." This would be a theme among freshmen from tough districts for Democrats. Every minute someone stays in Congress generally makes them long for another, but many of these new congresswomen had left decent day jobs. Losing might not have been their greatest fear.

Hill, a social progressive who has also fashioned herself a pragmatist eager to cut legislative deals with Republicans, the daughter of a cop and a nurse, a gun owner and a married bisexual, a dog *and* goat owner, a girl-next-door athlete who brags about her "resting bitch face," manages to seem less shape-shifter than simply a contemporary unfiltered product of her district on the northern edge of Los Angeles County. She was elected by her peers to be a leader of the class. This role, and her outspoken nature, also made Hill an early go-to for the news shows. "I go on Fox and I go on MSNBC and say the same things, and they both think I am with them," she said with a shrug. She also plays pickup basketball games on Monday night. One week she was the only woman. "And one guy was the only Republican," she said.

Katie Hill was an instant favorite of Nancy Pelosi, who liked her cheerful confidence and favored her laser-like questions in meetings about how to better market Democrats' ideas. How, Hill wondered, could freshmen let people back home know the goodies they got for them in appropriations bills? How were they supposed to talk about a potential pay raise for House members? Pelosi made her vice chair of the House Committee on Oversight and Reform, where Trump officials were expected to traipse through for questioning and chastening by the venerable Rep. Elijah Cummings (D-MD).

"I mean, WTF," Hill said with no small amount of awe as we chatted in a hallway off the floor of the House between votes. "I feel like, 'Wow, is this my life?'"

At the same time, she was quickly disenchanted by many of her colleagues, whose refusal to stop campaigning seemed to be getting in the way of some of the policy making she had hoped for. Republicans, short of tools in their newfound minority, would toss procedural measures known as "motions to recommit" on the floor to trip up Democrats. These measures, tacked on to bills at the very last minute, are full of inflammatory language meant to embarrass or shame people who wind up voting for what is otherwise a bill they support. But some new Democrats from Republican districts feared that voting against measures that called for things like denouncing anti-Semitism or curbing gun rights for illegal immigrants would hurt them back home, and so, imagining an easily cut thirty-second attack ad in the coming election season, they gave the measures a nod, at times giving Republicans victories on the floor, to the horror of Pelosi and other Democrats.

Hill had the Speaker's back on this. She would eventually be given the assignment to stand on the House floor and speak against a Republican motion that would have prevented transgender kids from participating in some school sports. It had been tacked on to a bill to extend long-standing federal antidiscrimination protections to LGBTQ Americans. In a fiery retort in the spirit of a much more seasoned colleague, Hill excoriated the amendment and addressed Republicans: "You, my colleagues, are on the wrong side of history," she said, "and we will be waiting for you on the other side."

Among her more moderate colleagues, not everyone was charmed by Hill's leadership. They worried she was too close to Pelosi to properly represent their interests. They were not sure their side of the story on these pesky motions to recommit was getting full consideration, or that she fully understood the challenges of districts where there were simply a limited number of Democratic voters. But many other members, and their young staff, were taken with Hill's fresh and casual manner—she met in the kitchen of a gun-control advocate, her sockless feet tucked under her on a stool—and the progressives loved her advocacy that they thought pushed back against some of the older leaders.

Katie Hill and Lauren Underwood were both candid and at times biting about their own whirlwind rides to the Capitol. Hill is the occasionally potty-mouthed, somewhat messy Oscar-ette to Underwood's preppy midwestern Felix-ette, a modern twist on the classic TV show *The Odd Couple*. Underwood once became flustered and apologized to staff members with whom she was stuffing envelopes while listening to Beyoncé, for a patch of R-rated lyrics; Hill's sex life would soon become part of the sometimes-messy narrative of her class.

In some sort of one-day-to-be-unraveled metaphor, the room-mates arrived in Washington and remained bedless for weeks. Hill's bed was delivered not once but twice to her California home. Underwood bought a bed on sale at Crate & Barrel before leaving Illinois, but the mattress slats arrived too short. Then came new slats that were too long. As she contemplated where to get a hacksaw (I mentioned to her they actually make furniture in the House, but she quickly pointed out that asking Capitol workers for said saw would be a potential ethics viola-tion), she slept on an air mattress on the kitchen floor. "So at eleven o'clock at night, we connect in our pajamas," Underwood told me. "And this is what we are."

For many of the new women, the thrill of victory was slowly being overtaken by the reality of the new job, both in its time-draining details and in the limits of their star power and nov-elty back home. The first time I met with Jahana Hayes, a few months into the new Congress, she was dressed in a Connecticut-neat yellow shift dress and matching cardigan. She settled into a comfy chair in her office and heaved a sigh, as if already exhausted by the week, the job, and me. Her outer office was filled with books about tennis, leadership, and black Americans in Congress. A map of Waterbury hung on the wall. She talked to me about the shocks of her entry into the DC world. It was hard, she said, after months of struggling to stand on a stage as a winner and a young, diverse majority maker, to find herself now subordinate to a group of septuagenarians who had failed to take back the House for nearly a decade and yet were calling all the shots. Minority women were left feeling isolated, their experiences back home with voters dismissed.

"There's this idea that you worked really hard to get here, and you're still trying to prove you belong here," Hayes said, sinking deeper into her chair. "Minority women ran very different elections. We engaged with a very different group. Then you get here, and it's like, 'Trust us— this is the way it's done. We appreciate you being here. Now, you need to change everything you did to get here.'"

Why, for instance, for every press conference, she wondered, do they have to line up by seniority, indicated by a number on the back of their member pin? Why was the length of term, rather than the difficulty of the race or the number of new voters brought to the polls, the measure of success and entitlement? And why, Hayes asked, was the Democratic leadership trying to prevent younger, insurgent members from joining their ranks?

It may come as a surprise, but House Democrats are more bound to tradition than Republicans. Under GOP control, committee chairmen (and they *were* virtually all men) were term-limited, guaranteeing fresh opportunities and frequent fights for supremacy. Democrats have stuck doggedly to the seniority system, largely because senior members are loath to jeopardize their primacy on committees. But that fealty to experience has consequences.

Before the class of 2019 was even sworn in, a fight had broken out over potential primary challenges to sitting members in 2020. Alexandria Ocasio-Cortez's bold pickoff of Joe Crowley was an inspiration to other young hopefuls across the country who wanted to take on the old guard. The House leaders, assisted by the Democratic Congressional Campaign Committee, which funds House campaigns, were seeking to tamp these upstarts down, and doing what they could to protect incumbents.

"If I waited my turn, I wouldn't be here," Hayes said. "There is a place for veterans in leadership, but there has to be a place for new members. They are telling us things to do to expand the electorate, and I am thinking, 'I didn't do any of these things.'"

Hayes offered insight about some of the specific sticking points dividing the generations. For instance, many of the older members were imploring the newcomers to tweet less, clearly unnerved by the platform's ability to stir up tensions. "Take social media," Hayes said. "They tell us to stay off. Well, that's how we engage people." There was also a lack of appreciation, she felt, for online fundraising, which was, she said, "a huge component and a huge reason we got here."

Senator Chris Murphy has kept in touch with Hayes and understands her frustration. "She has done everything her way her entire life," he told me. "She became a teacher her way. She built a campaign her way. And I think she is committed to being a congresswoman her way."

Even more challenging, Hayes said, is the fact that in spite of the constant celebrations of diversity, her race still felt at times like a liability. "My chief of staff is a white man," Hayes said. "So people ask me a question, then look at him." Controlling gun violence was one of her signature issues, she continued. "People assume that is because I represent Sandy Hook," she said, referring to the elementary school in Newtown, Connecticut, where in 2012, twenty children and six adult staff members were slaughtered in one of the most dreadful mass shootings in history. "But on my mind is also that I represent Bridgeport, and Waterbury," cities where gun violence is present every day.

Being a new voice in Congress, Hayes told me, "is both empowering and exhausting." Too often, she said, she would find herself expressing the views of a black member of Congress or framing issues around their impact on communities of color, only to find that perspective met with stony silence. At an education hearing, she turned a policy discussion toward how a proposal would impact young black boys. "You wait for someone else to see it and to agree with you. On the one hand, it's frustrating." She sat up a bit in her chair for the first time over our forty-five-minute discussion. "On the other hand, it's perfect. This is why I am here."

The new congresswomen were realizing that their days were more jam-packed than they could have ever imagined, and that control over their own time was often a luxury, their meals even less so.

A typical day for a House member is basically this: wake up, maybe go to the House gym. Most days, Rep. Mike Thompson, a California Democrat, will be leading a spin class. If it's Wednesday, the class will be taught by Senator Kyrsten Sinema, who once served in the House and whose spin class was very popular. A trainer would occasionally teach yoga. From there, the day is a block of fifteen-minute meetings with constituents and interest groups: *Hi, nice to see you, National Air Traffic Controllers Association, National Association of Chemical Distributors, National Association of Insurance and Financial Advisors, and National Association of Letter Carriers!*

In between, there are hearings, meetings with fellow Democrats, racing across the street to the DCCC office to make calls to donors (it is illegal to do that at the Capitol), and more meetings. Evenings bring receptions—with donors, interest groups, clubs, sororities, foreign policy panels. Usually, there is food, but members can't avail themselves of much more than a random goat cheese–stuffed date, lest their mouth be full when someone wants to meet them, bend their ear, take a selfie, or push a cause. Dinner is often a PowerBar and a handful of cashews. Ditto for snacks. "I try not to eat a bag of chips from the gas station," Angie Craig told me.

Members of Congress fly home at taxpayer expense when the votes are done for the week, which can change by the hour. (One of the hardest jobs on the Hill has to be that of the office schedulers, who live their lives with a Google Calendar that is a veritable Rubik's Cube, with multiple flight selections always on alt screen.)

Americans see very little of this. They assume that when members go home, they are sitting with their families in front of football games for a week, when, in fact, time back in the district usually means a grueling schedule of daily visits with local mayors and other officials, from health-care centers, chambers of commerce, and veterans' groups, along with attending events like kindergarten graduations and job fairs.

Many people accept the notion that when former TV host Jon Stewart comes to the Hill and goes viral-video ballistic, demanding to know why so few members have shown up to listen to him and 9/11 first responders testify on a health-care bill, that those members must be in secret meetings with shady donors. In fact, they are likely at one of many other hearings, which tend to be held simultaneously, another nod to a manic tradition of House scheduling, and a central complaint of many new members.

On nights without receptions or fundraisers, sometimes members work until 3 a.m., hashing out the rules for a bill, or poring over thick binders of policy notes over a microwaved Wawa burrito. It is arguably a ridiculous life, or, as one senior staff member characterized it, a frequent brew of "ambition, treachery, social awkwardness, and sexual frustration." But it isn't leisurely.

The challenges of the schedule are particularly hard for parents. A generation ago, members of Congress tended to move to Washington with their families in tow, returning to their home districts mainly at election time. Members got to know one another and each other's families, which at times created genuine bonds and helped to tamp down partisan rancor. That practice fell out of favor, however, as the public's desire for their representatives to show up in the district grew and the notion of "going Washington" became an increasingly pejorative term. Women with children were often frowned upon by their colleagues, constituents, or both. "Bella called me and said, 'I hear you have two children,'" Pat Schroeder told me, recalling, decades later, how her excitement in hearing from pioneering congresswoman Bella Abzug quickly evaporated. "She said 'I don't think you can do it.' And I thought, 'Oh my God, Bella doesn't think I can do it.'" (She did it, with a supportive husband and the time-management skills of a Martha Stewart calendar.)

A single mom of three children, Katie Porter has often noted that Congress "is not built for people like me." Her first move when she got to Washington was to hire a "manny," who lives with her kids at home in Orange County, California, during the week. She has an old-fashioned paper wall calendar in her office, on which she keeps meticulous track of how many days her children have her at home. In January, it was nineteen days "with mom" and twelve without. On the day that the first recess was canceled because of the government shutdown, there is a hand-drawn sad face.

In a House Financial Services Committee hearing one day, she was marking all of her days off, and two other freshman mothers sitting near her, Rashida Tlaib and Cindy Axne (D-IA), clucked with sympathy. "Having two moms on that committee, that is psychologically helpful to me," Porter told me. Tracking the days on her calendar also helps her manage emotionally. "I'm trying to be intentional about how this is unfolding," she said, "and not just letting this happen to me. I need to preserve the energy and passion that brought me here."

As difficult as it is to be a parent and a congressperson, the new cohort has it relatively good. The first congresswoman to give birth while in office was Rep. Yvonne Brathwaite Burke (D-CA) in 1973; she hung it up six years later to return to Los Angeles. "I didn't leave Congress because I did not enjoy it. I enjoyed it very much," she said in an interview with the National Visionary Leadership Project decades later. "But by the time my daughter got to be old enough to go to school in first grade, it just was going to be impossible, so I had to make some choices."

In 2019, Rep. Jaime Herrera Beutler, a Republican from the state of Washington, became the second woman to have three children while serving in Congress; the prior year, Senator Tammy Duckworth, a Democrat from Illinois, became the first woman to have a baby while serving in the Senate. Both births felt like tipping points to me. As I stood in the Speaker's lobby gazing at the House floor in June of 2019, Herrera Beutler walked onto the floor with her five-week-old baby in tow, something I had never seen before. She struggled to simultaneously vote on a bill while also removing her crabby newborn from her baby carrier, at one point gently settling her onto the floor. Members from both parties walked over to admire the squalling cutie. "She wants a boob," Herrera Beutler said to one of the women as she frantically bounced her daughter while staring at the timer on the vote. "She's had it."

An hour later, I walked across the steaming-hot Capitol complex to visit with Democratic senator Patty Murray, who ran for office decades ago as "just a mom in tennis shoes" and who also happens to be from Herrera Beutler's home state. She listened to my story with wide eyes. "Just the ability for Jaime to bring her baby on the floor, that never was allowed," she said. It was a small but stunning bit of progress, Murray said. She noted that just a year prior, there was a fight in the Senate to allow Duckworth to bring her baby on the Senate floor, because some of the male senators said they were afraid of being distracted by crying.

Men's and women's bathrooms now have changing tables, and in 2019, pumping areas for breastfeeding mothers were added to the House. Katie Porter had a provision written into a House bill that would codify a rule allowing working parents running for Congress to use campaign funds for childcare costs, a measure that the Senate will likely never consider under Republican control.

Children are slowly becoming a fixture on Capitol Hill. A decade ago, it was a novelty when New York senator Kirsten

Gillibrand had her young sons linger in the cloakroom while she voted. Now, kids can often be seen on the last days of the session, when school is out, wandering with their parents in the halls and sitting on the House floor, staring into space, while their parents debate the finer points of election law. Jahana Hayes won't let her staff schedule lunch meetings, because she uses the break to FaceTime with her daughter. She and the other women in the "Moms' Caucus" successfully pushed for the legislative calendar to more closely follow the school year.

The Senate, as ever, lags, with the leaders of that body prone to scheduling votes late at night or sometimes even on the weekends. "You can see in the women the stress of 'How am I going to balance that with what I told my kids—I would take them to dinner, because I've not been able to do that,'" Murray told me. "It's more often than not men who go, 'Yeah, we're gonna be here,'" she said, as if late-night votes were a signal of their tenacity. This is a hot topic at the bipartisan dinners that the women of the Senate attend nearly religiously every six weeks or so. "We really listen to each other," Murray said of those dinners, which were started decades ago by now-retired senator Barbara Mikulski, the longest-serving female senator ever. "You know, we talk about everything. How do you live in a place like this? Is it hard to be yourself? Where's the best place to get your clothes cleaned when it's midnight? How do you take care of your family? What do you like to do in the summer? Also heavy-duty policy issues, like what's happening in Iran. And how do you guys see this?"

The new freshmen also didn't know how good they had it in another important area: the ability to get media attention. Many had arrived on the Hill with a *Rolling Stone* cover, a glowing women's magazine profile, or a series of news program interviews already under their belts. They had no sense of how extraordinary this was, as some of their older colleagues had had to wait for years for reporters to come anywhere near them for a quote. A few freshmen were in the enviable position of already being household names, perhaps a boon not only for them but for an institution that attracted at best disinterest and more typically derision from average voters.

But long before they could pass a single bill, the freshmen arrived to a shut-down government and very little to actually do. The shutdown had begun in the prior Congress over a dispute over border-wall funding, which President Trump was seeking and Democrats and some Republicans were refusing to give him as part of a general spending agreement. In the new Congress, House Democrats had passed a variety of bills, absent wall money, to reopen the government, but because Trump insisted that he would veto any bill that did not appropriate money for a border wall, Senate Majority Leader Mitch McConnell refused to bring any bills to the Senate floor.

The impact on federal workers was devastating, particularly among Transportation Security Administration agents and air traffic controllers, who spent the December–January holidays working without pay. The shutdown went on so long that some US government employees, in Washington and all across the country, were forced to line up at food pantries.

Powerless freshmen wanted to help. Some had reached out to Republican members at a bipartisan government retreat early on, only to be rebuffed. They called Nancy Pelosi's office, to ask: How could they, a high-profile bunch of members, draw attention to the shutdown and make it clear to people who understand nothing about Congress that this was all the Senate

Republicans' fault? They were insiders now and wanted a piece of the action.

One day in early January, as the shutdown dragged into its third week, a group of freshmen, led by Katie Hill, decided the way to go about this was to hold a press conference outside the Capitol, and then go over to Senator McConnell's office and demand a meeting.

On cue, shortly after a midday vote, a dozen House members marched down the steps of the east side of the Capitol to the "Senate Swamp," a grassy area across the complex, outside the Senate door. They seemed mildly perplexed about what to do next. "How is the media going to find us?" asked one.

This was not a problem. Piles of photographers had lined up to catch the members walking through the icy afternoon across the cobblestones.

Katie Hill spoke first: "The dysfunction has to change," she said, before others took to the microphones to denounce Trump, McConnell, and the Republicans in general. "We were sent here to restore order," said Lauren Underwood. Ilhan Omar cracked, "This feels like a poorly scripted scene from *House of Cards*." A few more members spoke.

Everyone shivered. "I am starting to question my judgment here," grumbled one *Washington Post* reporter as the members droned on in the cold. (An outdoor press conference in the winter is rarely a crowd-pleaser, especially a long one.)

At last, Ayanna Pressley took to the microphone and the cameras focused in on her frame, coatless but perhaps owing to her Boston-ness seemingly impervious to the thirty-four-degree chill. "We are representatives of democracy," she thundered.

With that, the members turned to the right, intent on storming McConnell's office, which sits not far from the Capitol Rotunda. But first, they had to get there. None of them seemed quite sure of the route and looked to amused reporters, who were there to cover the story but not advise on it, to tell them which stairway to use.

As the members, their young staffers, and the media formed an odd-looking parade, an unanticipated bottleneck developed at the entrance; the members had not taken into account that their staff and the reporters chasing them would need to go through the metal detector. On top of that, Katie Hill's spokeswoman had forgotten her ID and had to have the congresswoman come back and dragoon her through. The media scrambled to keep up.

Finally, the new members marched into Senator McConnell's ornate office, where they were greeted by two staff members. The freshmen glanced around at the chandelier, the gilded rococo mirrors, and the silk-covered couches; the Republican majority leader's suite was the Ritz-Carlton to their freshman offices' Red Roof Inn. McConnell was not there. "He's on the floor voting," someone said.

After a few minutes, the jig was up. "We left a note," Ilhan Omar told the reporters, as if the members had popped in to see the principal about their errant teenager who had been caught skipping first period at Au Bon Pain. (A spokesman for McConnell, Don Stewart, seemed puzzled later. "No note," he said, looking around.) Hill then turned to walk back to the House side of the Capitol but went the wrong way. "Um, Katie, the House side is to the right," an aide said.

The next day, the group returned with an actual letter in hand, signed by scores of freshmen, demanding that McConnell, who had been largely silent for weeks, work to reopen the government. As they blasted through the Capitol, Senator Chuck Schumer of New York, the highest-ranking Democrat in the Senate, passed them in the Rotunda. "What's going on here?" he asked with amusement. No one appeared to recognize him.

The women, along with a handful of men, once again found their way into the yellow room with the giant chandelier, where this time McConnell's staff was ready for them with chocolate sea-salt almonds and an offer of coffee. The freshmen then realized that they had failed to make a copy of their letter. McConnell's scheduler gamely took the piece of paper down the hall and copied it for them.

Next, AOC, Hill, and Underwood ran around the Capitol creating the video meme "Where's Mitch?" while some of the more conservative members with military and service backgrounds, led by Rep. Abigail Spanberger (D-VA), got themselves an invite with some Republican colleagues to the White House to try to negotiate directly with Trump. None of these efforts had much impact, and Pelosi moved to cancel the president's State of the Union address.

In retaliation, Trump canceled the military plane that was meant to be used by Pelosi and other members to visit US troops in Afghanistan for the weekend. Rep. Elaine Luria (D-VA), a twenty-year navy veteran and the only freshman who had been invited to join that delegation, issued a starchy statement: "The President's comment that lawmakers visiting Afghanistan is a 'public relations event' is an insult to the brave men and women serving in harm's way. . . . It is my duty to support our troops and learn everything I can about their mission."

Pelosi's office was pleased, and promoted both efforts, #wheresmitch and the bipartisan Problem Solvers group. Pelosi joined the unified front to reopen the government in spite of significant policy differences over border security, because she believed that all the new members, led by women, were succeeding in embarrassing and cornering congressional Republicans and Trump.

Because of the shutdown, Democratic leaders canceled the week off, but members were permitted to go home for the Martin Luther King Day weekend. (Cue the benighted scheduler, clicking on the American Airlines website once again.) I followed Omar as she went home to Minneapolis. The shutdown had dragged into its thirtieth day. The airport and the TSA workers I encountered seemed dejected and angry. One got tears in her eyes as I expressed my sympathies. When I offered to buy coffee for the staff at DC's Reagan National Airport, a supervisor told me, "We have tons of coffee. What we need is to get paid." He stared angrily across his security podium. "Congress and Trump can fight over whatever they want, but why would you not pay people?" he asked indignantly. "I gave twenty years of my life to this country in the military, I guess stupidly." He turned away, disgusted.

On January 25, the shutdown ended. There was no new money for Trump's wall. The Congressional Budget Office estimated that it cost the US economy at least $11 billion. The hope was that now, maybe, at least some governing would begin.

FOUR

Whose Party Is It, Anyway?

This is a very headstrong group of freshmen.
—Rep. Katie Hill (D-CA)

EVERY MIDTERM ELECTION produces at least one underdog candidate who is ignored by the political establishment and written off by the distractible and fragmented news media, addicted to chasing close races—a person whose victory on Election Day causes observers to blink furiously at a board of elections website, wondering what they missed. My favorite example from my own reporting career occurred during a 2014 governor's race. When Larry Hogan, a Republican, was elected in the deep-blue state of Maryland, clobbering the Democratic lieutenant governor, an Iraq War veteran and the anointed gubernatorial heir apparent, I began my victory-day story with the words "Um, Larry who?" But it is hard to find a modern analogy to Alexandria Ocasio-Cortez, whose victory stemmed from a magical mélange of intense Kennedy-like personal dynamism, social- and digital-media savvy, and a singularly policy-focused campaign message that resonated with voters.

AOC's influence on her party has no recent antecedent for a freshman House member. In her first few months in office, she got normally skittish Democratic Congress members and some presidential candidates to sign on to her Green New Deal, forced a national conversation about marginal tax rates, helped tank a plan for tech company Amazon to build a campus in Queens, and catalyzed a vast rejection of corporate PAC money for incumbents who had just a year before eschewed that plan as impractical at best, unilateral disarmament at worst.

A June 2019 poll by one of the Republican Party's most respected pollsters found that Ocasio-Cortez had already become "the defining image of today's Democratic Party," surpassing Nancy Pelosi, who had served as the Republican antihero for a decade. For many Democratic House members, especially those of color, the arrival of all the new women in aggregate, with AOC leading the charge, had altered the landscape in a way they found animating and joyful. "I've been here a few years," Rep. John Lewis, a longtime congressman from Georgia, told me. "Their presence has helped to lift this body. They came with passion, determination, and they are very serious. They bring life when they speak." Many Republicans in Congress were instantly obsessed with Ocasio-Cortez, tweeting negatively about her while begging their colleagues to introduce them to her.

Stage one of post–Ocasio-Cortez politics began forthwith. She was one of a handful of progressive Democrats elected to the House in 2018, joining a group of senior progressives, like Rep. Barbara Lee of California, Rep. Lloyd Doggett of Texas, and Rep. Jerry Nadler of New York, who had been toiling on the margins of the minority for several years. Her victory had injected a steroid-sized dose of energy into their ranks. At the same time, however, she was proving to be a bit of a toxin, too—for some of the more conservative Democrats who had taken over Republican seats.

These tensions would surface during the government shutdown, but they were placed in stark relief right away during an early intense discussion over how Democrats ought to address climate change and, inadvertently, over two long-awaited gun-control measures. Many Democratic House members began to fret that the far left was going to do to them what the Tea Party had done to Republicans a few years back: run them out of town, one primary at a time. Pelosi, caught flat-footed by Joe Crowley's unexpected loss, nonetheless pooh-poohed the idea: "Nobody's district is representative of somebody else's district," she said. "They made a choice in one district. Let's not get yourself carried away."

The party was struggling to understand what "far left" even meant now, given that Republicans had been using the term with abandon for years to describe all Democrats, except perhaps the very few remaining antiabortion Democrats in the House. The Party overall was desperately trying to woo Republican and independent voters into the tent, while at the same time taking serious internal stock of its own voters. A January 2019 Gallup poll found that from 1994 to 2018, the percentage of all Democrats who call themselves liberal had more than doubled, going from 25 percent to 51 percent, perhaps underscoring Ocasio-Cortez's point that the party was starting to look and think more like her.

At the same time, there is ample evidence that more moderate Democrats pepper much of the party, though their positions are getting harder to define, as socially liberal but fiscally conservative now seems far too pat a notion. Rep. Max Rose, of Staten Island, a typical Democratic freshman to have picked off a Republican, is a pro-choice US Army veteran who earned a Purple Heart for his service in Afghanistan. He cares nothing about the deficit and is strongly against the Green New Deal.

Often, it seems that what pundits write off as regional differences in the party can be better chalked up to generational ones: younger people in both parties are by and large worried about climate change, supportive of gay rights, and skeptical of the powerful sway of corporate interests. And yet, in the 116th Congress, where the progressive and moderate caucuses both hit historic levels of membership, it seemed as if the progressives—pushing an aggressive climate-change agenda, Medicare for All, free community college and state college, and increased marginal tax rates for the superrich—were dominating the conversation and setting an agenda that may have been out of step with the broader electorate. This dichotomy would hang over the entire Democratic Party going into the 2020 election.

AOC's victory was considerably more complicated than the postelection analysis made it out to be, focusing almost completely on shifting demographics in her district. While the narrative of her win portrayed younger nonwhite and working-class voters as her secret base, in reality Alexandria Ocasio-Cortez had soundly beaten Joe Crowley in the areas of the district that were by and large whiter and wealthier, in particular parts of Queens filled with folks fleeing overpriced Manhattan. Crowley prevailed in most working-class corners of the district, including the district's Hispanic and African American enclaves; he beat Ocasio-Cortez by more than 25 points in her own Parkchester section of the Bronx.

Journalist David Freedlander neatly summed this up in his analysis for *Politico Magazine* soon after the race: "Ocasio-Cortez, the young Latina who proudly identifies as a democratic socialist, hadn't been all but vaulted into Congress by the party's diversity, or a blue-collar base looking to even the playing field. She won because she had galvanized the college-educated gentrifiers who are displacing those people." While AOC's former chief of staff, Saikat Chakrabarti, continued to characterize the victory as a result of a strong multiracial coalition, this was actually more true for other triumphant female Democrats that year, notably Ayanna Pressley, who won affluent whites and young people of all races in her district. But with AOC, "It was the Bernie Bros," one top Crowley advisor told Freelander as he surveyed the wreckage the day after the election. "They killed us."

Before casting a single vote or sitting through a single hearing, Ocasio-Cortez had begun to make her mark on Congress. During freshman orientation, not long after the November election, she entertained her Instagram followers with videos of new adventures in Washington. In another Instagram story, she fretted—while wearing something resembling sweats, making mac and cheese, and singing along to Janelle Monáe—about the media attention. "You're supposed to be perfect all the time on every issue and everything," she lamented. She also openly mocked the speakers at a leadership training event, many of whom were supplied by lobbyists (but who also offered some of the practical training for new members that some later complained was lacking from the official freshman orientation).

Between the election and the seating of the new Congress, she joined protesters outside Pelosi's office, demanding the establishment of a special panel to study and advise members on climate change. Pelosi had already agreed to the panel, and AOC's pro-test struck more senior members and donors as curious and worrisome: She was inside the tent now. Was she going to con-tinue to attack it from outside? The challenge was also met with some resistance from senior members of the leadership team, who wanted to take on the climate question the old-fashioned way, through committee work, hearings, and what is known as "regular order," in which bills are debated and adopted indi-vidually and passed between the House and Senate.

Rep. Frank Pallone (D-NJ), the incoming chair of the pow-erful House Energy and Commerce Committee, which has a lot of jurisdiction over climate legislation, criticized the panel idea, and in a meeting that included incoming freshmen, Ocasio-Cortez forcefully pushed back. This type of pushback again sur-prised more senior members, who were used to the freshmen keeping their heads down in the early days. It would also not be unique to Ocasio-Cortez. "This is a very headstrong group of freshmen," Katie Hill would tell me later. "We are just very unlike other classes."

Then, in mid-December 2018, the first battle of a war that would soon engulf the new group of House Democrats began. One otherwise sleepy day, while dejected Republicans were removing their nameplates from their palatial leadership offices, and losers were cleaning out their mini fridges, *Politico* popped a story that AOC (which she had now made her official Twitter handle) and the progressive PAC Justice Democrats were already gearing up for primary battles in 2020. In her crosshairs, the story reported, was fellow New Yorker Hakeem Jeffries, a well-liked rising star.

His crimes were apparently both political and interpersonal. Jeffries took corporate PAC money and, like most New York

City members of Congress, was friendly with the banking industry. Ocasio-Cortez had herself started her own leadership PAC
shortly after winning, and lots of folks—most, in fact—took
money from industries in their districts. This notion immediately
concerned many Congress members, who felt that eschewing all
industry money would mean only wealthy members could run.

Jeffries's other crime, according to *Politico*, was that he had
also just defeated an idol of Ocasio-Cortez's, Barbara Lee of
California, in the race to be House Democratic Caucus chair,
having run on the same new-blood principle that had helped
AOC herself win. Lee, who was in her seventies, was of great
importance to many of the new women, whom she quickly
moved to mentor. An African American representing the flats of
Oakland and the left-wing archipelago of Berkeley, she was one
of the earliest and most passionate opponents of the war in Iraq,
and she repeatedly authored legislation to empower Congress
to take more control of acts of war, which years later would be
embraced even by many Republicans. Some incoming members
thought Lee had been unfairly disposed of, even if Jeffries was
also black.

Poised to be the first black Speaker, Jeffries was popular
among his colleagues and to the left of many of them—and a
homegrown superstar in his Brooklyn district. Some colleagues
thought the challenge from a fellow New Yorker who had yet
even to be sworn in was unseemly. House Democrats had just
battled their way back from eight years in the wilderness, watching Republicans dismantle President Obama's legacy, reinstall
Styrofoam cups in the House cafeterias, defeat their ranks in
state house after state house, and then narrowly beat their first
female presidential candidate with one Donald J. Trump. They

were not eager to let their new triumph be soiled by infighting over who could be more liberal in districts as blue as the Caribbean Sea.

Roughly ten members—a group of Democrats that spanned generations, race, and geography—huddled around Jeffries on the House floor to assure him of their support. "People love Hakeem," Rep. Josh Gottheimer, a sophomore congressman from New Jersey, told me. "We thought attacking one of your own was outrageous. We went up to him, and everyone said, 'What can we do to help? We will do what we need to do.' It was a huge tactical error on her part."

Ocasio-Cortez limply denied the *Politico* story, even as Justice Democrats more or less confirmed it, and tried to put it behind her.

Shortly after she was sworn in, she got to work on promoting the centerpiece of her agenda: the Green New Deal. The deal was not a bill churned out after months and months of hearings, public comments, and legislative horse trading. In fact it wasn't a deal at all, but more like a list of resolutions or a set of goals that included an expansive array of government-supported economic policy ideas to address climate change, job security, poverty, and income inequality in one fell swoop.

The whole notion of the plan created a divide among Democrats. Some, either eager to get a little AOC stardust on their member pins, or merely afraid of her torching them on Twitter, signed on to the deal. Others quickly raced away, knowing that the last Democrat to represent their district had been tossed out over perceived government overreach. One of Pelosi's biggest mistakes during her first term as Speaker was when she demanded in 2009 that the Democratic majority in the House approve a controversial cap-and-trade bill to address climate change, even though she knew the Senate would never pass it. The Democrats had dutifully walked the plank. The Senate never even took it up. And several Democrats in coal country lost their seats the next year. But many of the newer members had no memory or even knowledge of this decisive failure.

The rollout of the Green New Deal should have been a slam dunk for both Alexandria Ocasio-Cortez and her cosponsor, Senator Ed Markey of Massachusetts, one of the most senior Democrats in Congress and long a leader on climate change. Their proposal—essentially a ten-year plan to get to net zero greenhouse gas emissions through a revolutionary rethinking of the nation's electricity and transportation systems—represented decades of research and activism that had forced a conversation on the subject, which had been dormant since the cap-and-trade debacle. But earlier in the day, before their joint news conference, a document had emerged out of AOC's office with a whole new set of goals that had never been run by Markey's office. They read like, according to one policy expert on the Hill, "something that a bunch of kids in a dorm room passing a big bong would come up with." The document called for the eventual elimination of air travel, the suggestion that cows, whose belches and flatulence emit greenhouse gases, had to go, and an economic-security package for those who are "unable or unwilling to work."

The Green New Deal had been a by-product of both offices, with the hope that it would catalyze a strong congressional climate debate, but this new document kneecapped the entire effort. Markey, having never seen it, could neither defend it nor explain it. "What about the cows?" reporters kept asking him. On the one hand, this generated a slew of news stories, helping to bring the climate debate to the fore. On the other, the new document was almost totally dismissed, often with derision. "It will be one of several or maybe many suggestions that we receive," Pelosi said, making it pretty clear that the resolution would never take the form of a bill on the House floor. "The Green Dream, or whatever they call it, nobody knows what it is, but they're for it, right?"

Then after the new climate advisory panel was formed, the one that Ocasio-Cortez had agitated for, she refused to join it, citing her commitment to other committees. Only months later, in a podcast interview with *New Yorker* editor David Remnick, did she admit to what most of her colleagues had suspected all along: "I had made very specific requests," she told him, "which I thought were rather reasonable, for the select committee on climate change. I asked that it have a mission to try to draft legislation by 2020, so that we essentially have a two-year mission to put together, whether it's a Green New Deal or whether it's some sweeping climate-change legislation, that the select committee have a legislative mission. I asked for it to have subpoena power, which most committees do. The last select committee had subpoena power, but now this one doesn't. And I asked for the members who sit on the select committee to not take any fossil-fuel money. And none of those requests were accommodated. And so I didn't join the committee."

Again, colleagues were amazed by the moxie of the freshman who had both made her name on the climate-change issue, lobbied the Speaker to make sure this committee was, and whom leadership had hoped would give it some credibility in her political sphere of influence. Perhaps more importantly: when the Speaker of the House believes she has given you a piece of cake, you don't dump it in the trash in front of her. "I think it was totally on-brand," one Democratic staffer told me. "She is say-ing, 'I won't participate in the traditional toothless congressional efforts. I have a movement outside.'"

Eventually, Ocasio-Cortez conceded that the launch of the climate plan had not gone as planned. "Our GND rollout was really difficult, and it was done in a way that it was really easy to hijack the narrative around it," she said in a Yahoo News podcast. "It was like, too fast, in some ways. I actually think the resolution itself is very solid, but between how it was rolled out—there were competing documents rolled out, some prema-turely, that muddied the waters."

One of the central components of the Democratic Party's agenda was to pass even modest gun-control legislation, a cam-paign promise many congressional candidates had made. Still, the fight for the soul of the party would cast a shadow over that effort as well. Rep. Lucy McBath, who had won a close contest in Georgia, was the only freshman invited to stand next to former congresswoman Gabrielle Giffords at a press conference early in the new Congress to announce one of the Democrats' first moves, a universal-background-check bill they had been waiting for years to bring to the House floor. McBath looked slightly nervous as Pelosi and her team touted the measure, eight years to the day after Giffords was shot at a constituent meet-and-greet in a supermarket parking lot in Tucson, Arizona.

McBath, while unknown to much of Washington, had come to town already a hero in the gun-control world and was well known among many of the black members of Congress with whom she had visited many times over the years. Her seven-teen-year-old son, Jordan Davis, was shot and killed in 2012 at a Florida gas station by a middle-aged stranger who said the teenager was playing his music too loud. Jordan's life, and the trial around the crime that led to his death, would become the subject of an HBO documentary called *3½ Minutes, Ten Bullets*, which examined Florida's controversial "stand your ground" law.

Not long after her son's death, McBath became a gun-control activist, working with the nonprofit organizations Everytown for Gun Safety and Moms Demand Action for Gun Sense in America. In October 2014, as her son's killer, Michael Dunn, was receiving a sentence of life without parole, McBath told him, "I choose to forgive you, Mr. Dunn, for taking my son's life. I choose to release the seeds of bitterness and anger and honor my son's love. I choose to walk in the freedom of knowing God's justice has been served. I pray that God has mercy on your soul."

Four and a half years later, there she was at a press conference on Capitol Hill, a new black congresswoman from a majority-white district in the northern suburbs of Atlanta, a district once held by a well-known Republican, former Speaker of the House Newt Gingrich. McBath had squeaked into Congress, beating the Republican incumbent, Karen Handel, 50.5 percent to 49.5; Handel would immediately sign up for a rematch in 2020.

A few weeks after that press conference, the bill was ready for a vote on the House floor. I was curious about how McBath would face this day, a culmination of her activism around an issue that had so deeply divided the country for decades. (It would become the first piece of major gun-control legislation to pass in the House in a quarter of a century.) I looked at a congressional schedule and discovered that before the bill would be voted on, McBath would be sitting in a subcommittee hearing on labor and education. I waited outside the door for an hour for her to emerge, and when she finally did, she was greeted by an aide while talking on her cell phone to another aide, whom she was instructing to find a photo of her son that she had left in her office.

The journey from the hearing to the House floor was a long one, and she began it by entering the members-only elevator, there to help perpetually tardy members speed to the underground tunnels and trains to get to the votes, which in general are meant to only be open for fifteen minutes or less. I broke a (rarely enforced) rule by joining her, riding in silence on an elevator mostly full of freshmen who did not recognize me. Then Rep. Billy Long, a loud Republican and former auctioneer from Missouri, gave me an icy glare. "There are people other than members on this elevator," he bellowed as the last few members squeezed in. "I am getting off!" Everyone packed tightly into the elevators looked around in mild shock; Ayanna Pressley raised an eyebrow in disgust. I stared at the floor, willing myself to become invisible.

When we emerged, I began, gingerly, to talk to McBath, who was swathed in an orange scarf, the color used by the movement against gun violence, as she jumped on the members-only subway. (Rep. Debbie Dingell had recently given every woman in the House four scarves—orange against gun violence; red to promote heart health; pink against breast cancer; purple in support of the Violence Against Women Act.) I followed McBath onto a final elevator that would take her to the floor to vote. She looked at a few of her colleagues. "Thank you, thank you, thank you for this," she said, her eyes welling with tears.

Then she walked to the House floor and settled into a seat among a sea of other orange scarves, next to Jahana Hayes. This is when the trouble began.

Moments before the bill to require universal background checks was approved, Republicans offered one of those tricky motions to recommit. These motions usually fail along party-line votes. The rule: thou shalt not vote for the minority's procedural motions! They are not subject to normal committee vetting, and surface at the last minute, a procedural practical joke of sorts. Members tend to use the short time they are debated to go to the bathroom or make a call. Most Republicans, of course, were furious with the gun bill, and added their best version of a motion to recommit, one requiring Immigration and Customs Enforcement to be notified when an illegal immigrant tries to buy a gun. This was a double stick in the eye, since ICE was the progressive members' most hated agency, the equivalent perhaps of the Internal Revenue Service for Republicans.

I knew that Democrats had been voting for these motions to recommit over the last few weeks, but they were being attached to meaningless bills concerning the shutdown, which went nowhere. As I watched the vote in the House gallery above the House floor, I leaned over to a fellow Hill reporter and said, "I think this thing is going to pass."

"No way," he said, scrolling absently through Twitter. It would be a massive black eye for the bill and not a great look for the nascent majority. Why would they allow that to happen?

House members vote with an electronic card similar to a credit card, and as they vote, their name and position lights up on a screen in the back of the gallery. We watched as Republicans quickly voted yes for their own motion, and as a handful of Democrats slowly but surely pushed the measure toward victory.

A furious scrum could be seen in the well of the House as Pelosi and others urged their colleagues to knock it off.

Ocasio-Cortez went into a sea of gun-control activists who had come to watch the vote, and told them she would have to choose between voting for McBath's, in her view, now-bespoiled bill or against the historic measure, in order to protest the ICE addition.

In the end, Democrats—and a handful of Republicans— voted for the legislation to tighten background checks. Ocasio-Cortez was among those who gave the bill the nod, but then took to Twitter to vent that she had been forced to explain to gun-control advocates after the fact that "the gotcha amendment pinned gun safety against immigration advocacy. Its intent was to divide."

But the fact that Democrats had voted for a nuisance measure written by the minority, which was meant to be ignored, had embarrassed their caucus and forced members to choose between their dislike of ICE and a bill they supported. Most chose the latter—perhaps out of respect for McBath, perhaps because they understood the bill would go nowhere in the Senate. McBath, clutching the photo of her son, looked on ruefully. She had won, but the victory exposed a widening early rift in her party.

After the vote, I caught up with Abigail Spanberger, the former CIA officer, who was among the twenty-six Democrats who voted with the Republicans for the ICE measure. Spanberger, who had endured a brutal campaign in Richmond, Virginia, beating the Republican incumbent by roughly sixty-six hundred votes for a seat that had not been held by a Democrat in nearly fifty years, had already made it clear she would side with Republicans on a variety of security issues. The fact that members historically voted against these motions did not matter to her, she said as she dashed past the East Front of the Capitol. "I am looking at every one of them just like I would any piece of legislation."

Dozens of gun-control activists and families had gathered on the steps to have photos taken with Lucy McBath in the freezing cold. She stood with them for a good hour, taking group shots and selfies, and hugging the dozens who had brought their own photos of relatives and friends killed in gun violence. "So many people lost their lives to get us to this point," she said as she made it at long last back to her office. "I know why I am here. Some of my colleagues who told me to my face, 'I've got your back' in the end were not there. But I will always take the hard votes." McBath looked out into the street, where a few activists were still straggling. Her bill, which she knew the Senate would never vote on, was tainted. Still, she said, "Today was an amazing day. I hope we have many amazing days. But they won't all be like this."

The next day, in an emotional meeting with Democrats, Pelosi let it be known that her tolerance for members of her party voting with Republicans on these nuisance measures was waning. She had not raced around the country helping to recruit, raise money for, and elevate all these Democrats, had not regained the gavel and stared down Donald Trump, only to be felled on the floor by a bunch of B-list vanquished Republican bros who had just overseen the biggest loss of women in their ranks in recent history. Another gun-control bill would be coming that day, one that would extend the waiting period from three days to ten for would-be buyers at gun shows who don't quickly pass a federal background check, and she did not want a repeat of the day before. The party had to have unity, she said, even when it meant taking hard votes, as she had been pressing her colleagues to do as their leader for a decade. "This is not a day at the beach," she snapped. "This is the Congress of the United States."

Flexing her considerable political power, she noted that those who continued to vote with Republicans would become a lower priority for party leadership and campaign assistance in the future. Ocasio-Cortez, in this case a helpful ally to Pelosi, upped the ante, suggesting that she was on a text chain with activists and that there were lists being kept of errant Democrats who voted with Republicans, and that liberal groups, ever on the hunt for transgressive Democrats to target, would be waiting.

At that emotional moment, Xochitl Torres Small, an eloquent but understated congresswoman from a conservative section of New Mexico, decided to speak. Her smile was usually as bright as a supernova, but now her voice choked with tears. Not every Democrat in the room came from a district where the ICE measure would be unpopular, Torres Small explained. She, like others in the room, had feared a vote against it would give Republicans ammunition in the next election.

The Second Congressional District of New Mexico is roughly sixty times the size of Rhode Island, and is as rural as it is massive. The Republican incumbent, Steve Pearce, had held the seat for much of the last fourteen years, fending off Democratic challengers, election after election, before resigning to run for governor. Torres Small, a former Hill staffer, had run a traditional anti-Washington race, focusing on the specific needs of her district, where 5 percent of the residents don't even have cell service and many live with no doctor nearby. She repeatedly suggested that DC had given the back of its bureaucratic hand to the rural Southwest. Rather than focus on the glories of the Affordable

Care Act, she emphasized that health care was too expensive, and still hard to access for rural residents. In a clever ad that drew a bit of national attention to her campaign, she depicted her fidelity to the district's public lands with a video showing her in a camo-esque blouse, shooting a gun while duck hunting.

Only the third Democrat in the last half century to prevail in her district, she eked out 50.9 percent of the vote, making her instantly one of the most vulnerable members of the freshman class. "The voices that are most often heard are not coming from districts like mine," Torres Small told me later. "One way that AOC and I are similar is that we both reflect our districts. We just happen to have very different ones." She added, "Being a member of Congress is lonely in all sorts of ways."

When the second gun bill came to the floor, Republicans tacked on another measure to amend the bill—and muck it up procedurally—by excluding victims of domestic violence from the lengthier waiting period. Again, this is how motions to recommit work: The minority comes up with language that sounds too good to pass up, springs it on the majority at the last minute, and the majority, understanding the game, rejects it. Later, the minority makes videos that no one watches, which say things like "So-and-so congresswoman voted against domestic violence survivors!" Republicans, fresh from their last victory, were offering up a dare: Could Democrats stomach voting to withhold a firearm from a desperate abused wife?

Democratic leaders sent out one of their most experienced women to argue against the measure. Debbie Dingell, the Michigan lawmaker whose husband, the legendary John Dingell, had recently died, walked to the podium to speak. There were three freshman women in her state—one conservative Democrat,

Elissa Slotkin; one liberal, Rashida Tlaib; and a popular middle-of-the roader, Haley Stevens—all of whom had leaned heavily on Dingell for help in their new jobs. They in turn had comforted her in her grief. Dingell recounted her mentally ill father menacing her family with a gun, but she said she feared a weapon gotten in haste by a victim of domestic violence could end up in the abuser's hands. "I have spent more time thinking about how you keep guns out of the hands of abusers, more probably than anybody in this chamber," she proclaimed. "I know better than most the dangers they pose. I will be honest on this floor—my father was mentally ill. I had to hide in that closet, with my siblings, wondering if we would live or die. One night, I kept my father from killing my mother. He shouldn't have had a gun."

Shaking as her fellow Democrats roared their approval, Debbie Dingell stood down and the motion failed. The underlying gun bill passed easily, though without Xochitl Torres Small's vote.

Democrats were starting to see Nancy Pelosi's point. In short: Lucy McBath and gun-control advocates had won the day, but at a cost, with one bill tainted by the ICE measure. "I was the last vote on that gun motion to recommit," Angie Craig told me some months later over coffee in Minnesota. "I think we saw the consequences. Lucy didn't get her big day."

At the time, it may have seemed a mere symbolic issue, since Senate Republicans had made clear they would never even consider both of the passed bills. However, months later, after the mass shootings in Dayton, Ohio, and El Paso, Midland, and Odessa, Texas, these bills would take on a new urgency.

The fight over these Republican measures would simmer down in the short term. Pelosi, aided by some freshmen, had done a good job impressing upon her group that they needed to hang together, that the point of being in power was never to give it away. But those first few weeks were not simple growing pains, they were tremors before a major tectonic shift that would affect how these newly empowered Democrats would govern—and set the stage for the critical 2020 battle for the White House.

Alexandria Ocasio-Cortez and her sort of shadow political operation was making some of her colleagues feel they were being watched and graded for sufficient loyalty to an emergent brand of progressive politics. Several members grumbled to me that her ability to challenge any of them was overstated; after all, Justice Democrats had lost every single primary race in 2018 but hers. (The PAC would later take credit for Pressley, but it had not touted her as one of its candidates until the very end.)

Over breakfast last winter in Naperville, Lauren Underwood—who, let's remember, had bested a half dozen primary challengers and smoked a Republican in the Chicago suburbs—dug into a pancake half the size of our table at her favorite diner and talked about how many of the freshmen had done something decidedly harder than Ocasio-Cortez in her decidedly quirky New York primary contest: they won tough primaries and then went on to clobber sitting Republicans. "Most of us got way more votes in our primaries than Alex," Underwood told me. "We are not afraid of her."

It is technically true that Ocasio-Cortez's power as a new member of Congress was equal only to her own vote, and she generally would prove unable to bring many colleagues along. She was, at the end of the day, no legislative force. She and her staff would soon alienate all but a handful of other offices. But playing politics was a different matter, and on that field she showed unbelievable savvy. She understood instinctively what language to use to get a message across, and whom to use it with. She was friendly and accessible to reporters, even as her staff was distant. She was disinclined to work with her New York colleagues on prosaic matters like local transit annoyances, but knew how to appeal to a mass audience on the global issues of the day.

With millions of followers on social media and an electrified base of voters unmatched by anyone else's in the House, she had more potential to influence those running for president than any colleague she was trying to woo to support an amendment. She was an object of fascination to the political media and to the often-smaller news outlets to which her staff doled out most interviews. And her fans continued to be dazzled by her TV appearances, even as some of her fellow freshmen and senior members of the party steamed that she was hardly the spokeswoman for all House Democrats. Where was *their* invitation to the Stephen Colbert show?

Privately, scores of members and their staff said AOC was sharp, informed, and far more humble than her antipathetic tweets might suggest, usually keeping quiet in the weekly meetings with the entire Democratic team. But with an outsized audience and many more media demands than most new lawmakers have, she was also prone, early on, to factual stumbles, which earned her dings on nonpartisan fact-checking sites. For example, she overstated polled support for Medicare for All, the amount of money Republicans spent in certain races against her colleagues, and said, falsely, that ICE was "required to fill 34,000 beds with detainees every single night," and that the Pentagon had engaged in massive accounting fraud between 1998 and 2015. In the era of Trump, however, a political base is not dissuaded by the sorts of fact checks that used to hobble politicians. "I think that there's a lot of people more concerned about being precisely, factually, and semantically correct than about being morally right," she told Anderson Cooper on *60 Minutes*.

From the Republican side of the aisle came fascination and derision. Ocasio-Cortez quickly learned she could leverage their obsession to her advantage. "Early on, I walked up to her on the floor to talk to her about signing on to a prescription drug bill," longtime progressive congressman Peter Welch told me. He was elected in the last massive Democratic wave in 2006, and had found a wistful fellowship with the new class, given that most of his classmates had since been vanquished or quit. "I wanted a freshman on the bill. I told her I had a Republican cosponsor named Francis Rooney." (Rooney is a Florida lawmaker who has long supported requiring the federal government to negotiate lower drug prices for older Americans in the Medicare Part D program.) "She said, 'Who is he? I'd like to meet him.'"

Democrats sit on one side of the House chamber, and Republicans, on the other. Physically crossing over was not unheard of, but it is notable. As the freshman walked with Welch, the Republican men stared. "They were all agog," Welch said as we stood one afternoon in the ornate Speaker's lobby off the House floor, where members traipse through to use the restroom, chat with reporters, or sit in front of a fire to read the newspaper. "Some of them hate her. Some of them are attracted. Some don't know what to think of her. But they all want to see her. First, she walked up to another Republican member, who she assumed was Rooney, and that member started smiling. He was very disappointed when I said, 'No, that's not the guy.'"

Finally, they got to Rooney, and as other Republicans attempted not to stare, the three discussed the Medicare bill. "I told her later, 'That was very savvy of you,'" Welch said. "'Do things like that and you will be very successful here.' She showcased real political instincts in that moment."

In the class of 2019, Welch saw the thrills of newly earned power, and the potential pitfalls down the line. "They remind me of our class, in 2007, that was also a majority changer," he said. "When you come in and change power, it's a real bonding experience. Of course, all my friends are now gone."

One night, I sat in my yoga clothes watching AOC's latest Instagram hit, the comments and heart emojis flowing by as she put together her IKEA furniture, chomped on popcorn, and talked climate policy as well as savory seasonings. "I've been living, like, a completely depraved lifestyle," she said, staring at the Swedish hieroglyphics and otherworldly screws and bolts that have felled millions of American apartment dwellers. Chomp. Chomp. Too busy to put her Washington apartment together, she had been sleeping on a mattress that still had the manufacturer's plastic on it, she confessed, while also noting that Republicans "lack moral grounding" as it pertained to cutting emissions. Handful of popcorn. "Someone asked me a similar question earlier today, just like, 'How do you stay grounded and focused on issues?'" she said, as eight thousand fans watched. "I am putting these things together." A table gets assembled. "*Boom!* I did it," she said, then shared her popcorn secret: ground pepper for a "savory dimension."

As I watched this interaction, one that would dazzle both my teenage daughters as well as most of my fiftysomething friends, I felt: (1) grateful for the man in my life who assembles all my

IKEA tables, and (2) an overwhelming need to make microwave popcorn, which I then doused with black pepper and ate for dinner with a glass of white wine. Then I licked brownie crumbs off a knife. Was I living my best old-person AOC life?

For millennials and Generation Z, AOC has the magical alchemy of position and reliability, and for younger women, whose beacons of inspiration had been largely confined to people at least twice their age—Hillary Clinton, Ruth Bader Ginsburg, Stacey Abrams—here was one of their own: someone who has struggled with student debt, underemployment, and a collapsing natural world; someone with agility with social media and the Instant Pot and modern sketch comedy; someone who also loves Drake.

For baby boomers and the often-forgotten Generation X, Alexandria Ocasio-Cortez was a riveting figure and, to those on the left, a ray of light pushing through the clouds of contemporary politics. She was, like it or not, the new face of the Democratic House majority. But this radically contemporary phenom, a bartender of color with working-class origins who was a former Ted Kennedy intern became a sort of symbol of the millennial generation, whose problems the older generations had helped create but whose response to them could sometimes feel baffling.

Baby boomers and Generation Xers both note that casual ageism is the one ism that does not seem to discomfit the progressive millennials' cultural critique, and this was emerging as a divide in the high-profile workplace of Congress, too. Ocasio-Cortez and her less famous colleagues were posing a threat not just to the left-of-center policy positions that Democrats had been using as safe havens to regain power, but also to assumptions about seniority, paying dues, and the value of senior wisdom. Having waited for decades for the boomers to finally vacate their positions of power and authority, Gen Xers now had to contend with impatient and assertive millennials who wanted to leapfrog into those posts.

Colleagues saw the risks that Ocasio-Cortez posed to them, and potentially their majority, even as they understood she might herald the future of the Democratic Party. "If I am winning young people by thirty points, then that changes the way we think about policy," Katie Hill told me. She, like AOC, had relied on younger voters to win, and as freshman leader, she was meant to be a bridge between her class and the older leadership team. She sat with the leadership in weekly meetings, offering the views and concerns of her classmates, though Pelosi at times would cast them off.

Dismissive or not, Hill said, "I truly believe the older leaders have been waiting for this. They have been looking for someone to hand things off to." Her view was that the more conservative members of her party, whom she sometimes joined on matters like military spending and defending the police, and the left, with whom she agreed on health care and social policy, would adjust to and accept each other, as the broader Democratic Party becomes the diverse, dominant force that demography will inevitably deliver. "Let's face it, if you look at the views of young Republican voters, the old Republican Party is dying off," Hill said. "[Democrats] Max Rose and Elissa Slotkin will be the new conservatives. So it is AOC and Ilhan's job to push us to the left, and our job will be to push back from our districts. We are just a new generation of leaders, and finding the middle ground is where democracy lies." For Hill, the story would soon become more complicated.

FIVE

Reclaiming Their Time

I think I'm exactly where I'm supposed to be.
—Rep. Ayanna Pressley (D-MA)

TO BE HONEST, my heart went out to Ben Carson one breezy May afternoon as I watched Katie Porter shred him like a ten-year-old bank statement. In her pointed, precise manner, during a House Financial Services Committee hearing, the freshman congresswoman asked President Trump's secretary of housing and urban development why it was that loans from his agency tended to result in high rates of foreclosure, turning properties into REOs, or real-estate-owned properties.

"Do you know what an REO is?" she asked Carson, once an acclaimed pediatric brain surgeon, somewhat pedantically.

"An Oreo?" he responded, apparently guessing that the conversation had turned to a sandwich cookie.

"No, not an Oreo. An R-E-O," Porter said. "REO"
Carson began to sound out the phrase. "Real-real-real estate."
"What does the 'O' stand for?" she asked.
He didn't know. "The organization."

The exchange was devastating.

Lawmakers in both parties have always used hearings to grandstand. But the women of the 116th Congress instead started using hearings to share expertise from their prior careers or personal trials (rather than relying mainly on the notes prepared by legislative staffers, as is common), to question deeply and intelligently, and, yes, at times to fillet administration officials and corporate executives, giving the lawmakers' work an investigative flair and showcasing both their preparation and professional knowledge.

These moments also seemed designed to give an emotional release to their voters, who enjoyed seeing such snippets of hearings flashed around social media. In the era of NowThis, a website dedicated to sending videos of liberal lawmakers into the political bloodstream with treacly music and dramatic slow motion, many of these exchanges, once limited to the C-SPAN set, went viral. The Firsts were making Americans pay attention.

When witnesses in 2019 came before the House Oversight Committee, a historical hotbed of partisan rancor, three members of the Squad—Alexandria Ocasio-Cortez, Rashida Tlaib, and Ayanna Pressley—often sat together, a gauntlet of inquiry, helping elevate not just their profiles but also the oversight work of the House. The committee assignment was a good one, at least for freshmen; it put them at the tip of the spear of clashes with the White House, providing high visibility.

In questioning Federal Reserve chair Jerome Powell on the curious coexistence of low inflation and low unemployment, Ocasio-Cortez dropped the Phillips curve on him, a theory positing that low unemployment will inevitably bring higher inflation. Even Larry Kudlow, Trump's senior economic advisor, with whom Ocasio-Cortez agrees almost never, was impressed. In an interview with Fox News after the hearing, he gave a "hats off to Ms. AOC" for her question, saying, "She kind of nailed that," suggesting that the administration shared her view.

When Michael Cohen, Trump's former personal lawyer and fixer, appeared before the committee, Ocasio-Cortez held her rhetorical fire and instead went into fact-finding mode. "To your knowledge, did the president ever provide inflated assets to an insurance company?" she asked Cohen.

He replied, "Yes."

"Do you think we need to review his financial statements and tax returns in order to compare them?" she asked.

Cohen said that indeed they should.

AOC had just cleverly opened up an entire new avenue for congressional investigation—a rare turn of events in a high-profile hearing, where members usually prefer to lecture witnesses and show off for C-SPAN.

When Ocasio-Cortez, Tlaib, and Pressley returned from a visit to detention centers at the border, they used a hearing to provide powerful testimony about the conditions, keeping the pressure on the Trump administration but also displaying their own personal styles and backgrounds.

Ocasio-Cortez insisted on being sworn in, which is something not normally done for committee members and was a tad bit of grandstanding, because she said Republicans too often accused her of lying. She then used her Spanish-language skills as she interviewed a woman whose daughter had died shortly after being released from ICE custody and who testified, "I watched my baby girl die slowly and painfully."

Rashida Tlaib, a former community activist who often leans emotional when describing children and families, wept as she talked about a child who had died in custody and the unbathed and suffering people she saw at the border facility. "I've been so deeply haunted by the unforgettable image of a four-year-old boy . . . [who] asked me in Spanish where his papa was," she said.

As Tlaib wiped her eyes, Ayanna Pressley, a seasoned local lawmaker whose soaring and extemporaneous speeches were becoming her trademark, said, "Today, I do not speak on behalf of anyone, but I make space for the stories our nation so desperately needs to hear in this moment. . . . I cannot unsee what I've seen, I cannot unfeel what I experienced. I refuse to, although admittedly it robs me of sleep and peace of mind."

Pressley has used hearings to raise issues that affected people with limited means, noting, for instance, that an online census process would be difficult for those who could not afford a phone and otherwise lacked access to the internet. She also worked over members of the Trump administration, who often interrupted her or declined to answer her pointed yes-or-no questions, at which juncture she would shoot back, "Reclaiming my time," usually to an aged white man on the other side of the dais.

When Trump's commerce secretary, Wilbur Ross, came before the committee to discuss the 2020 census, she took her dig, demanding to know if he had a generous-enough budget to conduct a canvassing of the entire country. Ross insisted he had requested a sufficient increase.

"Was it your testimony earlier," Pressley said, "that Mr. Trump prepared a budget that did not include your input for what would be required . . . and that you had also not read it?"

Later, a flustered Ross replied, "I believe you're out of time, ma'am."

The Oversight Committee has been more than a just vehicle for members of the Squad to show off their questioning prowess; it became a place they could highlight their policy areas of interest. Now, in addition to the usual array of hearings on veteran health care and facial-recognition technology the committee was exploring childhood trauma and the threats posed by white supremacy.

The committee has also been a bit of a refuge. The freshman congresswomen had each other, of course, but for most of 2019 they also had the chair, Elijah Cummings, a veteran lawmaker from Baltimore, who took apparent delight in giving these young newcomers broad latitude and a platform. "Elijah Cummings has said, 'I get so much energy from you three being on my committee,'" Tlaib told me. "There is something about us three that gives us all more intent and direction and passion. He has taken me and said, 'Tlaib come here,' and I think, 'Oh no, I'm in trouble,' and he just says, 'You did a good job.' What has been written about makes it look like we are isolated, but there are some incredibly thoughtful colleagues who are thrilled to have us here." (Cummings, perhaps the greatest mentor to many of the new women, died at the age of sixty-sight in October 2019, in the middle of helping to lead the impeachment investigations into President Trump.)

Pressley told me, during a visit with her in the conference room of a public-housing complex outside Boston, that the childhood-trauma hearing was a highlight of her overall legislative career, because the topic was informed by her own experiences. "By the challenges of being raised in a single-parent home, in a neighborhood that often felt unsafe, regularly facing the threat of eviction, my father's addiction battles and experience in the criminal-justice system, my being a survivor of a decade of childhood sexual abuse and, later, campus sexual assault. So it is not hyperbole, it's not, you know, abstract for me, the impact of all of those issues," she said. "With every fiber of my being, I'm in alignment with the contribution I seek to make. And I think I'm exactly where I'm supposed to be. And so on the hardest of days, I don't have any regrets. I'm so glad I'm exactly where I am. And glad to be doing it with who I'm doing it with."

Katie Hill and Lauren Underwood have leaned on their backgrounds in advocacy and health-care policy, to flex their muscles at the sorts of companies that many Americans suspect are maximizing profits at taxpayers' and consumers' expense or at government officials overseeing policies that it often seemed they did not fully understand. In a May committee hearing for the House Education and Labor Committee, Underwood, who worked for years in public health, demanded of Alexander Acosta, then Trump's labor secretary, whether he knew the cost of contraceptives or if he knew about uses for birth control pills other than preventing pregnancy. He did not, so she gave him a list. (Acosta later resigned amid an uproar over the sweetheart nonprosecution deal he cut as US attorney in Miami with the late convicted sex criminal Jeffrey Epstein.) Hill worked over a pharmaceutical executive, juxtaposing his $30 million signing bonus against the high cost of the HIV drugs he was selling, while Ocasio-Cortez looked on, grinning.

In one striking moment, during a hearing before the House Committee on Homeland Security, Underwood accused the acting head of the Department of Homeland Security of taking part in the "intentional" deaths of migrant children held in detention centers. When the official, Kevin McAleenan, countered that she had made "an appalling accusation," Underwood dug in, saying that the deaths were the result of "a policy choice being made on purpose by this administration." Republicans on the committee made the rare move of demanding a vote to condemn her remarks.

They were joined by freshman Democrat Elissa Slotkin of Michigan, who was sitting right next to Underwood as she cast a vote against her (a small but telling harbinger of an emotional debate over the border crisis that would soon come to a head). "Lauren is a friend of mine, and I respect her, and I thought most of her questions were good ones," Slotkin told me a few hours later as she rushed to meet her chief of staff. "But at the end of the day, you have to do what's right."

I thought she was done, as Slotkin is not generally one to waste words, but she stared at me intently, her (mildly frightening) way of letting me know we were still having a conversation.

"As a former CIA officer," she said, "I know what it's like for people to think the worst of you." She then zipped off into a waiting car.

Slotkin has proved to be a tough questioner herself; she just does it drawing on her own national security background and is careful to avoid any sort of hyperbole. When the previous Homeland Security secretary, Kirstjen Nielsen, came to a hearing on border security to discuss the family separation policy, Slotkin did a careful windup before she began gently to chastise the secretary. "I'm also a former CIA officer and DOD official," she said, "so I'm a big believer in border security and have spent my life preventing homeland attacks. But I also believe we have to be a country of morals and values." Pointing out that the influx of migrants had also been a problem under the Obama administration, she said: "It didn't matter who you were, where you got your news, the vision of a small child in a cage, separated and crying, I think just hits everyone's heart, and we cannot be a country that perpetuates that."

When Secretary Nielsen demurred, Slotkin leaned in further, but she never raised her voice. "I understand it's complicated . . . ," she said. "When you saw those pictures of babies in cages, what did you do? What did you do to just scream bloody murder up the chain to the president to say 'I cannot represent an agency that is forcing its border patrol to do this?' What did you do?"

Nielsen gave no real answer.

Likewise, Abigail Spanberger, who gathered intelligence and recruited foreign intelligence assets for the CIA, often prefaced her questions with the phrase "As a former intelligence officer." During a House Foreign Affairs Committee hearing on an $8 billion arms deal to Saudi Arabia, Spanberger sharply questioned the Trump administration's decision to circumvent Congress and authorize a new emergency sale of high-tech arms to the Saudi-led coalition fighting Houthis in Yemen. Spanberger pushed the witness, Assistant Secretary of State for Political-Military Affairs R. Clarke Cooper, to unpack the plans for their use.

"Can you explain to me the disconnect to why we're providing offensive and extremely lethal weapons for apparently defensive purposes?" she asked, later noting that based on her experiences abroad, "These are not tool kits for diplomatic returns."

Addressing Cooper's complaint that Congress was taking too long to greenlight weapon sales for a war that an increasing number of lawmakers wanted no part of, she said, "I would remind you, sir, that the protracted process you are bemoaning is in fact the constitutional process that we as members of Congress have a responsibility to exercise when we are selling our weapons systems that are this lethal to countries abroad." (Congress would later pass a bill to deny the weapons, which Trump promptly vetoed.)

But Katie Porter has really been the singular star in hearings. Early on, she became known for her ability to slice through an argument with the precision of a sushi chef, impressing her colleagues, and in some cases, terrifying them with her command of the issues and her sharp questioning, often supplemented with posters, calculators, or whiteboards.

Porter has often said she got her first taste of professional inspiration from the bankruptcy class she took at Harvard from then-professor Elizabeth Warren, now a US senator and presidential candidate, who was so impressed with her student that she hired her to help direct a research project that would eventually result in Warren's book *The Two-Income Trap*. Porter later edited her own collection of scholarly papers for a book called *Broke: How Debt Bankrupts the Middle Class*, and Warren contributed a chapter. In 2012, now–fellow US senator and presidential candidate Kamala Harris, then California's attorney general, tapped Porter to oversee the distribution of a $25 billion settlement with big banks for the fraudulent foreclosures that helped tank the state's economy in 2008. Porter's meticulous command of her material set her apart, but she was not above a bit of preening and what could sometimes smell like manufactured outrage.

There was the time she worked over Consumer Financial Protection Bureau director Kathy Kraninger about her plans to ease regulations aimed at predatory payday lenders. When

Kraninger seemed flummoxed by the difference between the interest rate and an annual percentage rate, Porter said, "I'll be happy to send you a copy of the textbook that I wrote," brandishing her own monograph on contemporary consumer law. When Kraninger could not puzzle out a math problem involving a two-week payday loan for a car repair, Porter offered her a calculator.

When Jamie Dimon, the CEO of JPMorgan Chase, the largest US bank, came before the Financial Services Committee, Porter pushed him to explain how a bank teller could live on take-home pay of $35,070 a year. "I don't know," Dimon replied. "I'd have to think about that."

"Would you recommend that she take out a JPMorgan Chase credit card and run a deficit?" Porter asked.

"I don't know. I'd have to think about it," Dimon replied, distinctly uncharmed.

Porter asked the head of Equifax, a company that once released the personal credit information of 143 million Americans into the world, to spit out his social security number at the hearing. When he declined, she said: "If you agree that exposing this kind of information . . . creates harm . . . why are your lawyers arguing in federal court that there was no injury and no harm created by your data breach?"

Among all the freshman women, Porter has always seemed to me to be the one most torn between her liberal proclivities as a lifelong consumer advocate and her Orange County, California, congressional district, where she was the first Democrat ever to win the seat. She can look back on her pre-politics life as a law professor elegiacally, not so much the happy political warrior as the harried political worrier. She can be seen at times alone on the House floor, poring over papers, or storming through the hallways with the determined yet frazzled look of a commuter about to miss the last train.

Although her skills in the hearing room have raised her profile, especially among television producers, she has not always been comfortable with the spotlight. Running as a Democrat in a traditionally Republican district was difficult enough, but Porter had something in her biography that she was terrified would come to light: she was the victim of domestic violence. By her own account, which has not been disputed by her ex-husband, she was repeatedly abused as she tried to end her marriage, forcing her more than once to call the police. Her ex-husband pushed her into a wall, she said, called her a "dumb bitch" in front of their three young children, shoved their one-year-old daughter across the kitchen in her high chair, and held open the door of Porter's car to stop her from driving away from an argument. She filed for a protective order against him in 2013 and was granted custody of their children. After a short prison sentence for domestic battery, her ex was given some limited custody rights and now lives in Oregon.

Democratic advisors told me that Porter was extremely worried about discussing her abuse during the campaign. But once one of her primary opponents brought the restraining order to light, she found that many women and families related to her experiences, both with domestic violence and with her subsequent struggles as a single mom. She spoke through tears about her ordeal as she advocated for the renewal and expansion of the Violence Against Women Act, remembering how she faced the threat of her children being taken from her if she were to call the police repeatedly.

In the course of working on this book, I heard about and witnessed many tears shed over policy making, sometimes as the lawmaker recalled personal experiences connected to the policy at hand, sometimes over the draconian choices that policy makers face, sometimes just because the women were sharing their stories. Rep. Susan Wild, a new Democratic congress-woman from Pennsylvania, held back tears when she went to the floor in June to talk about her partner, who had died by suicide only weeks before. "We all need to recognize that mental health issues know no boundaries," she said as she encouraged anyone who feels suicidal to seek help. Rashida Tlaib cried during numerous press conferences and hearings as she described the harm of children in government custody and the plight of undocumented immigrants.

Staff members told me they often witnessed tears that first year when various pieces of landmark legislation passed, even when they had no shot of becoming law. Veronica Escobar could not hold back her tears on the House floor describing the death of a migrant child, and several women, and men, wiped their own tears away as she spoke. In these cases, it struck me that the tears stemmed from a sense of momentousness: the lawmak-ers were highlighting issues that had for so many years been marginalized in the legislative discourse. I also witnessed "stress response" tears, congresswomen getting choked up in meetings with fellow Democrats when they felt attacked.

For women in the workplace, crying has never been a boon, and the workplace of politics is no exception. Many male voters often cite women's penchant for being "emotional" as a rea-son not to elect them. But emotionality didn't seem to affect the prospects of former Speaker John Boehner, who during his time in Congress, from 1991 to 2015, was frequently mocked for his bursts of tears, which were usually triggered by the testimony and celebrations of others. He cried generally, but not exclusively, at things related to kids, US troops, his parents, and, at least once, the pope. Boehner, a pristine white hankie always at the ready, was also often set off by Congressional Gold Medal ceremonies. His sobbing was so extreme as he awarded the astronaut Neil Armstrong with the medal in 2011 that Armstrong looked abashed; a *Washington Post* colleague of mine in the Senate press gallery pinned a photo of the moment above his desk. "He just had a soft spot for kids and anything that harkens back to the American dream," one aide recalled. Tlaib addressed the issue of visible emotion once on Twitter: "I rather lead with compassion and show vulnerability," she wrote. "We stay connected to the people we serve when we allow ourselves to feel their pain."

Though Boehner was at times taunted for these displays, he was never penalized for them. Notably, Nancy Pelosi, who has been visibly choked up from time to time over the death of a colleague or a tragic news event, was never known for openly weeping at news conferences or difficult junctures with colleagues. (Indeed, Google the image of her sitting next to Boehner as Obama unveiled a statue in honor of civil rights activist Rosa Parks in 2013 to see which lawmaker is sniffling.) Her path was different than most of the new crew; she knew the business of politics, the good, the bad, and the ugly, and the pressures of making tough decisions.

And maybe, too, times have changed, and stoicism—not to mention a kind of female be-seen-but-not-heard deference—is no longer necessary. Katie Porter often moves between cheerfully

harried and visibly cranky, from wry and amusing to biting and
mildly unpleasant, like an underripe fruit that might be more
inviting another day. I've watched her be warm and engaging
with staff one minute, then swiftly move to note their failure
to make the correct meeting a priority. She posts endearing and
vulnerable photos of herself surfing—including ones showing
near face-plants in the ocean—but can also be cutting in a way
that seems designed to show off her law professor credibility,
like during an appearance with the comedian and commentator
Bill Maher on his talk show. When Maher admitted to Porter
that he was "a little squishy" on the issue of abortion rights,
because after his mother's difficult delivery with his sister, his
mother had been told "she shouldn't have another one," she
shot back: "Look, your mom made her choice, and we're all here
with the consequences of that choice." When I am sometimes
confused by her seeming mercurial nature, I try to imagine her
weekly commute across the country, accompanied by an hour
plus drive in Southern California traffic, where she arrives home
to kids who probably have unknowable questions about earth
science and other homework conundrums.

Among her peers, Porter is deeply respected for her transparency both about her experiences with domestic violence and for
the way she handles the difficulties of caring for school-age children while trying to serve in Congress. Porter is certainly not the
only mother in Congress, but it is a major part of her identity,
and she and other new moms have embraced that identity and
worked to find ways to make Congress more inviting to parents.

The first time we met in her DC office, Porter was eager to
show me her new shoes. "They're Cole Haan," she said, tug-
ging open the box with the sort of enthusiasm that many people

reserve for high-end chocolate and bourbon. "I'm superexcited!" She tried on the notably sensible low-heeled numbers and did a small strut around her office. "This is not something guys have to worry about," she said, and mentioned her commute but also the miles she clocks racing around the Capitol all day. (Of all the overlapping things female lawmakers told me over the years, a need for comfortable shoes was high up there.) The shoes will stay in DC, so comfort will always be an arm's length—or more likely a call to an overworked aide—away.

Among Porter's congresswoman-mom coping strategies: always keep a hanger in your purse and minivan to hang your jacket on when you need to switch back to mom mode, and keep your watch on East Coast time, even when on the West Coast, though it's not a cure for the constant strain of jet lag. "That's why I want to kill my children at seven p.m.," she said. "That usually happens at nine." She also has an airtight network of friends back in Orange County who have created a system for picking up her kids from sports when her flight is delayed.

As we talked about school calendars, public policy, and footwear, a staff member tried to cut our conversation short. "In a minute," Porter said somewhat testily, noting that little patches of time were some of the few things she was learning she could control in her nascent congressional life. "There is a huge swath of things you have no control over," she said, and her own time was often one of them, perhaps her most precious commodity. She thought back for a second to the lottery that is held at the beginning of every new Congress for member offices. "I cling to something that Ayanna Pressley said to me when people were drawing their offices," Porter said, recalling that people were getting increasingly annoyed about their lot. "She would shout

out, 'Still in Congress!' I try to stay in that moment. If you spend all your time here worrying, you forgo the opportunity."

When I visited Porter in her district a few months later during a House recess, the push and pull of her life as a single mom and a fairly liberal Democrat representing a traditionally Republican area were front and center. Her day began at 6:30 a.m. with a CNN hit—after what had already been a week of laundry, coupon clipping, grocery shopping, school drop-offs, and endless calls about legislation she was working on. Next stop, a visit at a hospital center, where she provided the staff with details about her emergency appendectomy, which would be the foundation for a bill she would introduce later to stem surprise hospital billing. She looked at her aides: What had happened to her coffee? Ugh. Whatever. She took a plastic cup of fruit off the buffet set out by the hospital staff. This would be lunch.

In the car on the way back to her district office, Porter did what most members do when they aren't on the phone with donors, begging for money; she contacted constituents who have called her office, often with a complaint. (Yes, congressional staffers do indeed carefully take down every call and record the needs and opinions of constituents; no, they don't care what you think about their votes if you do not live in their district.) She looked down the list and dialed while her district manager turned their Prius toward one of Orange County's many highways, each connecting to yet another through a string of towns just inland from the Pacific Ocean.

"Hi, this is Congresswoman Katie Porter. I got your message about SALT," she said, referring to the new tax policy that had hammered many residents of blue states by reducing their state and local tax deduction, a dagger in the heart of heavily burdened Southern Californians. Her Republican predecessor, Rep. Mimi Walters, who was so convinced she was going to beat Porter she had already begun to angle for a House leadership role before the votes were counted, had supported the tax legislation, which, it seemed, had cost her a vote with this caller. "Yeah, well, Mimi never called me after I won either," Porter cracked.

She stuck a clipboard in front of her driving district manager, unnerving me (not the supremely unflappable staffer) slightly. "Is this person calling about the Green New Deal? Yes? Well, let's call Marjory. She's a frequent caller."

Marjory was also mad about SALT, and she wanted some new gun-control laws.

The next call was to Brandon. "I heard you called about the Consumer Financial Protection Bureau," she said to him, before correcting his many misconceptions about how the agency raises its money.

"I appreciate you calling me," I could hear Brandon telling her. "That says a lot. I am of the opposite party, but I can see you do care about the job you're doing and you have integrity. That goes a long way."

Her district manager slid the Prius into a one-hour parking spot. They would be there longer than an hour, so Porter directed her to move. "I'm a rule follower," she said, to no one specifically.

Back in the office, it was time for a meeting with pilots from United Airlines, where the discussion turned to her beloved local John Wayne Airport, which does not have direct flights to Washington. She mentioned the Quiet Skies Caucus, a group of lawmakers dedicated to reducing airline noise. "Where they hear noise, I see economic opportunity," she said. "So, yeah, dude, I will not be joining the Quiet Skies Caucus."

One of the pilots was a mom friend from one of her kid's schools, who asked Porter how she liked the new gig. "I had a good thing going as a professor," she said, looking a tiny bit sad. "This is a mixed bag."

Porter was running late for her next meeting. But first, a photo with airline pilots. Done. Now, a photo of her holding the flag of a university in the district. She smiled tightly. Done. An assistant takes the flag and hands her a Nowruz basket in celebration of the upcoming Persian New Year. Click. Photos taken, to be sent to the university and the Persians of her district.

Off to the elevator, she waved goodbye to her office staff. I asked her gingerly if she had time for coffee later. "No! I have been going since six a.m." Into the elevator. Gone.

Some months later, Porter would become the first freshman House member from her state to call for Trump's impeachment, and one of the few from a district previously held by a Republican. Because of her legal background and the respect she has among her colleagues, this move was considered a small turning point in the caucus that Pelosi had been carefully trying to prevent from leaning to impeachment. "I have not come to this easily," she said in a video that felt half law professor lecture, half hostage tape. "I come to this decision after much deliberation, and I know, deeply, what this means for our democracy."

Impeachment was a slow-motion crisis, and for someone like Porter, this type of decision was especially thorny. She was, after all, someone who, both personally and professionally, had on some level spent her life fighting against "the Man," and now, as a member of Congress, in a way she had become the

Man. But beyond that was the mystery of California, where Democrats had run the table, destroying Republicans in a manner unprecedented in the modern era. Had Porter been given permission by the changing demographics and sentiment in her state to embrace the positions favored by the base of the party, or did she need to be careful not to alienate the Republicans who helped put her in office in a fluke of a year?

Indeed, for members like Porter, killing it in an oversight hearing was never going to be enough to keep their seats in marginal districts. The so-called moderates had the numbers on their side to win policy victories in the House, but unlike the liberals who enjoyed strong support at home, they were often torn between the potential wrath of their various constituents. Their base voters wanted them to uphold party principles while their conservative voters expected them to cling to middle-of-the-road positions. It was a constant struggle, and many of them had fought hard to get there, fighting off primary opponents, then slaying Republicans, leaving behind exciting careers, only to find themselves cut off from the kind of alliances that had sustained them in their old professional lives.

Being a member of Congress is more like being a golfer than a football player—at the end of the day, there is only you back in the district, answering to thousands of people who sent you there and many who did not. There is also the undeniable addiction to power that hooks so many new members almost instantly. There is the power of making a difference in your community, of meeting interesting and compelling people, of having someone bring you a panini, of breezing past TSA agents at Washington's airport, of getting invited to elegant events at the Library of Congress, of sitting on a parade float, of walking into a room back home and being the most prominent person there, the one for whom they have set up an entire table full of coffee and fruit cups and pastries—even if you don't have time to eat.

Once in Congress, no one wants to lose. And for centrists, every day is borrowed time. After listening to a lengthy disquisition from one of the more liberal members of her conference one day on the need to never vote with Republicans, Native American congressman Sharice Davids of Kansas stood up in the meeting. "I may only be here for two years," she said, according to people in the room, and which Davids later confirmed. "During that time, I want to do the best I can to live out my values."

SIX

Crisis at the Border

I will never stop speaking truth to power.
—Rep. Rashida Tlaib (D-MI)

KATIE PORTER STOOD on the House floor, about to strike one of her grievous blows.

A group of freshman Democrats had gathered nearby, embroiled in an intense discussion focused on what to do about the crisis at the southern border of the United States. For months, migrant workers from Central America had been pouring into Texas, seeking asylum, and immigration officials had been detaining them en masse, a "zero tolerance" deterrence policy that had divided the nation. Several children who had been in detention camps after being captured and separated from their parents by US agents had died. Just that week, in late June, a heartbreaking photo of the corpses of a man and his toddler daughter who had drowned in the Rio Grande had surfaced, and newly published reports attested to horrific conditions at some of the centers.

Democrats, with strong advocacy from the Congressional Hispanic Caucus, had passed a spending bill that would fund the agencies maintaining the shelters, helping to alleviate the squalid, unsanitary conditions. With a push from the Progressive Caucus, the bill included a number of conditions on the money, such as forcing the Department of Homeland Security to draft and implement standards of care and to allow unannounced inspections by members of Congress. Left-wing advocacy groups mounted a campaign to block the bill under the banner "Not One Penny," but only four Democrats opposed it: Alexandria Ocasio-Cortez, Ilhan Omar, Ayanna Pressley, and Rashida Tlaib—a.k.a. the Squad.

Until that moment, the Squad had not really been considered a legislative bloc akin to the Republicans' Freedom Caucus, which voted together in a cohesive force great enough to upend its party's agenda. In the beginning, the group had seemed more like an ongoing progressive sleepover party, but with Audre Lorde poetry readings and kombucha making instead of face masks and Truth or Dare. The name "the Squad" originally came about when Ocasio-Cortez shared a photo on Instagram, captioned simply "Squad," of the four newly elected women during an orientation event, and it stuck.

Unlike the female veterans, who had campaigned together extensively during the election, these four did not really know each other, Ayanna Pressley told me, but she said, "We had an immediate kinship in that experience of being women of color challenging twenty-year incumbents," she said.

The Massachusetts congresswoman had bristled at first when lumped together with three other nonwhite women, and she was irritated when media reports would evince surprise when they did not vote or legislate in unison. "I used to say, please do not publicly challenge and pit us against each other," Pressley said.

"This is not a sorority. What are we? Thought leaders and policy makers. So please give us bandwidth and runway to uniquely govern ourselves."

During their initial few months in Congress, the four women often sat apart on the floor and did not always vote the same way. Alexandria Ocasio-Cortez, for instance, was one of only two members of the House to vote against the package of rules that would set standards for the 116th Congress, citing her objection to a budgetary rule, and her influence over other Democrats on votes was minimal at best. She was the biggest social media star and talked almost exclusively about national policy issues. Ayanna Pressley was the only one of the four to vote for a bipartisan resolution condemning the boycott-Israel movement. She was quietly regarded as the most experienced and reliable lawmaker of the four by her colleagues, even if they found her socially remote. She tended to stay out of the Twitter fray. Ilhan Omar was the one most often in the (at times unwanted) spotlight over her positions on foreign affairs. And Rashida Tlaib mainly focused on issues of importance to her district.

"So many members can get swallowed up by what happens within the boundaries of the Hill," Rashida Tlaib told me. "When I come home, I am reminded constantly of why I ran in the first place. Children being caged at the border, that is so important, but my district doesn't want me to forget about the high rates of car insurance."

So the Squad's vote as a unit in late June against the House border bill was notable. The bill was then rejected by the Senate, which instead overwhelmingly passed its own bipartisan measure, one that senators hoped would give money to get beds for migrant children held in detention centers but with fewer strings attached to make sure conditions actually improved. Democrats were torn: pass that bill so that they could go home for the July 4 recess and at least deliver money to the agencies that were badly in need of it, or fight a likely hopeless battle to attach more conditions.

Abigail Spanberger, who had barely won a heavily Republican seat in Virginia once held by former House majority leader Eric Cantor, was joined on the floor by other freshmen in an intense debate over how to proceed. "It was a gut check," one aide told me later. "It was clear that the more progressive wing of the party was going to be very loud in opposition. We thought it was better to give money for food and water to the border now, rather than be seen drinking beers on the lake without having attended to this crisis."

Katie Porter wandered up to the group and confronted Spanberger, who had been tapping intensely on a pile of papers, asking her: If she was going to be all in for a bill passed by the Republican-controlled Senate, why not just become a Republican herself? Spanberger stormed off the House floor, blowing through the swinging glass doors and past bewildered reporters. She, like so many of this class, had young children at home and was deeply disturbed by the crisis. But Spanberger, who had taken her oath of office before Nancy Pelosi moments after voting against her for Speaker, also came from a district with mixed opinions about immigration, and where President Trump was still popular in some pockets.

Things got worse: Rep. Mark Pocan (D-WI), cochair of the Progressive Caucus, singled out a group of twenty-three moderate Democrats and twenty-three Republicans—the self-named

Problem Solvers Caucus—who had lobbied lawmakers to accept the Senate measure. "Since when did the Problem Solvers Caucus become the Child Abuse Caucus?" Pocan jabbed on Twitter. Ocasio-Cortez's chief of staff, in a remarkable breach of decorum for a staff member, took to his own Twitter account to compare moderate Democrats to "new Southern Democrats," who "certainly seem hell bent to do to black and brown people today what the old Southern Democrats did in the 40s." That wasn't just out of line; it was wholly provocative, since there were black and brown people included in the Democrats he had tarred, from Rep. Sanford Bishop, a veteran African American from southern Georgia, to the two freshman Native Americans.

The fragile unity that had been formed largely in response to Trump, whose immigration policies had been so central to the country's divisions, was fraying in broad daylight. Pelosi moved to marginalize the Squad. "All these people have their public whatever and their Twitter world," she told *New York Times* columnist Maureen Dowd. "But they didn't have any following. They're four people and that's how many votes they got."

Ocasio-Cortez's legislative influence did indeed seem to have an inverse relationship to her social-media presence. Most of the measures she introduced failed; one that would have prohibited Trump from deploying troops on the southern border for immigration enforcement and another to block funds to detain undocumented immigrants in Department of Defense facilities died unceremonious deaths in no small part because many of her colleagues had no interest in helping her out.

The nasty fighting among Democrats offended many of them. "It was just astounding to me to watch adults in positions of collective leadership act as they acted," Spanberger told me later. "Not just name-calling, like ridiculous, like personal name-calling on Twitter. Not to mention mischaracterization of facts, you know, saying that anybody who voted for the Senate bill is writing a blank check to the president. Actually, the description of the money was clearly defined, it was clearly focused on what it could be used for. It was just disingenuous." (It was true that the conditions were delineated. It was also true that the Trump administration had a poor record of following orders from Congress.) As for Porter's confrontation, Spanberger said: "Katie walked into a conversation. She didn't know what she was walking into. And it didn't work out well."

Pelosi's decision simply to drop the House version of the border emergency bill and take up the Senate's was her first big defeat. She had opted to cut her losses. As members slunk onto the House floor to vote, Rep. Maxine Waters (D-CA), the fifteen-term Trump antagonist beloved by the left, told the Speaker there needed to be a moment of silence to honor the migrants who had died. Pelosi agreed, and gave the task of introducing that moment to one of her favorite freshmen, Veronica Escobar from El Paso, who would become a leading voice from the border for Democrats.

"The photograph that all of us saw this week should tear all of us up," Escobar said as she began to weep in the well of the House. "For those of us who are parents, to see a toddler with her little arms wrapped around the neck of her father"—she paused—"there is nothing that we wouldn't do for our children, nothing, to give them a better life. Oscar and Valeria [the father and toddler] represent tens of thousands of migrants who have died as they have tried to build a better life for themselves, only to find that they are demonized and locked out of the promise that those of us who are natural born citizens are so fortunate to enjoy. In their name, let us never forget their sacrifice and the sacrifice that so many parents make for the most vulnerable among us."

Ilhan Omar was standing next to Pelosi as Escobar spoke. "Wasn't that so moving?" Omar said the Speaker asked her. "Yes, it was," Omar replied. "But we need more than words."

Escobar told me later that she had never imagined when she ran for Congress that she would face such a draining fight. "I thought for a minute that I would be able to compose myself," she said about her short floor speech. "But then I saw some of my colleagues crying, and it made it harder for me to." As for the substance of the fight, Escobar, who had been Pelosi's loyal ally, felt no bitterness toward her "There was no leverage for the Speaker," she said.

After the vote, Porter left as wrenched by the conflict as everyone else, and she and Spanberger hugged it out off the floor. "The passion we brought to the discussion reflects our sense as mothers of the harms and risks facing these families," Porter said in an email to me later. "I'm grateful that many of my colleagues, like me, are parents to young kids and that we bring this perspective to Congress. While that was a tough vote, it helps to remember that despite potential disagreements about policy, there is much more that unites us than divides us."

Of course, efforts to unravel the nation's complex immigration issue has eluded lawmakers for a generation, vexing presidents of both parties. Congress had tried lawmaker policy "gangs." Huge ambitious bipartisan immigration bills got through the Senate in 2006, with President George W. Bush's blessing, and later under President Barack Obama, which would have given immediate legal status to young immigrants brought over as children and offered a pathway to citizenship for eleven million other undocumented immigrants, in exchange for tougher border controls and moderate changes to the balance of legal immigrants. Those bills died in Republican Houses.

Now, just six months into the new Congress, the incendiary debate had begun anew, dividing the party that had long promised to solve the problem. But the freshman women, notably Escobar and Ocasio-Cortez, kept the issue of detention centers front and center. While Ocasio-Cortez stoked the passions of her followers around the country, comparing crowded, filthy detention centers with Holocaust concentration camps, Escobar leaned on House colleagues to pay attention to the issue. Because she is from the border region, knows the subject intimately, and cares about it passionately, she was careful not to demonize US Border Patrol agents or engage in hyperbole.

Talk to any woman who ran and won as "the first" of anything from her district, and she will tell you that she longs to elevate people from her district who feel voiceless or unseen. In the case of Escobar, one of the first female Latinas elected from Texas, those voices would soon extend beyond her voters. The stories of Escobar and the Squad converged over a hot weekend in El Paso, where reports had surfaced about negligence and worse at a facility housing migrant children.

Veronica Escobar, then forty-nine, a third-generation El Pasoan who grew up on a dairy farm, has a master's degree in English literature from New York University and is an expert on Chicano literature. Before winning the seat vacated by Beto O'Rourke, she served on the governing body of El Paso County, first as a county commissioner and then as judge. She used the oversight authority of her judgeship to try to curb corruption in the area and rebuild El Paso's ailing downtown, as well as to secure primary-care clinics and a children's hospital at the border.

When she arrived in Congress, she held back her votes for leadership until she knew the position of each Democrat running. She was not prone to heated oratory or angry rejoinders to opponents—the closest she had come on the House floor was her moment-of-silence speech for deceased migrants. Coming from a majority Republican state, she had long worked with the other side of the aisle, and her radiant smile and warm manner made it difficult for opponents to renounce or demonize her. As such, she had stayed out of both the spotlight and the crosshairs. Despite that, or perhaps because of it, Democrats recognized her as a credible and appealing messenger for their immigration policy message.

When we first met before the new Congress convened, Escobar's goals were as lofty as they were difficult in divided government, but like every other member who had just spent months making promises to voters, she refused to give them up. "People expect comprehensive immigration reform," she said. "I think we will get gun safety done in the House, and then it will be up to the American people to say basta, and it will take Republican constituents and families who have been touched by gun violence to finish it." She went on. "There will be many tests for all of us. Tests of courage, tests of courage over party. There will be a lot of interests trying to prevent us from doing what is right."

After the ugly floor fight over the border bill, Escobar returned to Texas, crushed but furious, for the July 4 holiday recess. She had invited a bevy of lawmakers, including the Squad, to tour detention facilities—which members of Congress and others had been barred from visiting. They wanted to verify for themselves the stories of children languishing in soiled diapers, deprived of showers and other basics, like soap and toothpaste, left to wash themselves with the occasional baby wipe and eat junk food and cold bologna sandwiches.

That week, the news organization ProPublica had reported about a private Facebook group for Border Patrol agents where they shared inflammatory comments about migrants and mocked and threatened the female lawmakers who were coming to tour one facility, even suggesting that people should pelt the women with burritos during their visit.

The lawmakers confirmed that the conditions at the camps were indeed horrifying; one woman informed them that she was told to drink water from a toilet. The tours, the Facebook group, and the defeat a week before on the House floor all culminated in a news conference outside a facility in Clint, Texas, not far from El Paso, where pro-Trump protesters stood alongside the congresswomen, screaming taunts. "We don't want Muslims," yelled one protester, as another said something about loving pork, forbidden food for Muslims, among other insults.

"Racist words and venom for racist policies, very apropos," bellowed Ayanna Pressley over the din as Alexandria Ocasio-Cortez stood next to her, rubbing her back. "This is about the preservation of our humanity," she went on. "I learned a long time ago that when change happens, it's either because people see the light or they feel the fire. Today we are lifting up these stories in the hopes that you will see the light. And if you don't, we will bring the fire!"

Rashida Tlaib stepped up to the mic next, and the barbs became sharper. As she attempted to describe conditions in the detention facility, someone yelled, "Boohoo!"

Red in the face from the heat and the harassment, Tlaib yelled back. "I will outwork your hate," she said. "I will outlove your hate! I will always put my country first." Moreover, Tlaib said, defending the congresswoman from El Paso who was being heckled in her own backyard, "And I'll tell you this! Veronica Escobar is the best goddamned Congress member from this district. You all can outscream me, but I will never stop speaking truth to power."

There, under the hot sun, was the story of the United States in 2019: two political experiments on a collision course, Trumpism and multiculturalism—a reverence for a mythical white American past, embodied by the mocking protesters, and an impatience for a multiethnic egalitarian future, embodied by this new troupe of congresswomen, black, Arab American, and Latina. Both groups were determined to shape the future of their respective parties and the country's trajectory. More than anything, the gap was generational, youth and color versus an aging, shrinking white majority that felt both disenfranchised by a contemporary and shifting nation—a nation that, as their T-shirts proclaimed, was FULL—and emboldened by the Trump presidency to express a racism that many Americans had believed was outmoded after eight years of a black president. The United States of these first women of their generation and race to represent their communities in Washington, DC, was a pluralistic one, striving toward egalitarianism and sustained by, rather than suspicious of, government. It was integrated into the world around it, which held riches to be embraced and absorbed.

To them, the gulf felt insurmountable and demoralizing. "This is such a frightening and troubling time," Escobar told me the week after the trip. "It's very difficult to find hope."

Yet for so many millions of Americans, the world does not feel so starkly rendered. Many people outside the Beltway (and political Twitter) live lives defined by prosaic decisions: Mow the lawn or watch Netflix? Brave the traffic or use public transportation? Pay their medical bill or buy some groceries? Yoga or Orange Theory? Onion rings or fries? Their dealings with members of Congress are rare and generally to be avoided, as such an interaction would likely signal a problem with their social security check or a shakedown for a campaign donation.

The left and the right have taken turns over generations shouting, "Where's the outrage?" and demanding that someone "return" their country to them. But we are all the sum product of a nation that has been both taken from us and renewed. Just as twenty years before President Obama's election, his presidency would have been unimaginable, five years before Trump's, his presidency was perhaps even more so. Both of these eras resulted from the collective choice of US citizens, however divided and driven in part by the whimsical choices of a narrow swath of voters who chose to show up on Election Day. But the scene in Clint, Texas, made the choice feel more stark: not one between political parties or theories of philosophies, but rather the core of the nation's identity.

Back in Washington, the fight remained within the Democratic Party. Members of Congress, especially newcomers, always have a hard time accepting the limits of their control in divided government. But their leaders often contribute to their frustration in trying to make every faction feel heard, then overpromising about what can be achieved. This template had been set by John Boehner when the Tea Party Republicans—most of them driven out by 2019—took over the House years before.

After the recess in a meeting with her caucus, Nancy Pelosi warned against allowing political disagreements to become a toxic force in the party, creating the sort of purity tests that had driven away moderates from Republican ranks. "Some of you are here to make a beautiful pâté, but we're making sausage most of the time," she said as members laughed, according to a transcript released by House aides. "And we just have to get the best we can get. Fight for it. Not settle for anything. But understand that every fight is the beginning of the next fight. This is a team. On a team, you play as a team. . . . We are up against a Republican Party, in the administration and in the Congress, that does not believe in governance, in honoring its responsibility to the people, does not believe in science, data, truth, evidence, fact to act upon."

She added, "So don't play into their hands. Every day some of our members have to fight the fight for their reelection. It's easy for me in my district, right? I never have to worry about whether a Democrat will represent that district, whether it's me or somebody else. But, in their districts, it makes a difference for what we can do for the American people if we have the majority." She went on: "We have important fish to fry. We have a major opposition to our very value system about what America is. We must win this next election, and it is no foregone conclusion that we will."

Alluding to her many years as one of the Republicans' favorite women to attack (along with, of course, Hillary Clinton and Elizabeth Warren, and now AOC and Ilhan Omar), Pelosi said to bring it on. "I'm happy to be anybody's target," she said. "I've been the target all along."

She finished with this plea to her fracturing caucus: "You got a complaint? You come and talk to me about it. But do not tweet about our members and expect us to think that that is just okay."

A few weeks later, Pelosi would meet privately with Ocasio-Cortez to talk about, among other things, the increasingly toxic role that her chief of staff, Saikat Chakrabarti, had taken on in the caucus. His tweets alone were not greeted with joy, Pelosi had already noted in the caucus meeting, and attacks by other AOC staff members on fellow worker bees on the Hill, calling them, essentially, capitalist losers, had already frosted many of her colleagues. Ocasio-Cortez may have been as popular as ever outside Washington in her role as architect of the progressive left agenda, but among many of her colleagues, she was to be avoided.

Shortly after that meeting, Chakrabarti quit his job, and Ocasio-Cortez's spokesman, Corbin Trent, left to work on her reelection campaign. Advantage, Washington.

For women elected in areas where their political future depends on Republicans, the outlook seems less clear. "There are some people who don't really seem to understand the math of the majority making," Spanberger told me after a particularly frustrating week on the Hill. "Some people think that we're out of touch, and that if we just worked hard, more Democrats would come out of the woodwork and so we should just try to say all the things that excite all the Democrats. Well, you can say that until you're blue in the face. There are just not that many Democrats in my district."

In early August, Pelosi joined Omar and other members of the Congressional Black Caucus on a long-planned trip to Ghana to commemorate the four hundredth anniversary of the American slave trade. Omar, who sat with the Speaker on the plane for a long stretch of the trip, tweeted a photo of the two of them in Africa, the freshman in a lovely flowing sky-colored jumper and the Speaker in one of her signature elegant suits. Perhaps the purpose of the photo was to demonstrate their unity—or more likely, their respective power.

The president, meanwhile, had been watching all this unfold from his cloistered perch in the White House, his own Twitter account at the ready. Fearing that Pelosi would unite the Democrats and lessen the pressure on the Squad, Trump decided it was time to take his next shot.

SEVEN

This Is What Diversity Looks Like

I want everyone to know that we will keep fighting.
—Rep. Ilhan Omar (D-MN)

IT WAS MID-APRIL, and spring had finally arrived in Washington. A pink curtain of cherry blossoms drooped over a group of lawmakers and religious leaders who had gathered for a press conference outside the Capitol to announce a bill to undo President Trump's ban on travelers from some Muslim-majority countries. Standing a bit to the side was Ilhan Omar, one of just three Muslims in the House. For weeks, she had been at the center of the earliest and what would become one of the most lingering conflicts among Democrats, underscoring the complexity of a truly diverse Congress.

Khizr Khan, a Pakistani immigrant whose son had been killed in the Iraq War and who had been attacked by then-candidate Trump after the Democratic National Convention, spoke first. Khan had become a fixture in the Muslim rights world, and he seemed to wear his son's loss freshly every time I saw him, a man less animated by his fights, as some of the women in Congress clearly were, than burdened by them. Hunched over and soft of voice, he introduced Congresswoman Omar, calling her "my dear sister."

Omar stepped to the mic, wiping a tear from her eyes as she recalled her campaign promise to fight the travel ban. "When I was twelve years old, I myself came here as a refugee," she said, referring to the four years she spent in a refugee camp in Kenya after escaping civil war in her birthplace of Somalia. Describing the current ban, Omar choked up. "It's meant mothers cannot be at the bedside of their dying children," she said, alluding to a woman who had been unable to travel to see her gravely ill child in her last days.

Over the last several weeks, the freshman lawmaker from Minneapolis had had altercations with her Democratic colleagues, had been attacked by both anti-Muslim groups and Jewish organizations, and had become the topic of an official legislative rebuke on the House floor for her critiques of Israel and its supporters in the United States. Slight as a doe, with big dark eyes and a lilting voice that somehow evokes melting ice cream, Omar did not fit the image of villain that her detractors made her out to be, and she had done a good job of keeping a poker face in public. Now, among her allies, she allowed a few cracks to show in her usual steely composure.

"I want everyone to know that we will keep fighting," she said before turning from the mic and hugging Rashida Tlaib, the only other Muslim congresswoman.

Minutes later, a group of Republican members of Congress gathered on the steps of the Capitol to denounce the "socialist" Democrats now in charge of the House.

One Capitol, two very different realities: Omar's foreign

policy views, shaped by her experiences both as a refugee and a Muslim, had been an object of fascination and controversy before she even got to Congress, particularly her views on Israel. Over the last decade of the strongly conservative Likud Party government's control of Israel, a chasm has opened up among American Jews over continued US support for its historically unassailable ally. Many more liberal Jews, especially college students, have been feeling increasingly squeamish about the Jewish state after decades of that government's harsh treatment of Palestinians, the growing influence of powerful if very small ultrareligious groups on Israeli society, and the seeming futility of generations of peace processes in the region.

It did not help matters that Donald Trump had formed such a public, unctuous bond with Israel's right-wing prime minister Benjamin Netanyahu, who had been doing his level best for years to link the Likud with the Republican Party of the United States, even as American Jews remain by and large doggedly Democratic. The bond would culminate in the prime minister's barring of both Ilhan Omar and Rashida Tlaib from a visit to Israel in August, a move so ostentatiously political that even a number of Republicans denounced it.

Omar came to Congress determined to bring a Shirley Chisholm–style folding chair to the table on this topic. During her House campaign, a Twitter post of hers from November 2012, when she was still a nutrition outreach coordinator with the Minnesota Department of Education resurfaced: "Israel has hypnotized the world, may Allah awaken the people and help them see the evil doings of Israel. #Gaza #Palestine #Israel." That angered Jews in her home state and beyond, who saw in that tweet coded anti-Semitic language dating back to the death of Jesus. Omar alternated between defensive and apologetic, the beginning of her struggle to convincingly explain the difference between her foreign policy criticisms and standard anti-Semitic tropes, of which she often claimed to be ignorant.

"I don't know how my comments would be offensive to Jewish Americans," she told CNN. "My comments precisely are addressing what was happening during the Gaza War, and I'm clearly speaking about the way the Israeli regime was conducting itself in that war."

Later, in a tweet, she sought to clarify her remarks: "It's now apparent to me that I spent lots of energy putting my 2012 tweet in context and little energy in disavowing the anti-semitic trope I unknowingly used, which is unfortunate and offensive," she wrote. "With that said, it is important to distinguish between criticizing a military action by a government and attacking a particular people of faith. I will not shy away from criticism of any government when I see injustice—whether it be Saudi Arabia, Somalia, even our own government!" She added, "What is important to me is that people recognize that there's a difference between criticizing a military action by a government that has exercised really oppressive policies and being offensive or attacky to particular people of faith."

Omar's stated position on the conflict is in many ways in line with the mainstream—she supports a two-state solution, two sovereign nations, one Jewish, one Palestinian, side by side, which happens to be the official position of the US government. But she had also been open about her support for the BDS movement to boycott, divest from, and sanction Israel to pressure it to improve treatment of Palestinians. This movement, for the most part, had been confined to college campuses, but Democratic leaders feared it would wash up on the shores of a political party increasingly reliant on minority and immigrant votes. The Democratic Party may have been trying to up diversity in its ranks, but was it actually ready for a new dynamic around policies so long rooted in assumptions and traditions on the Hill? Omar's views on Israel would be an early test.

Ilhan Omar's journey to Congress was as unlikely as it was remarkable. Born in 1982 to a well-off family in Somalia's capital, Mogadishu, the youngest of seven siblings, her mother would die when she was two years old, and she and her siblings would be raised by her father and grandfather. Like many families, hers was caught in the cross fire of the Somali civil war, and when she was eight years old, they were forced to flee. The family spent four years in the Utanga refugee camp in Kenya, an isolated outpost where she and her siblings had no access to education.

In a 2017 speech at the United Way of Central Iowa's Refugee Summit, Omar described the refugee camp as "very segregated from other people." She said, "There were no schools, sanitation systems, or running water. To fetch water, we had to go to the next city over, carrying our buckets, every day. Because I was the youngest in the family, fetching water became my job. I would walk through the woods, carrying the buckets, and walk back with them full. On the way, I would often see the children from the city. I would watch them play and go to school, wearing their cute little school uniforms, and I would wonder why I could no longer do that. When I asked my father, he said that one day, one day, we would move to America and that everything would change. We would have access to everything that was available to Americans: free education, economic security— a normal life. America was a land of abundance, where everyone had these things, and my father dreamed that one day we would be in America."

Omar now often speaks of her high expectations for life in the United States, and of her gratitude that the country took in her family. "No one loves this country more than I do," I have often heard her say. She believes in the principle of free speech, and this is why, she says, she feels an obligation to criticize.

In 1995, the family was indeed granted refugee status in the United States, and two years later settled in Minneapolis, in a neighborhood full of other Somali refugees. After learning English, Omar came to feel like both a permanent outsider at school—she says she was often picked on by her American classmates—and an assimilator. While in high school, she worked as an interpreter at the local Democratic caucuses. She then attended North Dakota State University in Fargo, where she graduated with a bachelor's degree in political science and international studies, and where her interests in community organizing and politics grew.

Her first job, starting in 2006, was as a community nutrition educator with the University of Minnesota. In mid-2012, before she started working for the Minnesota Department of Education, she served as campaign manager for Kari Dziedzic, who was running for state senate. Eventually, Omar decided to give politics a try herself and ran for a spot in the Minnesota legislature in 2016, becoming the first Somali American Muslim legislator in the United States. She was so politically inexperienced that she did not return the congratulatory calls from some members of the state's congressional delegation; it was because, another House member told me, she had no idea who they were.

Green or not, in 2018 Omar quickly saw an opening to move up when Rep. Keith Ellison decided to leave his US House seat to run for Minnesota attorney general. His announcement came as the state filing deadline approached, and Omar had just three hours to decide whether to declare.

She entered a six-way primary, which included prominent Minnesota politicians. Her campaign mirrored those of many other young Democratic women who won that year, focusing on Medicare for All, increasing the federal minimum wage, and championing a standard progressive agenda. What endeared her to voters, it seems, was her backstory of perseverance against great odds.

Her campaign also had a massive organizing strategy: from the time she announced her candidacy that June until Election Day, her team reached out to more than 330,000 constituents via door knocking, texting, and calling, a textbook contemporary digitally driven campaign. She won the primary handily, and that November, she defeated the sacrificial Republican with 78 percent of the vote, more total votes than any other member in her class.

Omar, in many ways, is the contemporary face of modern female Muslims in the United States. She dresses modestly in stylish suits with large, often candy-colored necklaces, and the aforementioned colorful headscarf for every one of her outfits, including a fetching checkered scarf that she wore for a cameo, along with entertainers Mary J. Blige, Jennifer Lopez, and Ellen DeGeneres, in Maroon 5's video for its song "Girls Like You." She began wearing the hijab after the 9/11 attacks, she told me, less for religious reasons and more as a way of declaring her identity in the face of incipient prejudice against Muslims.

When she arrived in Congress, she feared a House ban on hats would prevent her from being able to wear the hijab on the floor, but she said Nancy Pelosi told her this would be "the one thing you will never have to worry about," and indeed the freshmen soon instituted a change to the rule, to expressly permit head coverings for religious reasons on the House floor for the first time in 181 years.

At the same time, Omar is a fierce advocate for gay rights and other liberal social positions not always associated with Muslims. Likewise, Rashida Tlaib moves comfortably between traditionally religious expressions in Arabic and the salty language of a marine. Most of the country was first introduced to her cursing the day she was sworn in, and the more animated she becomes in conversations, the more cursing she does.

Omar and Tlaib represent the attitudes of many American Muslims, particularly, the younger generation, according to Farhana Khera, the executive director of Muslim Advocates, a legal advocacy group and an ally of the new Muslim women in Congress. "Maybe the word I'm looking for, it's like 'rock stars,'" Khera told me, "a proxy for the community." Omar and Tlaib were not the first Muslims to join Congress, but as the first Muslim women, they carry extra burdens: they embody the hopes of other Muslim women seeking to run for office, while engendering suspicion in the broader diaspora, where some male Muslim officials from other countries have raced to criticize them—not to mention bearing all the cultural biases that continue to dominate US politics, in which outspoken women are overwhelmingly scrutinized, especially when they are not white.

Omar's predecessor in Minnesota's Fifth District, Keith Ellison, the first Muslim in Congress, had his fair share of controversies; some accused him of a coziness with the leader of the Nation of Islam, Louis Farrakhan, who is widely viewed by Jews as anti-Semitic, a relationship Ellison always denied.

Rep. André Carson (D-IN), the only male Muslim currently in Congress, hails from a Midwest district not quite as electorally safe as his female colleagues' districts. Like all other Muslims in Congress, he has faced criticisms, but he told me, "Ilhan and Rashida help provide a voice for the many Muslim Americans who feel underrepresented. I said a decade ago that one day we will see Muslim women in Congress, and they have come as powerful, outspoken women who are criticized for speaking their minds."

Khera sees it more starkly. "You've got a Muslim black refugee, and they're women, as well," she said. And so it's because of that confluence of factors that they're seen as a threat."

When Omar arrived in Congress, Pelosi assigned her to the Foreign Affairs Committee, which unnerved some Jewish Democrats who knew of her support for the boycott movement against Israel. The committee's chair, Rep. Eliot Engel of New York, was about as staunch an ally of Israel as there was in the House, and he made it clear early on he was watching—a member of the old guard representing traditional unconditional support for Israel sending a message to a new member with a different view.

"My colleague from Minnesota recognizes that her 2012 tweet was 'unfortunate and offensive,' which I appreciate," Engel told a Jewish news service shortly after Omar joined his committee. "In the days ahead, I hope to work with her and all members of the Committee to share my views about the importance of the U.S.-Israel relationship and the dangers of anti-Semitism."

Despite these pressures, Omar's early days in the House seemed joy-infused in large part thanks to her female colleagues. As a mother of three children ranging in age from seven to sixteen, she asked her fellow representatives for advice on how to be a good congresswoman mom. Rep. Grace Meng (D-NY), from Queens, said she would have her own children answer Omar; Meng's kids told her to make ample use of FaceTime to ask her kids lots of questions about what was going on back home. Omar was thrilled with all her new colleagues and their shared commitment to supporting one another rather than engaging in the rivalries that have often befallen women in politics. "Having more women in Congress matters," she said, "because we are more skilled at building relationships and nurturing them."

Those first weeks, her office buzzed with merriment. Omar smiled and laughed at every reception and press conference I saw her at, clearly enjoying the spotlight. She seemed to take in stride the more ominous attention she and other freshman women were receiving from Republican men, who went out of their way to find fault with them. When Alexandria Ocasio-Cortez cast her vote for Nancy Pelosi on the day the new House voted for Speaker, loud boos had risen from the Republican side of the aisle. "They are jealous," Omar told me, which may be the case, since many of those members had never before tasted the bitter brine of being in the House minority. "They wish they could be us."

Early on, House leaders warned members not to write their own tweets, which seemed quaint at best and anathema to some of the younger members who had spent their entire campaigns reaching out to voters on social media. AOC even gave some of her befuddled colleagues an official Twitter tutorial. That platform would soon set Omar greatly off course on the one issue for which she was already under the microscope: the United States' relationship to Israel.

The hypocrisy of attacking Ilhan Omar and Rashida Tlaib for their remarks about Israel was not lost on many in the House, especially members of the Congressional Black Caucus who had watched for years as some Republicans had made offensive statements. Rep. Steve King, a Republican from Iowa, made repeated racist and anti-Semitic remarks with little to no censure from his colleagues. In October 2018, then–house majority leader Kevin McCarthy (R-CA) accused Jewish billionaires George Soros, Tom Steyer, and Michael Bloomberg of trying to buy the election, a freighted charge in an era of rising anti-Semitism. Another Republican, Rep. Paul Gosar of Arizona, falsely suggested that the August 2017 white supremacist march in Charlottesville, Virginia, had been secretly funded by Soros. In January 2018, Rep. Matt Gaetz (R-FL) invited the notorious far-right internet troll and accused Holocaust denier Chuck Johnson to be his guest at Trump's first State of the Union. Not a word of admonishment came from the Republican leaders. Only in January 2019, after Steve King gave an interview to the *New York Times* in which he asked when the term "white supremacist" had become negative, did Republicans finally move to strip him of his committee assignments.

That action, belated as it was, paved the way for them to create a wedge issue out of the Israel question for Democrats. One weekend in February, the journalist Glenn Greenwald made the point on Twitter, arguing that there was nothing wrong with criticizing a foreign government. Omar replied in full public view, "It's all about the Benjamins baby," adding a music emoji to show she was referring to a popular rap song. In context, she seemed to be alluding to the influence of the American Israel

Public Affairs Committee, a nonprofit organization whose members donate heavily to pro-Israel lawmakers.

The backlash was almost instant. Centrist Democratic congressman Max Rose quickly rebuked her, pointing out that her language played off the long-standing trope that Jews seduce and control politicians with money. "Congresswoman Omar's statements are deeply hurtful to Jews, including myself," he tweeted. Criticism from other Jewish Democrats, and Republicans, was unrelenting.

Although she and her staff would often point out that she grew up among refugees and lacks awareness of anti-Semitic buzzwords, Omar quickly understood that she had made a grievous error. That evening, Josh Gottheimer, a moderate, called Pelosi to complain. He and other Jewish Democrats felt Omar had crossed a bright line. What were the House leaders going to do?

Seeking to avoid the horde of reporters who had gathered outside her office, Omar and her staff had retreated to her apartment near the Hill. The freshman congresswoman still seemed baffled. Her communications director, Jeremy Slevin, a young progressive who had grown up in a large Jewish family, quietly detailed to his boss his own father's upbringing in New York City, where non-Jewish classmates often hurled pennies at him, and the anti-Semitic bullying around money and its symbols that had followed him into college. Slevin suggested she apologize.

While this conversation was occurring, Pelosi had conferred with the rest of the leadership slate. She called Omar to tell her that she had been hearing from unhappy colleagues and that Omar was going to be the subject of a joint statement from leaders condemning her words.

Omar said she understood, but she was blindsided by the language of the statement, she later told aides, which was more pointed than she had expected: "Congresswoman Omar's use of anti-Semitic tropes and prejudicial accusations about Israel's supporters is deeply offensive."

She responded with a tweet: "Anti-Semitism is real and I am grateful for Jewish allies and colleagues who are educating me on the painful history of anti-Semitic tropes. My intention is never to offend my constituents or Jewish Americans as a whole. . . . I unequivocally apologize."

But, she added, she still believed the American Israel Public Affairs Committee had too much influence in Washington. "At the same time, I reaffirm the problematic role of lobbyists in our politics, whether it be AIPAC, the NRA or the fossil fuel industry," the tweet said.

As the reporters continued their vigil outside Omar's office, Max Rose stomped over to find her himself. She wasn't there, so he spoke to them instead. The fireplug congressman, a military veteran who often speaks with the edge of a New Yorker who has just been cut in line at Starbucks, admonished the reporters for failing to take on what he viewed as anti-Semitic remarks previously made by the former majority leader. "Their caucus stayed united and had his back, and none of you called him out on that," he growled. "That caucus can't be chickenshit in face of anti-Semitism either."

While some Democratic members also put out their own statements critical of Omar, others held their fire. "The smart operatives see that is where the energy is," one aide to a prominent member of Congress told me, referring to the base that is quick to defend Omar, Ocasio-Cortez, and others from attacks. "The new identity stuff is really important. I worry less these days about people thinking my boss is too nice to pharma than that he is a white dude tsk-tsking a young woman of color from Minnesota with an incredible story."

Republicans had the precise opposite view. Any chance to seize on anti-Semitism, both to distract from the alt-right followers of Trump who continued to help fuel his base and to force Democrats to have to answer to critics on the issue was a boon. So Republican leaders once again turned to a "motion to recommit," and moved to attach an amendment condemning anti-Semitism to the bill to end military assistance for the war in Yemen, a bill that Omar had been championing since she got to Congress.

Tlaib, Pressley, and Ocasio-Cortez looked stricken as the text of this amendment was read and fellow Democrat Eliot Engel announced that he supported it; once again, a debate over an issue close to their hearts had been enveloped in controversy. The measure was insidious in its blandness, because it made it hard to vote against; everyone in the House voted yes, including Omar. Then, Republicans voted against the underlying Yemen withdrawal bill anyway. Another day in Congress.

Later that week, on Valentine's Day, I stopped by Omar's office. The phones were ringing incessantly, while a Minnesota water group and civil servant advocates clustered in separate meetings in corners of the tiny office. It felt chaotic and cramped.

The young aide answering the phone was trying to nibble at her chocolate-covered doughnut, but the calls would not stop. "Okay, I will pass on the message," she said repeatedly.

"She never used the word 'Jewish,'" she told another caller, looking forlornly at her doughnut.

In the meantime, Omar and Tlaib faced continual threats to their safety. In Minnesota that March, a gas station restroom was festooned with graffiti: *Assassinate Ilhan Omar.* Later that month, at a celebration for the West Virginia Republican Party, someone hung a poster linking Omar to the 9/11 terror attacks, depicting her under a photo of the burning Twin Towers and the words "NEVER FORGET" - YOU SAID... 'I AM THE PROOF - YOU HAVE FORGOTTEN.

That same racial and religious animus continued to marinate, and play out publicly, in the minds of the president and his on-air Fox News supporters. At one point, talk show host Tucker Carlson sniffed, "Our country rescued Ilhan Omar from the single worst place on earth. We didn't do it to get rich; in fact, it cost us money. We did it because we are kind people. How did Omar respond to the remarkable gift we gave her? She scolded us and called us names; she showered us with contempt."

The Muslim Advocates group had been monitoring far-right buzzwords and codes for years. "It's the exact same messaging we've seen for well over a decade," Farhana Khera told me. "It's always about American Muslim values being inconsistent with American values, that we're going to bring Sharia law, that we're a threat. And then there's sometimes other submessages about we don't treat our women well, which they don't use as much with Rashida and Ilhan because they are actually exactly counter to the stereotype."

Khera explained that this messaging is now "currency," used by local communities to reject refugees and to inflame racism on a national level, as the president has been doing. "I would say it's probably more clear today than ever before," she said. "I think it's not just anti-Muslim, but people who are deeply threatened by nonwhites slowly gaining traction and power." But, she added, whether this was evidence of an ugly last gasp en route to a more just, diverse, liberal order remained unclear.

After the outreach Omar made to Jewish colleagues and the blows she had absorbed, she seemed to have gotten through the anti-Semitism crisis. But then in March, she delivered a message that tried the patience of even some of her most loyal advocates. Speaking at a progressive town hall meeting at Busboys and Poets, a famous Washington hangout, Omar spoke extensively about her life in Congress as a religious minority and her desire to advocate for the Palestinian people. "What people are afraid of is not that there are two Muslims in Congress," she said. "What people are afraid of is that there are two Muslims in Congress that have their eyes wide open, that have their feet to the ground, that know what they're talking about, that are fearless, and that understand that they have the same election certificate that everyone in Congress does."

But the one sentence that caught fire was this one: "I want to talk about the political influence in this country that says it is okay for people to push for allegiance to a foreign country. And I want to ask, why is it okay for me to talk about the influence of the NRA, of fossil fuel industries, or Big Pharma, and not talk about a powerful lobby that is influencing policy?"

It was the single word *allegiance* that once again strayed into dangerous historical language against Jews, who had long been accused of being more faithful to their own people and to Israel than to the United States, a dual-loyalty trope that goes back centuries.

Again, Omar claimed ignorance, but her claims began to strain credulity with some of her colleagues. "I am getting really frustrated with Ilhan," one House member with a background in national security, where the remark hit especially hard, told me. Jewish members of the Department of Defense, the CIA, and other agencies were always careful, for instance, to meet with Israeli officials with a translator in the room, lest the dual loyalty accusation ever surface.

Rashida Tlaib had also come under fire for previous remarks about Israel, and she took heat for association with some activists who were linked to anti-Semitic groups. But by and large, Tlaib's peers tend to view her differently. The daughter of Palestinian immigrants from the Detroit area, she is first and foremost an advocate for Palestinians. Her district is home to one of the largest Arab American communities in the country. When she arrived at her new office on Capitol Hill with her parents, they peered at the map of the world hanging in the outer room and put a Post-it note on Israel. "We should change that to Palestine," her father said.

In meetings with her colleagues, Tlaib spoke movingly of her grandmother, who was still in the West Bank, and of the harassment of Arab Americans, including her parents in Detroit by the FBI and protesters after 9/11.

During a short speech on the floor against a bipartisan measure to condemn boycotts of Israel, she said: "I stand before you as the daughter of Palestinian immigrants, parents who experienced being stripped of their human rights, the right to freedom of travel, equal treatment. So I can't stand by and watch this attack on our freedom of speech and the right to boycott the racist policies of the government and the state of Israel." The speech got far less criticism or attention than Omar's previous remarks, perhaps because members were focused on Israel's current government.

Several Jewish members in the freshman class told me they found Tlaib's narrative compelling and educational, and had the sense that she was learning from them as well, while they found Omar at best indifferent.

In addition, Tlaib's activism around Palestine was often subordinate to many other areas of public policy that had dominated her years as a street fighter, from civil rights to environmental justice to corporate malfeasance to the high rates of auto insurance in Michigan, one of her pet issues in Congress. From day one, she was one of the loudest voices in favor of the president's impeachment: at orientation, she gave each of her fellow freshman a copy of *The Constitution Demands It: The Case for the Impeachment of Donald Trump,* by Ron Fein, John Bonifaz, and Ben Clements, as a welcome gift.

"Rashida has always been Rashida," Debbie Dingell, who has known Tlaib since she was a young activist lawyer, told me. "I'm not going to speak for her. But I'm not sure this experience is what she thought it would be. I mean, people come here to make a difference. We each come here and we have issues that we care about, that we're passionate about, that we want to fix, we want to change. We have visions, and then suddenly you're in this pack of people." But at least with her old friend, Dingell noted, what you see is what you get. "Rashida will say to me, 'What did I do now?' She and I talk honestly if I think, you know, if she's done something or something bothers me. But we also support each other. I would rather have a Rashida, who will never lie to me. A lot of these people will lie to your face."

While Omar moves through the public sphere seemingly indifferent to the strife, Tlaib radiates more self-doubt. And Dingell was right that Tlaib was experiencing some disillusionment.

"It's love-hate, I guess," Tlaib said when I asked for her feelings about her new job. "One of my more senior colleagues sat next to me the other day, and he said, 'How do you like it, kid?' And I said, 'Do you ever feel there is a lack of urgency here?' and he said, 'That's how I felt my first term.' Then he stared out and said, 'I wonder if this place just beats it out of you.' Well, I hope it doesn't."

These differences—in personality, in framing—help to explain why Omar, more than Tlaib, found herself at the center of the Israel debate. If she had focused her criticism specifically on Benjamin Netanyahu, or on the hard-right drift of AIPAC in recent years, or that group's fealty to Trump despite his failure to criticize his anti-Semitic followers, Omar might have pushed the policy conversation in a direction already taken by a growing group of liberal American Jews and found her natural allies in the Jewish community. But her language continued to create the impression that her beef was not with Israel, but with Jews, and so she would continue to be a complicated figure.

Members of Congress and the Washington Jewish establishment with whom I spoke wanted to take her at her word about her ignorance of the tropes. At the same time, anti-Semitic sentiments are prevalent in her birth country of Somalia, a deeply conservative Muslim nation, and those sentiments ferment in refugee camps. Ayaan Hirsi Ali, a human rights activist and a research fellow at the conservative Hoover Institution, recalled her childhood in Somalia as steeped in disdain for Jews. "I never heard the term 'anti-Semitism' until I moved to the Netherlands in my 20s," she wrote in the *Wall Street Journal*. "But I had firsthand familiarity with its Muslim variety. As a child in Somalia, I was a passive consumer of anti-Semitism. Things would break, conflicts would arise, shortages would occur—and adults would blame it all on the Jews." She added, "We were taught to pray: 'Dear God, please destroy the Jews, the Zionists, the state of Israel.'"

Omar bristles at the notion that people from Muslim countries would have any particular biases against Jews, but the issue is likely steeped in the language norms of a culture, just as many Americans grew up hearing expressions like "Indian giver" but failed to consider its true impact until adulthood. She knew few Jews growing up in the land of the "frozen chosen," a term used locally to describe Jewish Minnesotans, who played a large role in welcoming Somali refugees, in much the way the Scandinavians welcomed the Jews a generation ago. But her views on Israeli and US foreign policy, she said, were clearly informed by her background as a refugee: "Clearly I am bringing a different perspective that not many of our colleagues share. There is an opportunity to understand these issues from a personal perspective at the most intense time of our nation's history. We're having an intensive conversation about who should be at the table. I'm quite okay with it. At the moment, what is important is being focused on shifting the narrative."

Indeed, given that she came from one of the world's most insular and conservative places to emerge as a symbol of American progressivism, her transition was fated to have its bumps. At the end of the day, to admire Omar is to live in conflict with her casual dismissal of Jewish concerns.

With Omar's "allegiance" remarks, Pelosi was once again under pressure, and she decided that the House would need an official resolution condemning anti-Semitism. That decision, which on the surface seemed targeted at a single member over a narrow if explosive issue, untapped a simmering anger of another sort among the sizable group of black Democrats. They had been listening to offensive racist language from Trump and his allies for the better part of two years, and had watched as a series of black youths were shot by the police, as white Americans targeted black neighbors with nuisance calls to the police, and worse. Where was the resolution for them?

The majority of House members did not even know the motion was coming until they showed up for a weekly meeting, which instantly turned tense. Rep. Cedric Richmond (D-LA), a former chair of the Congressional Black Caucus, angrily asked why no resolutions had been offered by Democrats in previous years to condemn instances of racism. Richmond, a former Morehouse College baseball player, cuts an impressive figure, charming and assertive. Since joining the House, he has single-handedly ensured the rout of Republicans by Democrats at the annual congressional baseball game. One of his best friends is the far-right congressman from his home state of Louisiana, Rep. Steve Scalise. Richmond's authority matters, and so he spoke for many of his colleagues when he demanded, "I want to know what the bar is."

The House floor on swearing-in day had been a visual tale of two parties, and one that Democrats had enjoyed highlighting. White men in navy suits had populated the Republican side of the room, while the Democrats' side was resplendent with women and people of color in a fashion rainbow, joyous in the growth in diversity that had been the cornerstone goal of the party's base. But months later, the Democratic leaders still didn't seem to grasp that many of their members had not come to Washington to convene under the old rules; they had come to adjust them. Jahana Hayes said the tensions surrounding the anti-Semitism resolution "brought to the surface uncomfortable conversations that people were not prepared to have."

There was more. Hayes told Pelosi she had not liked learning about the resolution via cable news. "It was the same thing when the Mueller report came out. I had people calling my office, and I had heard nothing," she said. "The question was, How are we communicating in an inclusive way?"

Other freshmen shared this view: they wanted to know what the Democratic leadership was up to, and they wanted it communicated in a more professional and regular manner. Pelosi expressed annoyance with Hayes's bluntness, but the freshman congresswoman was undaunted. "When Cedric said, 'Is there a hierarchy of hate?' the room went silent," Hayes told me. "I've heard questions like that in my community over and over. And nobody really answered that. The room went silent."

America's affluent Jews may be mostly Democratic and liberal, but they are a tiny voting bloc. Left unsaid was the obvious fact: Democratic leaders did not want to offend Jewish donors, or, worse yet, see them drift to the Republicans. Privately, black members complained that the largely white leaders came to them when they needed votes but had failed to be fierce advocates for the issues that people of color cared about most deeply.

In June, Lauren Underwood would be greeted at a parade near her hometown with a Nazi salute from a local Republican volunteer. The incident was met with silence once again, I noted, from both sides.

"What was a surprise to me is how consumed Congress had become about a colleague," Rashida Tlaib told me, referring to Ilhan Omar. "Newer members of all different backgrounds were all taken aback by [her] approach, even if they disagreed or were even pained by her statements. But, I have to tell you, I was in the Michigan statehouse for six years. One of my colleagues asked for my birth certificate in committee, and no one called him out. In another incident, he vilified Latino immigrants. Still, they never went that far," she said. "The policing of words from women of color seems to be stronger here. We do feel we are silenced and hushed sometimes, in the terminology we use, and the fact that we are much more direct. Our lens is different. If we are going to be diverse, we need to say we are diverse in opinions, too."

Just as women remain a minority on the Hill, so do black Americans and other people of color. While 2018 greatly broadened their ranks, the disparity remains striking; the majority of black people you will see on any given day are serving food in the many dining halls around the Capitol, and much of the place is filled with affluent white people who are dislocated from much of black America.

"As a black person in this business, you live this weird existence of being in this supposedly prestigious circle, and then going home and opening up the paper and reading a story about a fifteen-year-old who has been killed in Southeast who looks just like you," Michael Hardaway, a chief aide to Rep. Hakeem Jeffries and one of the Capitol's few black senior staff members, told me. "Black staffers here try to build a bridge through mentorship programs and other things, but it too often feels like there's a moat between that existence and ours. But it's on us to close that gap. We have to do better. And we will."

After extensive back-and-forth, the resolution, once clearly directed at Omar, was enhanced to condemn virtually every form of prejudice, making it both more palatable and yet more meaningless with regard to its original intent. Rather than unifying the body, it only exposed new rifts. Rep. Liz Cheney (R-WY) outfoxed the now–minority leader Kevin McCarthy, who saw the resolution as a political victory, when she voted against it, saying it should have been focused on Jews alone. Most everyone else simply voted for it with the wish to move on to actual bills. This was one of the myriad pointless exercises of Congress, designed as a balm to hurt feelings that only resulted in creating more of them.

Back in Minneapolis, where Omar is a bit of a folk hero among her supporters, she moves about cheerfully, seemingly unbowed by the controversies. At one point during that first year, I trailed her as she visited health-care clinics and employment centers and met with a group of local Muslim women from around the state, many of whom fretted about her life back in the Capitol. Omar assured them that she was just fine. "My message to you is, I've got this," she said.

While the issue quieted in Congress for the rest of 2019, it was notable that three Democrats—Elizabeth Warren, Bernie Sanders, and Pete Buttigieg—all said during their presidential primary runs that they were open to curbing US security assistance to Israel if it does not stop building settlements in the West Bank. Omar may have not moved her colleagues on the Hill much, but she was on the vanguard of a broader, significant trend.

That May, the Muslim Advocates group hosted an unusual event at the Capitol: an iftar, a sunset dinner celebration to break the daily fast during the Muslim holiday of Ramadan. The event was cohosted by André Carson, Ilhan Omar, and Rashida Tlaib. The guests came from a broad cross-section of Washington's progressive community: Khizr Khan, once again; leaders from Bend the Arc, a progressive Jewish advocacy group; a few women wearing T-shirts for Code Pink, a far-left activist group; Muslim professionals, in everything from fully covered hair to short skirts to business suits.

A set of prayer rugs had been laid out, and each table was covered with medjool dates, with which to break the fast. Tlaib and Omar were clearly the stars of the show, but other freshman congresswomen were there, too. Alexandria Ocasio-Cortez spoke, with Ayanna Pressley and Jahana Hayes sitting near the front of the room as well.

Rep. Steny Hoyer (D-MD), among the Democratic House leadership there, gave a somewhat cringe-inducing speech about how people should not be prejudiced, which, given that it was an event held by Muslims, the audience already knew. Then Omar spoke, calling herself and Tlaib "the two loudest Muslim women in the country" and gave an impassioned defense of her own patriotism, formed, she said, through her journey as a refugee. "I love this country more than anyone could ever love this country."

Hayes sat along the side of the room, nodding along with some of the remarks. "I've never been to an iftar," she told me on the way out. "In the short time I've been here, I have made it a priority to learn about Muslim and Jewish traditions."

It had taken the addition of two Muslim women to Congress to make an iftar celebration on Capitol Hill actually happen, and not just happen: it had become the cool kids' table.

Two months later, in mid-July, President Trump, increasingly agitated by the criticism of his administration's detention centers at the border, began the day by pounding out a series of incendiary tweets against the Squad, culminating in his now-infamous words: "Why don't they go back and help fix the totally broken and crime infested places from which they came. Then come back and show us how it is done. These places need your help badly, you can't leave fast enough. I'm sure that Nancy Pelosi would be very happy to quickly work out free travel arrangements!"

The tweets were as inaccurate as they were demagogic. Three of the four Squad members were born in the United States, and one represented a section of Trump's home borough of Queens. Even some Republican lawmakers, usually loath to challenge Trump, denounced his comments as racist claptrap. "There is no excuse for the president's spiteful comments—they were absolutely unacceptable and this needs to stop," tweeted Senator Lisa Murkowski (R-AK). "We have enough challenges addressing the humanitarian crises both at our borders and around the world. Instead of digging deeper into the mud with personal, vindictive insults—we must demand a higher standard of decorum and decency."

The day after Trump's tweetstorm, the freshman congresswomen piled onto a dais in a freezing studio in the Capitol where Pelosi usually holds her weekly press conference to face a room packed with reporters eager to hear their response. As usual, Ayanna Pressley stole the show, suggesting that members of the Squad were not interlopers or even a squad, but rather the voice of all Americans who were fed up with Trump's policies, rhetoric, and tweets, and any other drops of misery he seemed intent on raining down on the discourse of American life. "Despite the occupant of the White House's attempts to marginalize us and to silence us, please know that we are more than four people," Pressley said. "We ran on a mandate to advocate for and to represent those ignored left out and left behind. Our squad includes any person committed to building a more equitable and just world. And that is the work that we want to get back to. And given the size of this squad, and this great nation, we cannot, we will not be silenced."

EIGHT

Lived Experiences

Can you believe we are going to be members of Congress?
—Rep. Sharice Davids (D-KS) to Rep. Deb Haaland (D-NM)

ON AN OVERCAST day in April, a dozen high school girls gathered in a recreation room in Juniper Gardens, the oldest and largest public housing complex in Kansas City, Kansas. It was their weekly meeting with the Learning Club, an after-school program that offers tutoring and mentoring to some of the most marginalized students in this postindustrial city. As an intoxicated denizen stumbled past the probing gaze of a security guard, Sharice Davids finished up a call on the portico of the building, then walked in to join the girls waiting to meet her. Casual in dark trousers and a light-colored shirt, her face free of makeup, her long hair swinging behind her, the Native American congresswoman carried herself with an unstudied, casual pleasantness, and plopped herself among them.

Most Congress members adjust their outfits, their demeanor, their vernacular—even their accents—to conform to their audience, be it at a campaign stop, a committee hearing, a dinner with donors, or a town hall meeting in their districts. For months, I followed Davids to water treatment projects; to meetings with mayors and job seekers; to a confab with designer-accessorized members of the Wing, a high-end coworking space for women in Georgetown; and to see these high school students from families with an average household income of $8,184 per year. In each environment, she always seemed to be just Sharice.

"So, what's it like to be a role model?" Davids casually asked the girls, who were working with smaller kids at the center as part of a training workshop in childcare. What did they like to study? What did they want to do after high school? Did any of them want to run for office at some point? (Her advice if they did: take naps.) She didn't do so well in school all the time, she told them, especially the year her mother was stationed overseas for the army. Other times, high school went better.

They had questions for her, too: What was hard about her job?

Making big decisions, Davids said, like whether or not to ground airplanes involved in a series of crashes, even if the grounding would have an enormous impact on the airline business. "I get emotional and overwhelmed," she admitted.

She told them about how carpenters make furniture in one of the House office buildings, about how all of her meetings last approximately fifteen minutes, about people who come to her office to get issues with their social security payments unraveled.

One young black girl, her voice slightly shaking, quietly asked Davids, a former mixed martial artist, community college and law school graduate, lesbian, Ho-Chunk Nation member, and the only Democrat in the Kansas congressional delegation, if she faced discrimination in Washington.

Davids sipped from her water bottle, sipped again, and then jokingly went to take another sip, feigning avoidance of the question. There had been a local publication during her campaign that often targeted her with racist taunts, she told them. "I asked my staff to stop including their clips in my daily media binder," she said.

In Congress, she went on, things had been better, but not always. "Guys will grab me in one way or another. That stuff still happens. People say things that are unintentional and also overt," she said. "I have a go-to phrase: 'That's an interesting thing for you to say to me!'"

The girls, riveted by her candor, laughed.

"Now that I am a member of Congress, I have more authority," she added. "I depend on people to be good allies. It depends, though, because I don't like to escalate things. You know what that's like?"

The girl who had asked the discrimination question nodded.

Davids looked at her. "What do you do?" she asked the young woman, who looked back shyly. "You don't have to say."

I sat back in my chair at the edge of the room and closed my eyes, thinking of every male member of Congress I had ever followed around a district, from Rotary Club meetings to small-business forums to hospital centers to 4-H clubs, and tried to recall a similar moment, the kind that will never go in a campaign video or become part of the *Congressional Record*. There were no voters in this nondescript recreation room in Kansas City, no potential donors, no officials who needed Davids's assistance or could provide her help. It was a major chunk of time for a member of Congress to give up in the middle of an overscheduled day.

That moment, and scores of other unseen ones like it over that initial year, illustrated how the new women of Congress, many of them firsts from their racial or ethnic group to serve in their district (or, as in Davids's case, the nation) undertook their roles beyond lawmaking. They know that they are not just "representatives" in the constitutional sense; they also represent real inspiration for others, and they take that role seriously.

As she took her leave, disappointed to be pulled back into her car and the trappings of the adult world again, Davids had a reminder for her new young friends, whatever their paths were, whether college student, member of Congress, journeyman plumber: "You get to decide what success means."

There is a new current flowing through this diverse Congress that helps to redefine success as well. Along with experiencing the pure joy of once-silent voices being heard, the Firsts also want to build and maintain their power; to keep the momentum of diversity going. Taking the time, as Davids was doing, to be a role model, may not have been traditional politics, but politics in its own way, it surely is.

Political scientists have a term: "descriptive representation." It usually refers to elected officials whose gender, ethnicity, or racial identity resembles that of his or her constituents. In general, the term describes officials who are elected in minority-majority areas, in terms of race or ethnicity, but it can also extend to gender or sexual orientation, even occupation. Descriptive representation is seen as a thing of value to the community, in terms of the advocacy and policy making that comes with it. Ample academic evidence, for instance, points to Latino lawmakers from majority Latino districts proving more able to block legislation that is harmful to their communities than non-Latino representatives.

Clearly, though, a less quantifiable value of descriptive representation is the creation of role models, especially for younger voters and those too young to vote. It is all the more interesting where women of color are elected to represent majority-white districts. It is the political equivalent, if you will, of some of the more notable photographs that emerged during the Obama administration, like the iconic photo of a little black boy, the son of a staff member, touching President Barack Obama's head during an Oval Office visit, or of two-year-old Parker Curry standing in awe before the large-scale painting of first lady Michelle Obama at the National Portrait Gallery. It is the unpolled, unspoken, maybe even unconscious calculation, of a constituent realizing: "If her, why not me?"

"There is something symbolic in being the first Native American elected to Congress," Christian Grose, an associate professor of political science and public policy at the University of Southern California, told me. When he heard my description of Davids in the rec center that day, he noted, "She was not necessarily delivering something for those girls, but inspiring them."

Davids, thirty-nine, never really considered a career in politics before 2016. Although she was a White House Fellow under President Obama—a one-year program, begun in 1964 by President Lyndon B. Johnson, to give high-achieving young men and women a chance to try their hand in public service—she had spent much of her adult life as a professional mixed martial artist and lawyer. She neither overtly touts nor hides the fact that she is the first out lesbian to win a seat in Kansas. Several people who worked on her campaign or work beside her in Congress laud her for being a quick policy study, and for her deliberateness as she evaluates legislation.

Her political instincts are impressive. "Call every person you've ever met in your entire life, even if you don't like them, and ask them for money," she advised the group of women at the Wing about how to raise money for campaigns. "Just say, 'It's not about you and me—it's about democracy!'"

Davids tends to keep a low profile on the Hill, drilling down on legislation to help her newly Democratic district. She carries the burden, though a welcome one, of representing both her local district and an entire group nationwide. "There was a college student who was in here a little bit ago," she told me one day during an interview in her office. "She's Native, she grew up in Wichita, Kansas. But she was saying how important it felt to her that I was here, that Deb [Haaland] was here. I think it's usually when I'm actually talking to people where I have a moment to take a step back, that sometimes I get a sense of it. Because the day-to-day, it's so busy. And we're trying to make structural change, because that's what big-policy federal legislating is. And so it's not that often that I stop and think about it, which is probably good, because it feels very big."

When she feels the need to slow down, step back, and "be present and connect," Davids said, she goes to the floor to look for fellow Native American congresswoman Haaland. "I just want to sit by her, because I feel a connection and a comfort with Deb. I don't even need to be talking to her about anything specific."

The two attorneys, who both traveled through a prestigious program for Native American lawyers, have formed a tight bond, although they, and their congressional districts, are quite distinct from one another. Haaland, fifty-nine, represents a largely liberal district that encompasses most of Albuquerque and its suburbs; the majority of voters in her safe Democratic district share her progressive views.

A single mother who once ran her own salsa-canning business and later did legal work on behalf of the Laguna Pueblo tribe, of which she is a member, she has long been steeped in local and national politics. She ran unsuccessfully for New Mexico lieutenant governor in 2014, and later led the state Democratic Party. Elegant and slightly formal in her midcalf skirts and Native American jewelry, she speaks with the studied cadence of someone who has spent a long time thinking about policy. A climate activist, she is a fan of the Green New Deal and Medicare for All.

During her childhood in Winslow, Arizona, Haaland had only a vague awareness of her status as a Laguna Pueblo Indian. Her mother was a naval officer, and her father, a Marine Corps officer who had earned a Silver Star in Vietnam. "We were raised on green chili stew, and hot tortillas and fried potatoes and beans and things like that," Haaland said. "I guess I didn't really think about being the only Indian in the classroom."

Her mother did Haaland's hair every day, putting it into two braids. "Because we always had long hair, me and my sister. That was the only hairstyle I was ever allowed to have," she said. "I'd get comments about that from my teachers sometimes, about my braids and thinking that that was Indian, but it was just because my mom didn't want our hair flying around our face."

She started to reflect more on being the only Native in her classroom only years later—when she was tribal administrator for the Pueblo of San Felipe tribe, when she was state vote director for Native Americans for President Obama, and especially when she ran for Congress. "There was just so much attention being paid to identity during the time I was running my campaign," she said during one of our interviews in her House office, where a woven God's eye and posters for renewable energy decorate the walls. "I got accused of playing identity politics because one of our taglines was 'Congress has never heard a voice like mine.' I got comments like, '[You] play identity politics, and we should just vote for the person and their qualifications.' It made me feel like, if you've always been represented in this country, then, yeah, I understand what you're saying. But if you've never been represented, if you've never seen yourself, it's hard to call it 'identity politics.'"

Sharice Davids, on the other hand, told me she got an "early start" in recognizing that she was the only person like herself in the room. Her single mother served in the army for twenty years and did a stint in Germany when Davids was in elementary school. "I remember coming home and talking to my mom, and I think I said, 'What am I?' or something. Because she was like, 'What do you mean?' And I said, 'Well, at school, some people, they were asking 'What are you?' And she said, 'Oh, well, I know what they're asking about, because you're a Native American. And you're Ho-Chunk,'" Davids said. "My mom would come and do presentations about Native history and about our tribe and stuff like that. So it was interesting, because I was often the only Native American anybody had ever met. Which is, in some ways, a lot like what my professional life was—just going into a bunch of different spaces and being sometimes the only woman, sometimes the only nonwhite person, sometimes the only person who's a first-generation college student and coming from a not-wealthy family."

Davids's politics are more in line with her district, while also reflecting both her own biography and, in some cases, progressive leanings. Is she for expanding health care and addressing climate change? Yes. Medicare for All and the Green New Deal?

Not so much. Unlike Haaland, she voted for an appropriations bill that lacked strong protections for migrant children in overcrowded border shelters, leading Alexandria Ocasio-Cortez's then–chief of staff to tweet: "I don't believe Sharice is a racist person, but her votes are showing her to enable a racist system," a final harbinger of his demise.

While Davids and Haaland are not politically homogeneous, their identities were central to their campaigns, and later their friendship, and people took notice. "Part of what was so significant is that they ran aggressively as Native Americans," Kevin Gover, the director of the Smithsonian's National Museum of the American Indian and a citizen of the Pawnee Tribe of Oklahoma, told me. "That is not always the case with the Native guys who run for Congress."

Gover recalled a luncheon event at the museum honoring Native women that both congresswomen attended a month after they were sworn in. "The feeling in the room was hard to describe," he said. "There was this huge sense of pride among the women who were there. It's almost like—how would you call it?—a redemption. That finally someone understands the value of Native women who have been devalued in every way you can think of, from the mythology of Pocahontas and Sacagawea. So for all these women [to hear Davids and Haaland] saying 'We are still here, and we are powerful' was inspirational."

The two started to bond during freshman orientation, where at one point Davids grabbed Haaland by the arm and said, "Can you believe we are going to be members of Congress?" While many of the younger women have gravitated to others of their own generation, Davids and Haaland became close quickly despite their age difference, and they often check in with each other over the weekends when back in their districts. They also meet for dinner or walks after long days on the Hill.

After the last August recess, Davids tweeted a photo of the two of them, both wearing backpacks, making their way down a long tunnel under the Capitol. They are often seen sitting together on the floor, with a Native blanket sometimes draped over Haaland's seat to save it. "There will only ever be two people in history who have this shared experience that Deb and I have," Davids told me. "When you go through, like law school, or something intense, you know, like if you get into a car accident with somebody, you have that sense that something really big happened. And you're both in a very vulnerable place. So that's the sense of connection that I feel with Deb, and the multiple things that exist. One of them, I think, is that feeling of responsibility about the role that we play in Indian country. And then both being lawyers, who really understand not just the legal implications, but the real-life implications for tribes."

Reflecting a bit more, Davids added, "We've had eleven thousand plus people serve in the United States Congress, and the fact that there's never been a Native woman here before Deb and I got here is just, it's mind-blowing."

Haaland sees other connections with Davids. "It's interesting," she said when we talked later in her office. "Her mom was a single mom and raised her. And I was a single mom and raised my daughter. So, too, we understand the family dynamics of how we were raised. And so I just have a tremendous amount of respect and sisterly love for her." We progressed to other topics, but as I packed up to leave she circled back. "You know, I'm grateful I'm not the only Native woman in Congress. When you're the only one, I think things are hard."

Descriptive representation is not all emotional intangibles. Its two central goals are measurable: stimulating voter turn-out—think about Barack Obama and the activation of African American voters—and passing legislation that benefits the represented community, or at least stopping bills that harm it. In that sense, it is not so much descriptive as substantive.

There is early evidence that the Firsts have chipped away at this goal, at least on House-passed bills. The Violence Against Women Act has for years been mired in controversy as lawmakers have tried to address the crimes perpetrated against Native women on tribal land by non-Indians. Because non–Native Americans accused of crimes have questioned whether they are subject to Native law, they have often escaped justice.

"Haaland has made a point of saying that Native Americans were never fully represented," Georgetown University government professor Michele Swers told me. The law, for decades, has extended important protection to survivors of domestic and sexual violence, and such violence impacts Native American women at far higher rates than the general population.

"She has actually worked in that area as a lawyer, and the way that she spoke about it was so personally important to her," Swers said. "You can see how personal background influences how you spend your time and political capital."

In her short time on the Hill, Haaland has made sure to have tribal leaders at hearings concerning national parks; secured an amendment to the National Defense Authorization Act that required any military construction projects to have tribal consultation; helped organize a hearing on missing and murdered indigenous women, with a witness panel composed entirely of indigenous women; and requested a review of how Native

Americans are portrayed in artwork and statues around the Capitol, which could potentially change how millions of tourists in Washington see Native people.

Haaland is fully aware of the importance of her role to tribe members. "They don't have to explain things to me. They can just come in and talk about their issue," she told me, knowing that they have "a congressperson who understands what tribal sovereignty is, and understands what the three foundational cases of the Supreme Court are, and understands what the difference between an executive order and a treaty is."

Ayanna Pressley has taken a similar tack with some of her work on behalf of African Americans, from championing legislation that would ban facial-recognition technology in public housing to securing funding for school-based health centers; she was a "frequent flyer" at the school nurse as a child, she said, but rather than become annoyed by her near-constant presence, the nurse was able to detect Pressley's experience as a victim of sexual abuse.

"Women are very effective coalition builders, very effective truth and storytellers," Pressley told me. "Ultimately, that makes for more effective lawmaking." She points to the example of Katie Porter, a survivor of domestic violence. "During the Violence Against Women Act reauthorization debate, she introduced an amendment to cite economic abuse as a form of violence against women. Now, we all know anecdotally that victims will stay with abusers out of economic codependence. But by my quick read and study, this is the first time that amendment had been authored, and that it passed speaks to the power of lived experience, of identity, of representation." The idea also stemmed from Porter's work on bankruptcy issues, specifically a project that gathered data from bankruptcy filers who were abused.

At the end of the day, however, Congress is about power. And with every child who gazes upon the new freshmen in awe, with every elderly woman who had never seen a representative of her race or gender in her town, who grabs a female Congress member by the elbow in excitement, that power is amassing and accruing. The congresswomen may not have craved power in the traditional sense of how we think about electoral politics, but they certainly fought for it and intend to keep it.

Sometimes simply being there changes the way people in newly represented groups see themselves, and opens the notion of possibilities. On a morning in Minneapolis that was so cold I had to take shelter in a bus station after walking only a block, I watched as Ilhan Omar tried to move through a large banquet hall at a celebration for Martin Luther King Jr. She could not move more than a foot before a fan, often a girl in braces and a hijab, stopped her and begged for a selfie. Months later in the same city, a group of Muslim women gathered to meet with Omar, and listened raptly as she described her life in Washington. Some of them were inspired to ponder their own runs for office.

"Since 9/11 in our country, the heavy media focus, unfortunately, has been on the bad actors, whether it's been Al Qaeda, and then obviously the Iraq War, and just framing Muslims as the enemy," Farhana Khera, the executive director of Muslim Advocates, told me. "And now we have two high-profile Muslims in this country, who, if you even remotely follow politics now, you've probably heard of. And so they are actually helping to shape a more positive view of who Muslims in America are, and that we are people who care deeply about the future of our country, we care deeply about justice for all people. And I think, fundamentally, that's what I find so exciting."

Both Ilhan Omar and Rashida Tlaib have also provoked more than their share of negativity, but they try to emphasize the positive. In a video interview right after winning the election, Tlaib spoke of the impact she felt she was already having on young women. "I love when a Muslim father comes up to me and says to his daughter, 'She is a Muslim.' And I almost want to cry," she said. "We're constantly looking for permission to be in leadership roles. And we need to shake that out of our young girls and, in the meantime, keep asking women to run."

There is scholarly evidence that role-model representation yields results. "As younger people are still in the process of learning about the political world and developing political interests and habits, their behavior may be more susceptible to the impact of role models," wrote Christina Wolbrecht and David E. Campbell in a 2017 article "Role Models Revisited: Youth, Novelty, and the Impact of Female Candidates" in the journal *Politics, Groups, and Identities*. They found that "the presence of new female candidates" impacted women ages eighteen to twenty-nine, who could see themselves in those roles, and that could lead to greater political participation including voting and running for office.

That impact is not confined merely to the young and impressionable. It can overwhelm even the most storied of politicians. John Lewis, the legendary civil rights leader and congressman from Atlanta, recalled the first time he saw Deb Haaland sit in the Speaker's chair to preside over the House. That might sound glamorous, but it is a mundane task, time-consuming and procedural, mostly involving watching other members as they come to the floor to talk or debate a bill. It is thus often left to freshmen. But in this case, Lewis said, it was historic.

Rep. Rodney Davis of Illinois, the top Republican on the House Administration Committee, paused before beginning what would be a contentious debate over voting rights and campaign finance to note the moment. "Madam Chair," he said, "before I get started, could I ask for a point of personal privilege to have the members of this institution in the gallery recognize you as the first Native American woman to ever chair the House proceedings?" Congress members from both sides of the aisle rose and applauded madly.

"I shed a tear," Lewis said to me much later. "It reminded me of what we have had to go through as African Americans, bringing down the old ways, and creating new ways. It should inspire young girls, that they can do it, too."

Descriptive representation does not erase institutional obstacles for women or people of color, and it does not blunt the original sins of racism. But it does open the aperture of possibility.

As Sharice Davids and I wrapped up one of our interviews, an intense and, at times, wandering conversation in her always-five-degrees-too-cold office, she remembered the first time she considered being a lawyer. "There are some very serious, real barriers for people to get into those spaces," she said. "But in addition to those real barriers, there's the one of our people not even thinking about that as an option."

"This is the thing, why it matters to have so many different people serving in office," she concluded. "It is not just because of the policy changes, which are huge. This class of people won't even see the real long-term impacts, because we'll all be dead and gone. But how many people will have had their paradigm shifted because of the current times that we're living in now?"

NINE

The Lasts

We have got to rid ourselves of these
toxic characters who can't win.
—Former congresswoman Barbara Comstock (R-VA)

IN HIS FIRST State of the Union address to the 116th Congress, President Donald Trump delivered a few lines that brought nearly everyone to their feet: "Exactly one century after Congress passed the constitutional amendment giving women the right to vote," he said, "we also have more women serving in Congress than at any time before."

Speaker of the House Nancy Pelosi, sitting behind Trump, rose and began to clap, and the room quickly erupted into chants of "USA! USA!"

The irony of the moment was not lost on Rep. Cathy McMorris Rodgers (R-WA), one of the few Republican women who had survived the 2018 campaign. Trump, who had played a large role in motivating women across the country to dump candidates of his party in the midterm election, was lauding the record increase in female lawmakers. "The Republican women's message gets lost as one of the few women in Congress,"

McMorris Rodgers told me. "I would say it was more difficult to be one of the few Republicans among women than one of the few women among Republicans."

In a year of female firsts, 2019 was an unwelcome one for GOP congresswomen: a historic wipeout. Their numbers in the House fell from twenty-three to thirteen, the biggest percentage drop ever and the lowest number overall in a generation. The story was much the same in state legislatures, where Republican women's representation fell nearly 10 percentage points to 9 percent, even as women's total representation increased from about 25 percent to 29 percent.

Some Republicans had chosen to retire before voters could decide their fate. Then, just months into the new Congress, two Republican women, Rep. Susan Brooks, a former prosecutor from Indiana who was a key recruiter of women for the party, and Rep. Martha Roby, who came from a ruby-red district in Alabama and was deeply respected by her colleagues, announced they would soon be hanging it up, too.

In Ernest Hemingway's novel *The Sun Also Rises*, one character asks another, "How did you go bankrupt?" The reply: "Two ways. Gradually, and then suddenly." Without a doubt, Trump cost many Republican members of Congress their seats in 2018, especially in districts where Democratic presidential candidate Hillary Clinton had prevailed in 2016. His constant and pernicious attacks targeting a broad array of groups; his history of misogyny, of denigrating women's looks, of bragging about sexual assault and laughing off more than a dozen charges of sexual misconduct; his persistent humiliation of his own cabinet members; and his public disregard for basic comity toward veterans, members of his own party, and others had all become a proxy for the Republican Party, even for the few members who had tried to run away from him.

Many Republicans and their campaign managers told me tales of going door-to-door in 2018, only to be met by female voters who said that although they had voted for the Republican incumbent in 2016, they were not going to pull the lever for a member of Trump's party now. "The suburban woman voter cares about raising her kids as good citizens," said Mimi Walters, who lost her seat in Southern California to Katie Porter. "She wants them to have people to look up to, including the president, and she looked at Trump and she didn't like what she saw."

In fact, 2018 was merely the capper of a slowly deteriorating decade for Republican women. Myriad factors have contributed to this decline, including a fractured fundraising system that is far outmatched by the one fueling female Democrats; a historic allergy throughout much of the party to so-called identity politics; and too few senior Republican women pulling up newcomers into the ranks. "I can say with certainty that the problem of so few elected women in the Republican Party is not simply a Trump effect," Laurel Elder, a political science professor at Hartwick College and coordinator of its Women's and Gender Studies Program, told me. She has written extensively on women in both parties. "The problem is structural, and there are several overlapping causes."

Cathy McMorris Rodgers, who had recently relinquished her leadership seat to Liz Cheney, the daughter of former vice president Dick Cheney and one of the few other Republican women left standing, won her reelection in eastern Washington largely by appealing to female voters, and was eager to share her somewhat atypical campaign strategy—it included a lot of ads specifically targeting women—with her male Republican colleagues back on Capitol Hill.

They showed little interest, however. "A lot of women were saying, 'Hey, I need to do that in my district,'" she told me. "And when I told the guys this, I felt kind of like I was talking past them."

The lack of interest, she felt, illuminated problems ranging from too few female professionals running political campaigns to much larger philosophical issues in the party she says she loves. "I am very concerned that the Republican Party is sending signals that we are rejecting minorities, offensive to millennials, and not reaching out to women," McMorris Rodgers said. "As a party, we're foolish if we do not make sure that people see Republicans as part of the next generation."

File under "insult to injury": in the era of Trump, many Republican women in the suburbs have stopped voting for Republican women.

Within weeks of the start of the new session, McMorris Rodgers, now in the minority, out of her leadership post, and with a lot more time on her hands, began to take steps on her own to reach out to Republican women to take on the new female Democrats. "There are a lot of women in America who don't identify with marches and funny hats and anger," she said, adding that many women who are running in 2020 felt simultaneously motivated by the big wins among Democratic women and began calling her for help.

But while the party was looking narrowly at the Trump effect on the midterm elections, it is abundantly clear that Republican women were contending with a much broader trend: the increased polarization in contemporary politics that has pulled the bases of both parties to their most strident corners. That dynamic has in some ways benefited female Democrats, who can appeal to the liberal base's desire, even demands, for diversity, but it has been corrosive for female Republicans, whose base over time has moved further from this goal.

It was not always thus. From 1917, when Jeannette Rankin began to serve, until the 1970s, women in Congress were about evenly split between the parties, and at several points Republican women outnumbered Democrats. Rankin was a Republican who devoted much of her life to fighting for women's right to vote; more Republicans than Democrats voted for the Nineteenth Amendment, which codified those rights. The first woman to win an election to both the House and the Senate was Margaret Chase Smith, a Republican from Maine who tirelessly fought for the Women's Armed Services Integration Act of 1948, which gave women the right to serve as permanent regular members of the military, as well as the Equal Rights Amendment in the 1970s; she was a political maverick long before Senator John McCain of Arizona appropriated the term for himself. Republican Nancy Kassebaum of Kansas, served in the Senate for nearly two decades, and was the first woman ever to chair a major Senate committee.

The feminist movement of the '70s fueled the pace for female Democrats, however, as the Republican Party moved away from gender-based recruitment, and by the 1990s, Democratic women began to outnumber Republican women significantly.

This trend culminated in the 116th Congress, when 106 female Democrats were sworn into office, compared with twenty-one Republicans. "I'll be honest with you, when [my husband] and I made the decision to run both for the city council and for Congress, the fact that I was a woman never occurred to me," said Republican congresswoman Martha Roby in an interview in her large office on Capitol Hill. "I had taken my father's word that I could be anything I wanted to be." But, she told me, there have been things that have been said to her over the years that demonstrate the challenges female politicians face.

Roby first served in the city council of her hometown of Montgomery, Alabama, after its only female member retired. She was a lawyer at the time she decided to campaign for the seat. "I would get to my law practice at like seven in the morning," she said, "and then leave at three o'clock in a 'Montgomery Needs Martha' T-shirt and a pair of shorts, and go knock on doors by myself."

She announced she was running for Congress when her son, George, her second child, was twelve weeks old. People, often women, would ask her about that. "'Well, who's going to baby-sit the children? Is Riley planning to babysit the children when you're in Washington?'" she said. "I would say, 'Nooooo, he's their father, and we're raising these children together. And we actually pay a babysitter when we need after-school childcare or whatever the need may be. And I would guess that men don't get asked that question. If they have, I'd love to know."

Equally irritating was what people would say to Roby when she announced her retirement and said she had no set future plans. "'You can go home and be a wife and a mother.' You know, as though I have not been a wife and mother for the nine years that I've been doing this," she said. "I know people don't mean it maliciously. But if people could step back for a moment, and just think about the words that they're saying . . ."

While men often gaze into a mirror and find the best candidate for office staring back, women historically have had to be asked to run by others, often numerous times. Jennifer Lawless and Richard Fox, who have studied the "ambition gap" for years, have found that Republican women feel even less qualified to run than Democratic women, and that this has not been remedied by current events, nor by the tiny increase of women in boardrooms or C-suites, which are often a breeding ground for political leadership. After the 2018 election they found that 23 percent of women, compared to 38 percent of men, had considered running for office. "Nearly identical to the 16-point gender gap we uncovered in political ambition in studies of potential candidates from 2001 and 2011," they wrote.

There are also cultural gaps. Women in both parties fear neglecting family responsibilities or losing income when they run, but the Republican women I spoke to said they have encountered this more acutely over the decades. "When I first ran for office in 1996, I had women tell me to stay home with my kids," two-term California congresswoman Mimi Walters recalled in a telephone interview. "And that was for the city council, which was a part-time deal!"

Two-term Virginia congresswoman Barbara Comstock was an accidental candidate when she ran for the statehouse in 2009. A former senior aide to Rep. Frank Wolf (R-VA) and a conservative operative during the Clinton years, Comstock was working as a lawyer in private practice when Wolf encouraged her to take a run at the Virginia House of Delegates. As the primary breadwinner in her family (her husband is a schoolteacher), she feared the financial risk. Wolf recommended that she reach out to the Virginia House Speaker, Bill Howell.

Howell suggested that she attend an event for another candidate, where he would be speaking on that candidate's behalf. It was there, she told me, that Howell, not realizing she hadn't yet made up her mind, announced, "I want to introduce Barbara Comstock. She is running, too."

"Like a lot of Republican women, I had not thought of myself as a candidate," Comstock said. "But the Speaker announced I was going to run, and I really hit it off with him and liked him, so I thought, 'What the heck,' and I ran."

Later, when Wolf retired from his US House seat, it was a different story. "I didn't need someone to accidentally push me in the pool to run," Comstock said. "I jumped in and won a six-way primary, defeating five men with fifty-five percent of the vote."

Republicans often seem to forget their own history, it seems. "Thirty to forty years ago, it seemed like the party was prepping lots of women, and they were eagerly in the pipeline for positions at all legislative levels," Melanie Gustafson, a professor at the University of Vermont who has written extensively on political inclusion, told me. "It was the era when Republican women learned the power of wearing red suits. Now they are in grays, trying to blend in with the men, perhaps trying to go unnoticed. In the 1990s, I predicted that the first woman president would be a Republican. Elizabeth Dole's candidacy [in 2000], however, didn't seem to spark Republican women; she was too much the surrogate, almost as if she was in widow's weeds. Sarah Palin's vice-presidential candidacy didn't help, and Michele Bachmann certainly did not either."

Women in both parties often cite a fear of raising money, the engine of most successful political campaigns, even though they tend to be as successful as men in doing so once they put their minds to it. Most of the early women who entered Congress were financially secure, but as time went on, many had to depend on grassroots fundraising. The first time Senator Patty Murray ran for local office in the state of Washington, she and her husband held a garage sale rather than ask for donations. (She said that, sadly, he gave away an expensive lawn mower, leaving the fundraiser at a net loss.) Senator Amy Klobuchar loves to tell the story of her 2006 Senate run in Minnesota, which she financed by shaking down all her ex-boyfriends—to the tune of $17,000.

Seeing money as the key to political equity, Democrats in the late 1980s began to focus specifically on fundraising vehicles for female candidates in their ranks. EMILY's List, which is an acronym for "Early Money Is Like Yeast," started in 1985 with the specific goal of raising money for female Democrats who supported abortion rights. It was an immediate success, propelling Barbara Mikulski of Maryland in 1986 to run for the Senate from the House (she went on to become the longest-serving woman in Congress ever), and it has grown into a fundraising powerhouse that has helped to elect scores of female Democrats since.

"The Democratic Party is benefiting from an incredibly well-funded and well-organized external organization dedicated to recruitment and support of women candidates," Laurel Elder told me. "I interviewed women members of Congress, and they said it was EMILY's list, not the Democratic Party itself, that reached out to them when openings occurred and supported them every step of the way."

While there are now a few such organizations on the Republican side, none of them have the clout of EMILY's List, and sometimes they even compete with each other. "If all these different organizations pooled their money together, they'd be more effective," former Republican congresswoman Mimi Walters said. "You can't get them to work together. Everyone wants their own PACs, but you're not going to be as successful that way. Giving me twenty-seven hundred dollars, that doesn't do anything. You pool your money and do a hundred-thousand-dollar ad campaign—*that* is going to have an impact."

Often, female Republican voters simply won't put their money where their mouths are. "My biggest donors are Republican men," Congresswoman Brooks said. "Myself and others are trying to get the message out to Republican women about the importance of supporting Republican women. The Democrats have done a better job of that."

The story of the Republican women of Congress can be told through the tale of the Congressional Women's Caucus. For much of the 1970s, largely left out of leadership positions and with no real platform to leverage their role as women, a bipartisan group of congresswomen tried to form an alliance that would, they hoped, give them legislative strength in numbers. The launch was initially stymied by senior Democratic women, many of whom hewed socially conservative, who were either contemptuous of the goals of the caucus or fearful that having a legislative organization based on gender would only foment division along gender lines.

Then there was Bella Abzug, a polarizing figure many women wanted nothing to do with, according to political scientist Irwin Gertzog's fascinating book *Women & Power on Capitol Hill*. Abzug's aggressive manner, which worked on the West Side of Manhattan, did not endear her to other women in Congress, and this served as an impediment to a coalition.

At last, though, in 1977 fifteen women from both parties came together to form the congresswomen's caucus, with the goal of elevating legislative issues that they believed bridged party lines. The group insisted that its cochairs always come from both parties and that they focus on an agenda that all could agree on. Although the majority of the female Republicans in Congress before the mid-1990s were pro-choice, the abortion issue was left off the agenda.

In an oral history interview with House historian Matt Wasniewski, one of the founding members, Yvonne Brathwaite Burke, told him, "The creation of the Women's Caucus for the first time said to women of every ethnicity and every political party that there was a place for women in the process. . . . We were feminists, but we brought together women who weren't necessarily feminists. And I think that it had an impact on bringing more women to the House and the Senate."

During its early years, according to Gertzog, the Women's Caucus struggled to get its highest-priority agenda items on the congressional calendar, including help for single mothers, an increase in high-level jobs for women in the federal government, and improved health-care resources for women. The caucus also pressed for legislation to protect victims of domestic violence, a rape shield law to prohibit victims from being asked about their sexual history in court, and the Equal Rights Amendment, which then saw tremendous gains in congressional support, even if it ultimately failed.

The caucus managed to hold together in the 1980s, through the Republican administration of President Ronald Reagan, which was hostile to much of its agenda, serving as a refuge of sorts for what remained a small number of women relative to the legislative body.

"It was a great opportunity for women to come together," former congresswoman Connie Morella, a moderate Republican who was a key member of the caucus in the 1990s, told me. "We didn't talk about abortion. We talked about the Violence Against Women Act. We planned conferences. We just did all kinds of things. Whenever men saw women come out of the Women's Caucus, they would say, 'What are they conspiring about now?' It constituted a group of ideas and the sense that something was going to happen from them."

In 1993—after twenty-four new women were elected to the House, the post–Anita Hill cohort—the caucus began to see truly large victories in the areas of health care, domestic violence, and employment, and used its expanding numbers to push for better committee assignments. Their efforts, along with the support of the Democratic administration of President Bill Clinton, meant that, "The 103rd Congress produced more legislation addressing the needs of women and their children than any Congress in history," Gertzog wrote, citing the Family and Medical Leave Act; funding at the National Institutes of Health for women's health programs and making sure women were included in clinical research; free vaccines for kids on Medicaid; the Violence Against Women Act; and a measure helping single parents collect child support. Pressed by Republican women, there were also measures to assist in women's access to credit and business development.

The biggest blow to the Women's Caucus came with the Republican takeover of the House in 1995. The newly empowered Republicans did away with the funding for legislative groups, meaning that the Women's Caucus and other such groups were starved of cash for staff and research. Many new Republican women were hostile to the caucus's mission and, for the first time, tried to roll back its agenda, including even such petty but symbolic acts as refusing to allow the move of a marble sculpture that memorialized suffrage leaders to a more prominent place in the Capitol. And as more antiabortion Republican women joined the House, the abortion debate became a wedge issue.

Bipartisanship, once the bedrock of the group, fractured, and Democrats started their own separate group.

The Congressional Women's Caucus now has so few avenues for legislative agreement that its activities tend to be more ceremonial and social than anything else, reflecting an erosion of political cooperation writ large in the Congress and the country. If anything, many Republican congresswomen have come to resent their Democratic counterparts, believing, fairly or not, that they have specifically targeted them for defeat, and that the Democrats' desire to see more women in politics is purely limited to their own party. (This is basically true for both parties, but there used to be far more talk among women about the need for more of one another in politics regardless of party. That notion has fallen victim to partisan rancor.) "Make no mistake," one Republican staff member told me, "Democrats want more Democratic women in Congress, not more women in general. This is not a happy bipartisan scene you're seeing up there now."

It is becoming increasingly hard for a Republican woman to be a moderate—and still win. Some experts have found that Republican voters perceive women to be less conservative and doctrinaire, when voters actually want, as one GOP fundraiser put it, "someone to spit fire and tear the place down."

Connie Morella, who represented a swath of Maryland from 1987 to 2003, agreed with this assessment. "There is the desire within the party leadership that people who run for office must feel a certain way about key issues," she said. "So many women look at the platform and say, 'Do I have to come out and say I am against *Roe v. Wade* or background checks for gun buyers?' You must come out and pledge it, and that discourages them from running."

Even when they fit the hard-core GOP mold, however, con-gresswomen still face more challenges than congressmen. Joan Perry, a North Carolina pediatrician who was soundly defeated in a primary race for a special election in 2019, is a case in point. Perry was a very conservative, highly educated woman running in a soundly red district, and many Republican women, along with those who fund them, threw their weight behind her. It seemed to be a perfect opportunity for a party eager to expand its female ranks. But the male voters in the district weren't having it.

"Females are perceived to be more liberal, particularly on crime issues," Michael Luethy, who managed her campaign, told me. "In this environment, for the Republican primary voter there is no more important issue than illegal immigration, which shows support for the president and fits into the crime-issues set. I do believe that is why we lost."

"A man campaigning with me who could speak on behalf of my conservatism would have been a game changer," Perry told me, in retrospect. Her internal polling showed that older female and male voters rejected her on the basis of gender. "I would never play the woman card, and I never did," she said, "but you know the leadership of any organization needs to reflect the body that they are leading. Millennials are going to be looking at this and saying, 'Is there a place for women in the Republican Party?'"

Barbara Comstock, who lost her House seat in 2018 to a Democrat, did not mince words about the need to try and eliminate some of the more fringe male Republican candidates, especially in politically mixed districts. "We have these really ridiculous men who are unaccomplished and just nuts, who troll around and cause trouble," she said, citing as an example Corey Stewart, a Virginia politician associated with white nationalists, who won a Senate primary in 2018 only to get destroyed by Democrat Tim Kaine in the general election. She also mentioned her own 2018 primary challenger, Shak Hill, who associated himself with some of Stewart's beliefs. "We have got to rid ourselves of these toxic characters who can't win and they come in and make life worse for everybody," Comstock said.

The challenges GOP women face now could well turn into a vicious cycle for the future: senior women are necessary for recruiting, mentoring, campaigning for, and otherwise bringing along new candidates from the same party. "There are simply many more Democratic women actively involved in recruiting and supporting more women to run," expert Laurel Elder said. Running for office begets running for office. And as the numbers of Republican women decline at the state level, the national candidate pool shrinks.

Republicans must also confront a deep philosophical issue: while most Democrats believe that it is beneficial to have a big tent that includes women, Republicans in recent decades have become wedded to the notion of so-called meritocracy, over gender parity. For instance, Liz Cheney, the Wyoming Republican who more or less pushed Cathy McMorris Rodgers out of her leadership post, has been a fierce opponent of highlighting gender in Republican politics, often insisting that running on a strong national security agenda is enough to bring in female voters (perhaps failing here to acknowledge her own significant advantage of being named Cheney).

When the *New York Times* did a large photo essay of all the women in the 116th Congress, Cheney was the only member who declined to participate. Cheney is also one of the few Republican women whom colleagues seem to treat with near reverence. "I just think that one reason Liz Cheney is so successful is that she doesn't take crap from anybody," Mimi Walters told me. "If we want to compete with the big boys, we have to be tough. Cathy [McMorris Rodgers] is a really nice lady, but if she really wanted that position she would have fought for it."

If a party doesn't make an effort to care about gender equity, however, it won't "just happen on its own," as Elder noted. After the 2018 wipeout, Rep. Elise Stefanik, a Republican from New York's North Country, wrote a memo to her colleagues that suggested they work harder to elect women to their ranks and saying that she would start a PAC to do just that. She was instantly shot down by party operatives. "If that's what Elise wants to do, then that's her call, her right," said Tom Emmer, a Republican from Minnesota, who is in charge of the party's committee to elect House Republicans. "But I think that's a mistake."

"NEWSFLASH," Stefanik replied to him on Twitter. "I wasn't asking for permission."

Until the party makes systemic moves to help women get through primaries, the ladies' room off the House floor will likely feature few Republican women between votes. Martha Roby, who clashed early on with Trump when she retracted her endorsement of him after his "Grab them by the pussy" comments came out, insists that the current politics of the day did not lead her to become the latest Republican woman to flee the Hill. "It's just time," she told me. "I mean, look, there are frustrating days here, or just in this world that I live in. But the joy that I find in doing the work on behalf of the people I represent far outweighs any one thing."

In that case, I asked her, why has she decided to leave Congress, when Republican women need her in the ranks?

"We're just at a place where we're ready to see what's next," she said.

TEN

To Impeach or Not to Impeach

This is a grave moment for our country.
—Rep. Abigail Spanberger (D-VA)

ABIGAIL SPANBERGER CAME to Congress to do everything but impeach Donald Trump. Then came Ukraine.

She was sitting in the passenger seat of her Honda CR-V, watching the stupefying news unfold on her phone as a driver hustled her between weekend events in her suburban Richmond district. The former CIA operations officer, among the most conservative of the Democratic freshman women, prided herself on careful deliberation, especially around the issue of impeachment.

She had read the Mueller report more than once, and then, at the suggestion of a constituent, she listened to the audiobook—sometimes in bed, since it made her sleepy, sometimes in the car. "I am trying to take in this information in every way possible," Spanberger had told me over the summer, "because you just keep hearing more and more." She added, "And the more you're digesting it, the more there is that really needs to be discussed."

But the late September revelation that the president of the United States had called the newly elected leader of Ukraine after withholding hundreds of millions of dollars in much-needed military aid, and requested that the Ukrainian leader investigate one of the president's political opponents felt very different. Spanberger began furiously texting her best buddies in Congress, other freshmen, many of them women with a national security or military background, most of them from difficult districts where they had beaten a Republican not quite a year before, to see if they were thinking what she was thinking.

She discussed the matter with her husband, Adam, over 11 p.m. bowls of cereal. "We talked about it nonstop," she said. "If these allegations are true, this is a grave moment for our country."

About the same time, Democratic congresswoman Elaine Luria, the US Navy veteran who also had won a Republican district in 2018, was sitting on a folding chair in her outdoor den of sorts (really, her garage), sipping coffee with her husband, when they, too, turned to the news on their phones. "I said, 'This can't be true.'" she told me. "You know, this is the president. And he is now asking a foreign leader to conduct an investigation to dig up dirt in order to bolster his opportunities to win the next election?"

The development, in Luria's view, had "nothing to do with the previous things," such as the findings of the Mueller report, the accusations of obstruction of justice, the failure of the White House to allow witnesses to come to the Hill, or the payments of hush money to a Playboy model.

"This," she said, "was something separate."

She, too, took her feelings to the group chat with other freshman congresswomen on the encrypted texting app Signal. Also on the chat were former air force officer Chrissy Houlahan, former navy helicopter pilot Mikie Sherrill, and former CIA analyst and DOD official Elissa Slotkin.

The five women refer to themselves as the Badasses, their own sort of Squad. At times, they have infuriated that other "squad" and their progressive colleagues, especially those who had been pushing impeachment from day one. The Badasses had watched with increasing alarm as the message about Trump's infractions became muddled and confusing to their constituents, as the hearing with special counsel Robert Mueller fizzled like so many Pop Rocks, and as another hearing, this one with former Trump campaign manager Corey Lewandowski, devolved into a clown show. There was no unified message, they thought; there was no central goal. There were only spinning wheels.

"When we were sworn in we were not presented with facts that in my mind warranted a true and significant impeachment inquiry," Slotkin told me. "It was not that I agreed with Donald Trump, and I certainly didn't appreciate much of the tone, but that is different from the series of events that lead to an impeachment inquiry."

That was before Ukraine, however. Now, the text exchange was fast and constant. "It was, 'Have you seen this article? Have you heard this tape?' pinging back and forth," Slotkin said, adding that the words they all used seeing the leader of the free world essentially shaking down a security partner for dirt on a political opponent were, "This is something different."

Each felt it was time to make a move.

The power to impeach is one of the most awesome powers given by the nation's founders to the House of Representatives, one to be exercised in the case of treason or high crimes and misdemeanors. But it had been degraded by partisans in both parties over the last two decades. In 1998, Bill Clinton became the first elected president ever to be impeached—over lying under oath about sex with a former intern. Liberals had called for President George W. Bush's impeachment over the Iraq War, conservatives had declared any number of Barack Obama's missteps—from the deaths in Benghazi to a failed gun-tracing operation called Fast and Furious—to be "high crimes."

The question of whether or not to seek impeachment proceedings against Trump, or even to speak about the topic, had loomed over the new Congress from the day it was sworn in. Impeachment has been historically unpopular with American voters, especially in districts full of voters from the party of the person in the White House, and it was an issue that most Democrats who won Republican districts in 2018 had hoped to avoid, even as their progressive colleagues from safe seats pressed on. The liberals felt they had been elected in large part to rid the nation of Trump's presidency. Nancy Pelosi, well aware that moderates had given Democrats the majority and, in turn, handed her back the Speaker's gavel, knew whose political fortunes she had to protect. Trump appalled her. But she wasn't going to lose the House over him.

House Judiciary Committee chair Jerry Nadler, whom Trump had tangled with off and on for years back in Manhattan, was among the six committee chairs taking the lead on the early investigative efforts of an impeachment inquiry. Nadler and his staff—under pressure back home in New York from constituents who were angry that the House was not moving to impeach—pushed the effort past Pelosi's comfort zone, using terms like "formal inquiry" when that was not where she headed at the moment. In particular, according to several people involved in the impeachment discussions, Nadler's staff had personally called other members of the Judiciary Committee to press them to come out for said inquiry, greatly irritating the Speaker.

Pelosi, holding major decisions on how to move forward in her own hands, responded by pulling a series of rugs out from under him week after week (in the view of Nadler allies, slow-walking things like lawsuits, which the Speaker's office denied) and undermining him by bad-mouthing his process to fellow Democrats in a meeting, then encouraging people in the room to leak her ire to the press.

When the House left for an extended summer recess, pro-gressive groups declared it Impeachment August, fanning out to town hall meetings and lawmaker appearances to raise the pres-sure on the moderates. It didn't work. To add to the fears of wor-ried Democrats, the Judiciary Committee's first impeachment hearing on September 17, before the Ukraine issue had surfaced, was viewed by most Democrats on the Hill as an unmitigated disaster. Member after member failed to rattle the recalcitrant Lewandowski, making the Democrats look like feckless pea-cocks bested by an insect they were seeking to devour.

The Badasses had made their distaste for all of this known to House leaders. By September 18, everyone in Washington under-stood: impeachment was DOA.

Then came Ukraine. The whistleblower's claims fell clearly under the jurisdiction of Pelosi's fellow Californian Rep. Adam Schiff, chair of the House Intelligence Committee, on which Pelosi sat for years. Schiff was a respected and ambitious for-mer prosecutor with a deliberate manner and a disciplined and astute staff that understood the ways of Pelosi Land and how to succeed there. (Improbably, but somehow perfectly, Adam Schiff's wife is named Eve.)

The incident also had the benefit of being digestible. "This was a clean shot," a senior Democratic staff member told me. "This was clearly a national security issue, clearly a violation of oath and an effort at undermining the integrity of our elections. It was very simple and made it easier that this was the president's words. Schiff is insanely talented. He is almost the perfect person to pursue this."

After conferring over texts and the phone, the five national security freshman women agreed that moving to impeach was necessary, and they decided to make a public statement together—along with two freshman men, Rep. Gil Cisneros (D-CA) and Rep. Jason Crow (D-CO), who came from similar national security backgrounds. The seven had a conference call on September 23 with Pelosi, who was in New York for a panel related to the United Nations General Assembly. They warned her of their decision, and told her they were about to publish an op-ed in the *Washington Post* that concluded Trump's actions were "an impeachable offense."

"Of course we made a point of informing the Speaker before the op-ed came out," Elissa Slotkin said. "We practice the doctrine of no surprises, which comes from our military background." She said Pelosi was interested in their approach and willing to meet with them.

The op-ed was a bombshell. "Our lives have been defined by national service. We are not career politicians," wrote the seven. "We are veterans of the military and of the nation's defense and intelligence agencies. Our service is rooted in the defense of our country on the front lines of national security.

"We have devoted our lives to the service and security of our country, and throughout our careers, we have sworn oaths to defend the Constitution of the United States many times over. Now, we join as a unified group to uphold that oath as we enter uncharted waters and face unprecedented allegations against President Trump."

Nancy Pelosi read the published piece on her 9 p.m. flight from New York to Washington, DC, and took furious notes. She spoke to some congresswomen individually, encouraging them to follow their own instincts on the impeachment issue.

The next day, in a meeting with the entire Democratic caucus, the national security women made their case. Where the progressive Squad had brought passion and righteous outrage to Twitter, TV, and press conferences, the Badasses brought an almost affectless cool, like contract killers about to take care of business.

"I laid out what I thought would be important points to get across if we were going to do this," Slotkin told me. "We need the inquiry to be qualitatively different than the processes that came beforehand, where we largely confused people. It needs to be strategic, clear, and efficient . . . I believe Democratic leadership has heard us on this."

Other moderates had come along as well.

In the spring of 2019, a constituent of Angie Craig's named Kim Westra had sat, frowning, in the bleachers of Cottage Grove Middle School outside Minneapolis, where the congresswoman was holding a town hall meeting. Mueller had just released his report, and Westra had asked Craig her views on impeaching the president.

"I believe the next step is for the committee chairmen to call a number of folks forward to testify, to fill in the facts for the

American people," Craig said, demurring. "I am very troubled by the number of potential areas of obstruction of justice that are mentioned in the report."

Westra found the answer wholly unsatisfying. If this was going to be the response of Democrats, what really was the purpose of electing them to begin with? she asked me.

Six months later, on that same Monday that the op-ed was released, Craig was mulling her decision on a plane from Minnesota. "At the end of the day, I asked myself, if this were a Democratic president with exactly the same set of admissions, or behavior, would I have the courage to stand up and call for an inquiry on my own Democratic president?" Craig told *Politico*. She decided she would.

A tsunami of other House Democrats joined the fray that Tuesday, including many members of the Congressional Black Caucus, who had until then held their fire under Pelosi's direction. "They come from a sense of extreme credibility," New Orleans lawmaker Cedric Richmond said of the national security women, with their nod to impeachment. "A lot of them are not very progressive, so for those moderates who were looking for some subject expertise to validate them, they gave it to them." Richmond was among the scores of members to join the impeachment wave.

Politically, impeachment would begin when Nancy Pelosi said so. Now, at last, on September 24, the troops were on board, not just the committee chairs or the elected leaders, but also the rank and file, helped along by the Badasses. "The op-ed was the inflection point," a senior aide told me. "There was no Pelosi coming out without it. They are security eggheads. It's their issue. Them doing what they did gave everyone else cover. The silent majority want him impeached."

Drew Hammill, Pelosi's deputy chief of staff, said that Pelosi came to her conclusions independent of other members based solely on the underlying facts, though he noted that the Badass group had been key in influencing the messaging.

The next day, Abigail Spanberger stood in front of a camera near the Will Rogers statue in the Capitol, waiting for her hit. She bounced on her toes and tapped her fingers together nervously while her spokesman gave her reassuring head nods from behind the videographer.

A few feet away, fellow freshman Rep. Debbie Mucarsel-Powell (D-FL) stood regally in spike heels, bellowing, "This president is undermining our national security!" to a different disembodied voice piping through a tiny earpiece as she looked into another television camera.

When it was her turn, Spanberger spoke carefully. "This is a different set of circumstances," she said.

For some of the freshmen, this was supposed to be the Congress that focused on health care and clean drinking water and prescription drug prices. But the impeachment fight was inescapable. "This is not why we ran for Congress," Mikie Sherrill told me. The New Jersey congresswoman looks like that mom at school that other moms want to resent, because she has four darling children, an amazing résumé, perfect teeth, and is a member of Congress, but is impossible to dislike, because she is so incredibly warm while also being extremely practical. She is, in short, the sort you would turn to for good legal advice and a hearty casserole if your spouse were to leave you. But, Sherrill said, as we stood a few days later in the autumn sun on the East Front of the Capitol, "The threat was so great that we had to act."

That reasoned, agonized tone fits the gravity of the task ahead, the third impeachment proceedings in the history of the nation. But it is all the more remarkable when considering how the House of Representatives got there. Just nine months before, Rashida Tlaib had been the first to raise the battle cry "Impeach the motherfucker!"—and the Squad had carried the torch in the intervening months. And then the Badass women finished the job, influencing what would almost certainly be the most monumental move of the Democratic majority in this Congress, and possibly of Pelosi's storied career.

Five years ago, most of the key players in this most conse-quential drama had never even seen themselves in public office— and the Badass freshman women told me it was equally unclear where they would be five years from now. Still, they stand firm on impeachment.

"I understand that this could have implications about my reelection," Elaine Luria said. "I was chosen by the voters in my district to make tough decisions. And I think part of the reason they chose me to do that is because they know I spent an entire career, twenty years in the navy, making tough decisions, deploy-ing six times on combat ships and operating weapons systems and nuclear reactors."

By early October, Elissa Slotkin already had a Republican challenger, whose central campaign theme out of the gate was anti-impeachment. Others would certainly follow.

"It's a really solid and grave responsibility, central to who I am," said Chrissy Houlahan, calling the vote among the most difficult things she had ever done. "We do things as a collective, we try to work together. This is not an insignificant event. I hope it's an indication of things to come."

ELEVEN

Paving the Way

I don't know if I have fulfilled what I set out to do.
—Rep. Alexandria Ocasio-Cortez (D-NY)

IN THE END, the 116th Congress may be less about the laws that are passed than the reinvigoration of an institution that many Americans have written off as dysfunctional and intellectually bankrupt—activated by a diverse group of women who are often in significant disagreement with one another about the political course of the nation. It may be a Congress judged less for what it did than for what it was.

House women made the case against President Donald Trump, even at a possibly high political cost to themselves. The Firsts—sometimes the progressives, sometimes the moderates—led the way on the most important policy debates, yet often it was less about their particular political convictions than what they brought to the table: a collective moral clarity. Whether or not the Senate would ultimately come along for the ride, these freshman congresswomen, captained by a flawed but indomitable political veteran, have made Congress essential again.

In just one short year, this group of women, as both products and drivers of a dynamic new political era, have helped reframe the national debate over impeachment, climate change, gun rights, foreign policy, and electoral politics, all with an extraordinary presidential election looming. Those people privileged enough to look out onto the House floor on any given day can see plainly that the Firsts have begun to change what power actually looks like, as blue suits and ties have given way to flowing scarves and member-pin necklaces, and the faces in the seats have begun to look a tiny bit more like the United States.

The Bibles they were sworn in on have been long tucked away, the magazine cover stories have slowed, and the lonely single pieces of art on office walls have been joined by photos, district maps, appreciation certificates, and Post-it notes. Frequent-flyer miles have been accrued. Secret routes traversing the Capitol have been memorized. No longer insurgents, the new women would soon be using their institutional advantage to keep their power as incumbents. This is the Washington story.

At home, things have remained mundane: town hall meetings, events to promote the Census, roundtables on prescription-drug costs, one-on-ones with local mayors. To the best of their ability, the new members have tried to serve the needs of the communities they represent both electorally and descriptively, by working to end the use of facial-recognition technology in public housing, improve black maternal health, protect poor people from predatory lending and high auto insurance rates, shore up legislation to shield victims of domestic violence and, as ever, get more money to their district's projects. Given the deliberately nonfunctioning Senate, most of those legislative efforts have not made it into law. But here was a start.

The new women were also faced with the reality that unconventional biographies could hamper them, and that their gender—key as it was to their election—was still a liability in a fundamentally sexist institution.

In late October, RedState, a far-right blog, unleashed photos and texts that exposed an intimate relationship between Katie Hill and a campaign aide. In one photo, Hill was depicted naked, brushing the campaign aide's hair. As Capitol Hill sex scandals go, this one was unusual. Hill's aide was a woman—Hill was an out married bisexual—and the affair has included her husband. The story also said that Hill, by then embroiled in a bitter divorce, had also had an affair with her legislative director, which would be a clear violation of a rule change in the new Congress, one written with the help of Hill's roommate, Lauren Underwood, barring lawmakers from engaging in sexual relations with anyone who works in their congressional office or committees on which they serve.

The House Ethics Committee announced that it was opening an investigation into the allegations, but Hill—who denies the affair with the congressional staffer—quickly announced that "with a broken heart" she would resign and focus on ending "revenge porn." The poster child for power among freshmen had become the poster child for cautionary tales. "I made this decision so my supporters, my family, my staff, and our community will no longer be subjected to the pain inflicted by my abusive husband and the brutality of hateful political operatives," Hill said in a video message. She added, "I never claimed to be perfect, but I never thought my imperfections would be weaponized and used to try to destroy me and the community that I have loved for my entire life. And for that I am so incredibly sorry."

Many wondered how it was that Rep. Ken Calvert, a veteran Republican congressman from California, could still be in the House twenty-six years after he was caught in his car with a known prostitute by two Corona, California, police officers, and how Rep. Duncan Hunter (R-CA) could continue to represent his district after being indicted on sweeping campaign finance violations, yet Hill couldn't survive her sex scandal for two weeks. Hill's biggest booster, Nancy Pelosi, quickly dismissed her in a starchy statement akin to an expulsion letter from Sunday school, noting that Hill's "errors in judgment" made it "untenable" for her to remain in office. "We must ensure a climate of integrity and dignity in the Congress, and in all workplaces," Pelosi wrote.

In a sense, the fact that one of the first to fall under new post-#MeToo rules on Congress was female is a demonstration of equality, but it is just as clear that the evolving gender roles in Washington were still evolving. While blaming her demise on gutter politics and misogyny, Hill still acknowledged her mistakes in her final speech on the House floor. "I wanted to show young people, queer people, working people, imperfect people, that they belong here," she said. "To every young person who saw themselves and their dreams reflected in me, I'm sorry."

The increase in the number of women in Congress in 2019 was symbolically important, of course. But during this tumultuous year, I came to believe that the congresswomen's diversity—of age, race, religion, and economic status—could be even more transformative than their gender alone.

"The diversity of the caucus goes a long way in creating potential new leaders," said Alexandria Ocasio-Cortez as we walked together one day between votes, while she nibbled at what often seems to be her late lunch, a cranberry muffin. "I do think geography and culture and background play a big role. People from my community understand me more than other people from other areas who happen to be women."

She cited the example of Elijah Cummings, at the time chair of the House Oversight Committee, on which she and other new women sat, who was constantly giving them chances to schedule hearings on topics close to their hearts. "I think that as much as people don't want to admit it," she said, "leaders with a vested interest in the next generation of leaders tend to gravitate toward younger versions of themselves."

A month or so later, I caught up with AOC again. (Same pastry, different day.) Did she believe she was making an impact herself? I asked her.

"I feel like there is some real woo-woo here," she said, referring to the traditions and rituals of Congress. "I do feel I answered a calling in the larger sense by running, but I don't know if I have fulfilled what I set out to do."

This was a remarkable statement from a woman whose power and influence already far exceeded her age and experience; it was at once self-aware and prematurely self-deprecating.

For many Americans, the 2016 election marked the beginning of a truth-telling era. The country under President Trump has experienced not simply the faltering of American exceptionalism but a full unleashing of its most dangerous and base instincts, which had been set to simmer for generations. Many white citizens had believed they were living in a "post-racial" nation, whose scars had been smoothed by eight years of a black president, but Americans of color, aided by cell-phone cameras and social media, have started peeling back that blanket of self-assurance to reveal ongoing police brutality, inequities in the criminal-justice and education systems, and the enduring open wounds of the nation's original sin.

White Americans have come face-to-face with symbols and pedagogy that academics and activists have been grappling with for decades. Confederate monuments have begun to come down, even in places like South Carolina, and state flags featuring the "Southern Cross" have been removed from a long hallway of the Capitol, where Democrats, led by black members from the South, beat back a Republican push to allow such symbols at national cemeteries on Confederate Memorial Day. The need for a deeper understanding of the role of slaves in the foundation of US culture has taken on a widespread urgency. All of this has been met with pushback.

Many southern plantations, including President Thomas Jefferson's famous Monticello, have begun to include slave stories in their guided tours. Most visitors are moved and engaged by these additions, and in the case of black visitors, validated. Others, however, clinging to racist proclivities, post negative Yelp reviews, wondering why their garden tours have been tainted by an education into the dark truth of history.

Nonwhite Americans, understandably, were not particularly surprised by the surfacing of white nationalism in the Trump years, having absorbed the inner message of Tea Party slogans like "We want our country back" during the Obama years. But they may have been surprised by the rise of millennial and Generation Z voices, of social-media platforms and shifting political mores, of the surge of energy generated by the 2018 midterm elections, which has made people less afraid to yell back. One can peer out at the mass of furious climate-strike kids and see the future, one that some of the new congresswomen helped create an architecture for.

Indeed, the new class of women in the House, from its one-time refugee to its former CIA officers to its single moms to its former bartender, have formed a collective mirror of the broader cultural and economic shifts in American life—in which those previously toiling at the margins have found their voices and, in some cases, real institutional power.

The counterrevolution has come with its own verities, often demanding conformity of belief or silence, with the left creating its own tribes and criteria for belonging. In many workplaces, older workers have been marginalized and substantively suspect "cultures" have replaced traditional markers of measurable success. Most Americans sit comfortably in their silos of worldview self-selection and bias confirmation. But, oddly, as polarized as it is and as poorly as Americans view it, Congress sometimes feels like the last spot in the country left for authentic daily debate—where Republicans and Democrats, conservatives and liberals, must sit literally side by side in committee rooms, windowless offices, and the well of the House, and hash things out, however imperfectly. There are enforced rules against the ad hominem attacks so common on cable television and Twitter. Not all ideas are acted upon, but they are all heard.

In a nation that seems hopelessly cleaved, preaching for unity may feel somehow hollow, if not preposterous; Americans may feel the need to pick a side. In the Trump universe, this has come with a set of declarations: *Send them back. Lock her up. Make America great again.* On the other side, the rejoinder comes, yes, with some sloganeering, but also with a vivid manifestation of beliefs in human form: the group of women in these pages, and many others, including men, who are unapologetically out-spoken, culturally modern, telegenic, intelligent, and fearless. Their lack of legislative power is inverse to their political capital among base voters.

"Since we launched our Black Maternal Health Caucus, every Democrat running for president has talked about black maternal health," freshman congresswoman Lauren Underwood said during one of our winter chats. "Elizabeth Warren has a plan for it, and the Ways and Means Committee just had a hearing today. These things don't just happen in this place. There are not political upsides for someone like me. I am just grateful that we are able to make a difference, because that is how I know we can still do great things here."

During this past year, sometimes as an unseen observer of the class of 2019 and at other times as a question-asking irritant, I always felt like both a witness and a stalker, eager to find meaning in the journey of the Firsts. How will the women of the 116th be remembered in thirty years? No matter the long-term policy—and impeachment—outcomes, many of them, without a doubt, have been the sparks for progress. It remains to be seen whether the influence of money, the quest for endorsements, or the desire to rise in the institution will chip away at the Firsts' initial distinctiveness. The desire to effect more than incremental change may prove frustrating to some, who may come to find themselves better situated on the picket line than in the Rayburn Room.

Among the many overlooked pieces of remarkable monuments on the grounds of the US Capitol is the Statue of Freedom, a bronze female figure who looms majestically atop the Capitol dome. Between dusk and dawn, the dome is illuminated, bathing

Freedom, with her flowing hair, dramatic helmet, and cast-iron pedestal inscribed with E PLURIBUS UNUM, in haunting yellow light. Below her, the tholos, a round lookout, also lights up when one or both chambers are in session, a reminder that the nation's business goes on well after dark.

Freedom's journey to Washington, DC, was arduous. The American artist who had cast a plaster model of the statue in Rome died suddenly in 1857, leaving his widow to send it in crates on a journey across the sea, during which the ship leaked, causing the crates to be hopelessly late. The casting of the final version was delayed by the Civil War. Finally, in 1863, the statue was installed in full, saluted by scores of guns near the Capitol and from twelve forts nearby.

This female warrior, constructed almost six decades before women were permitted to vote in the United States, has stood above the nation's legislative branch as generations of Congress members have debated legislation about suffrage, abortion, child labor, equal pay, family leave, and women's sports, and scores of other laws that have changed the lives of all Americans. Many of these laws were championed by women, more than half the nation's population but still a perpetual minority in Congress.

Now, a new generation of lawmakers has come along to lay another brick in the country's path toward self-actualization, with the hopes that others, too, will follow behind, to pave it forward, wisely, and on.

Acknowledgments

No ONE WRITES a book alone, and the value of moral and professional support in a lonely journey can never be overstated. I am forever grateful to my supersmart and kind agent, Alia Hanna Habib, who believes in me when I lose faith in myself. I deeply thank my formidable editor Betsy Gleick and the fabulous team at Algonquin Books, who worked so hard to bring this together under an intense deadline. Elizabeth Johnson, especially, is the copyeditor we all dream of.

I would be nowhere without my super readers, most especially the brilliant Andrea Levine, who carefully pored over every chapter and managed to never say "Who taught you to spell?" as well as Helene Cooper, who held my feet to the fire to do better, while also feeding me, and Carl Hulse, from whom I have always learned so much about Capitol Hill. Peter Baker, Ian Fisher, Mike Ricci, and Ed Wyatt also offered important and thoughtful input. Susan Davis introduced me to Otter, a lifesaver.

I owe a special well of gratitude to House historian Matthew Wasniewski, who spent hours helping me to get my history right, and Albin Kowalewski, who also took time to weigh in. Wasniewski is one of the Hill's many unsung subject experts. He can speak extemporaneously about the history of women's fashions on the Hill as well as that of African American congressmen after the Civil War and dueling and brawling among male members earlier in the nineteenth century. No one should ever try to cite significant congressional historical references without calling him.

Anyone need a fact-checker? Hilary McClellen is in a class by herself. Any errors in this book are mine alone.

For kindness and moral support, I am indebted especially to Frank Bruni, as well as to Lynn Steinhauer, Alissa and Hannah Weisman, Paul Kane, Robert Draper, Jake Sherman, Thom Shanker, Sabrina Tavernise, Abby Goodnough, and Kate Zernike, and to Annie Tin, for her hospitality in the House Press Gallery. To the many "senior aides," even though I can't name you, you were invaluable.

For historical references, I drew heavily on history.house.gov, in particular its fascinating oral histories, as well as *Women & Power on Capitol Hill* by Irwin Gertzog, *The Class of '74* by John A. Lawrence, and the various academic works of the peerless Jennifer Lawless.

Shout out to the baristas at DC's Emissary coffeehouse, Compass Coffee, Philz Coffee, and Pizza Paradiso, where I wore out my welcome before my Wi-Fi password.

Last—because they could never be least—I am forever and deeply indebted to Jonathan Weisman, whose editing notes, support, patience, and love know no bounds even when my gratitude did not match them, and my astounding children, Hannah and Sadie, who have watched women in power in Washington, DC, and tried to learn from them.

Endnotes

Introduction: The New Arrivals

4 **"Impeach the motherfucker"** "Rashida Tlaib's Expletive-Laden Cry to Impeach Trump Upends Democrats' Talking Point," *New York Times*, January 4, 2019, https://www.nytimes.com/2019/01/04/us/politics/tlaib-impeach-trump.html.

6 **"We have to fix this shit"** Rep. Katie Porter, interview with the author, March 1, 2019.

6 **"A new breed of politician"** John A. Lawrence, *The Class of '74: Congress after Watergate and the Roots of Partisanship* (Baltimore: Johns Hopkins University Press, 2018), 5.

7 **In the 2017 report *The Trump Effect*** Jennifer L. Lawless and Richard L. Fox, *The Trump Effect* (Washington, DC: Women & Politics Institute, June 2017), https://www.american.edu/spa/wpi/upload/the-trump-effect.pdf.

Chapter One: French Heels, Kidney Punches, and the Dead Husbands' Club

14 **"Professional attire"** Senator Amy Klobuchar, interview with the author, December 13, 2018.

16 **"The best lemon pie in Montana"** "First Congresswoman Makes Debut Here," *Baltimore Sun*, June 4, 1917, https://www.newspapers.com/clip/27070587/the_baltimore_sun/.

17 **CONGRESSWOMAN RANKIN REAL GIRL** "A Womanly Woman with Womanly Ambitions," Whereas: Stories from the People's House, Office of the Historian, US House of Representatives, April 17, 2017, https://history.house.gov/Blog/2017/April/4-17-Womanly-Rankin/.

17 **"'Did she wear a hat?'"** Matthew Wasniewski (House historian), interview with the author, January 28, 2019.

17 **"How shall we answer their challenge"** *Congressional Record*, vol. 165, no. 99, June 13, 2019, https://www.congress.gov/congressional-record/2019/6/13/senate-section/article/s3457-1.

18 **"As a woman I can't go to war"** "Rankin, Jeannette," Office of the Historian, US House of Representatives, https://history.house.gov/People/Listing/R/RANKIN,-Jeannette-(R000055)/.

18 **"They just weren't going to hear her"** Oral history interview with Rep. John Dingell Jr., Office of the Historian, US House of Representatives, February 3, 2012, https://history.house.gov/Oral-History/People/The-Honorable-John-D--Dingell,-Jr-/.

18 **"Never for one second"** "Rankin: Courage Finally Honored," *Washington Post*, May 18, 1985, https://www.washingtonpost .com/archive/politics/1985/05/18/rankin-courage-finally-honored/ af69ee33-0e4b-4be1-95c0-a170a81897f4/.

18 **Bootlegging jailed spouse** Hope Chamberlin, *A Minority of Members: Women in the U.S. Congress* (New York: Praeger, 1973), 64.

19 **"I am no lady"** "Norton, Mary Teresa," Office of the Historian, US House of Representatives, https://history.house.gov/People/Detail/ 19024.

20 **"Deviation from the expected"** Wendy Mink (daughter of Rep. Patsy Takemoto Mink), phone interview with the author, May 31, 2019.

22 **"A man's voice"** "Chisholm, Shirley Anita," Office of the Historian, US House of Representatives, https://history.house.gov/People/Detail/10918.

22 **"Unbought and unbossed"** "Lauren Underwood on Stunning Upset Against 4-Term GOP Congressman: 'Together We Have Built a Movement,'" *Chicago Tribune*, November 7, 2018, https://www .chicagotribune.com/politics/elections/ct-met-illinois-14th-district-randy-hultgren-lauren-underwood-20181106-story.html.

22 **"A celebrity so like AOC"** Barbara Winslow (Shirley Chisholm Project founder), phone interview with the author, April 25, 2019.

22 **Neither the black movement nor women's liberation** "Shirley Chisholm," Say It Plain, Say It Loud: A Century of Great African American Speeches, American RadioWorks, http://americanradioworks.publicradio.org/ features/blackspeech/schisholm.html.

23 **"When I ran for the Congress"** "Shirley Chisholm, 'Unbossed' Pioneer in Congress, Is Dead at 80," *New York Times*, January 3, 2005, https://www .nytimes.com/2005/01/03/obituaries/shirley-chisholm-unbossedpioneer-in-congress-is-dead-at-80.html.

23 **"Bring a folding chair"** "Before Hillary Clinton, There Was Shirley Chisholm," BBC News, January 26, 2016, https://www.bbc.com/news/ magazine-35057641.

23 **"A soul tie"** Rep. Ayanna Pressley, email exchange with author, June 7, 2019.

24 **"Not running in the midst of a feminist movement"** Debbie Walsh (Center for American Women and Politics director), phone interview with the author, April 19, 2019.

24 **"Talk softly and carry a lipstick"** "Bella Abzug Was 'Alive to Her Fingertips,'" *Toronto Star*, April 12, 1998.

24 **"This woman's place is in the House"** "Abzug, Bella Savitzky," Office of the Historian, US House of Representatives, https://history.house.gov/ People/Listing/A/ABZUG,-Bella-Savitzky-(A000018)/.

26 **"This is about Chivas Regal"** "Patricia Schroeder," *Los Angeles Times*, December 1, 1996, https://www.latimes.com/archives/la-xpm-1996-12-01-op-4631-story.html.

27 **"Even though we wanted to scream"** Oral history interview with Rep. Ronald V. Dellums, Office of the Historian, US House of Representatives, April 19, 2012, https://history.house.gov/People/Detail?id=12109.

28 **"I'm sure it was just an oversight"** "Lindy Boggs, Longtime Representative and Champion of Women, Is Dead at 97," *New York Times*, July 28, 2013, https://www.nytimes.com/2013/07/28/us/politics/lindy-boggs-longtime-representative-from-louisiana-dies-at-97.html.

30 **"The ladies understand"** "Members Only," Whereas: Stories from the People's House, Office of the Historian, US House of Representatives, March 20, 2017, https://history.house.gov/Blog/2017/March/3-20-Members-Only/.

30 **"'The [women's] gym equipment is terrible'"** Oral history interview with Rep. Nancy Lee Johnson, Office of the Historian, US House of Representatives, December 3, 2015, https://history.house.gov/Oral-History/Women/Representative-NJohnson/.

32 **"'We don't tell personal stories on the floor'"** Senator Patty Murray, interview with the author, June 26, 2019.

33 **"An airhead"** Marc Sandalow, *Madam Speaker: Nancy Pelosi's Life, Times, and Rise to Power* (New York: Modern Times, 2008), 79.

33 **"It is clear to me"** Sandalow, *Madam Speaker*, 80.

33 **"Proper preparation"** "From the 60 Minutes Archives: Nancy Pelosi," 60 Minutes Overtime, April 14, 2019, https://www.cbsnews.com/news/from-the-60-minutes-archives-nancy-pelosi/.

Chapter Two: They Did It Their Way

36 **"'Girl, it's you,'"** Rep. Lauren Underwood, interview with the author, January 30, 2019.

37 **Men are 15 percent more likely** Jennifer L. Lawless and Richard L. Fox, *Girls Just Wanna Not Run: The Gender Gap in Young Americans' Political Ambition* (Washington, DC: Women & Politics Institute, March 2013), https://www.american.edu/spa/wpi/upload/girls-just-wanna-not-run_policy-report.pdf.

39 **"Bring it up naturally"** Rep. Angie Craig, interview with the author, January 22, 2019.

42 **"I aim to be the very best congresswoman"** "In 14th District, Political Newcomer Underwood Defeats GOP Rep. Hultgren," WTTW News, November 6, 2018, https://news.wttw.com/2018/11/06/14th-district-political-newcomer-underwood-defeats-gop-rep-hultgren.

44 **"Booty calls"** "Katie Hill's Most Millennial Campaign Ever: She's Running Ep. 1," VICE News, YouTube video, May 14, 2018, https://www.youtube.com/watch?v=B2MeTpDByEw&feature=youtu.be.

44 **"I invested a lot more in field"** Katie Hill (former congresswoman), interview with the author, June 5, 2019.

45 **Sniffed one reporter** "Katie Hill: Can 'America's Most Millennial Candidate' Win?" *Guardian*, October 23, 2018, https://www.theguardian .com/us-news/2018/oct/22/millennial-candidate-midterms-katie-hill-25th-district.

47 **"Two hundred fifty incarcerated black men"** Pressley, interview with the author, March 7, 2019.

48 **"The people closest to the pain"** "Ayanna Pressley Upsets Capuano in Massachusetts House Race," *New York Times*, September 4, 2018, https://www.nytimes.com/2018/09/04/us/politics/ayanna-pressley-massachusetts.html.

48 **"I was at a bar"** Amy Pritchard (campaign consultant), phone interview with the author, May 29, 2019.

49 **"It's not just good enough"** "'Change Can't Wait': Ayanna Pressley Defeats 10-Term Rep. Michael Capuano in Democratic Primary, September 4, 2018, Boston.com, https://www.boston.com/news/politics/2018/09/04/ayanna-pressley-defeats-michael-capuano-massachusetts-democratic-primary.

49 **"You devalue the life of the immigrant"** "Rep. Ayanna Pressley Rips into Trump in First House Floor Speech," *Essence*, January 9, 2019, https://www.essence.com/news/ayanna-pressley-house-floor-speech/.

49 **"Refrain from engaging in personalities"** "Rep. Ayanna Pressley," *Essence*.

50 **"You just need to settle down"** "Jahana Hayes Was Told She 'Had No Chance.' She, and Voters, Beg to Differ." *New York Times*, August 15, 2018, https://www.nytimes.com/2018/08/15/nyregion/jahana-hayes-democrat-connecticut-primary-congress.html.

51 **"I found it maddening"** Senator Chris Murphy, phone interview with the author, May 13, 2019.

52 **"When I saw these kids"** Speech by Rep. Jahana Hayes, 2019 John F Kennedy Jr. Award and Lecture, Watson Institute for International and Public Affairs, YouTube video, May 23, 2019, https://www.youtube.com/watch?v=iKT3jPA7YBU.

53 **"People are strong"** "Viral Videos Are Replacing Pricey Political Ads. They're Cheaper, and They Work." *New York Times*, September 10, 2018, https://www.nytimes.com/2018/09/10/us/politics/midterm-primaries-advertising.html.

54 **"Force people to think differently"** Rep. Jahana Hayes, interview with the author, April 2, 2019.

56 **"Women like me aren't supposed to run"** Alexandria Ocasio-Cortez (@AOC), Twitter, May 30, 2018, https://twitter.com/AOC/status/1001795660524457985.

57 **"They see themselves"** Rep. Peter Welch, interview with the author, January 30, 2019.

58 **"Identify stories and literature"** Alexandria Ocasio-Cortez, "Brook Avenue Press," YouTube video, October 16, 2011, https://www.youtube.com/watch?v=-pFAayEMqDM.

58 **"Rather than think of it as somewhere to run from"** "Diverse Group of Startups Thriving at City-Sponsored Sunshine Bronx Business Incubator in Hunts Point," *New York Daily News*, July 17, 2012, https://www.nydailynews.com/new-york/bronx/diverse-group-startups-thriving-city-sponsored-sunshine-bronx-business-incubator-hunts-point-article-1.1115489.

59 **"Social entrepreneur in residence** "The Surprising Entrepreneurial Roots of the Democrats' Rising Star, Alexandria Ocasio-Cortez," *Inc.*, July 20, 2018, https://www.inc.com/zoe-henry/alexandria-ocasio-cortez-surprising-entrepreneurial-roots-run-for-congress.html.

59 **"I felt ready to dedicate my whole self"** Alexandria Ocasio-Cortez, interview with the author, June 11, 2019.

60 **"People who really led"** Saikat Chakrabarti (Brand New Congress cofounder), interview with the author, June 11, 2019.

60 **"America can be so much more"** Alexandra Rojas (Brand New Congress cofounder), phone interview with the author, February 7, 2019.

60 **"Looking for leaders"** "Our Mission," Brand New Congress, accessed October 14, 2019, https://brandnewcongress.org/nomination/.

61 **"We realized things are fucked-up"** Hill, interview, June 5, 2019.

62 **"Something special there"** Corbin Trent (Brand New Congress cofounder), phone interview with the author, June 12, 2019.

65 **"This is for Alexandria Ocasio-Cortez"** "Watch Rep. Joe Crowley Pick Up a Guitar and Dedicate 'Born to Run' to Primary Winner Alexandria Ocasio-Cortez," *The Week*, June 26, 2018, https://theweek.com/speedreads/781483/watch-rep-joe-crowley-pick-guitar-dedicate-born-run-primary-winner-alexandria-ocasiocortez.

65 **".@repjoecrowley stated on live TV"** Alexandria Ocasio-Cortez (@AOC), Twitter, July 12, 2018, https://twitter.com/AOC/status/1017394155268575232.

Chapter Three: Now What?

68 **"The first day of high school"** Rep. Sharice Davids, interview with the author, January 2, 2019.

68 **"Pretend I was there to see Amy"** Craig, interview, January 22, 2019.

69 **"Basically a small business"** Rep. Donna Shalala, interview with the author, January 10, 2019.

69 **"Pretty content-free"** Rep. Chrissy Houlahan, interview with the author, January 23, 2019.

71 **"Trump got elected on her watch"** "For Rashida Tlaib, Palestinian Heritage Infuses a Detroit Sense of Community," *New York Times*, August 14, 2018, https://www.nytimes.com/2018/08/14/us/politics/rashida-tlaib-muslim-congress.html.

72   **"The first thing we do is we thank"** "Is Nancy Pelosi's Fight to Become
     Speaker Again a Referendum on Gender?" *Time*, November 16, 2018,
     https://time.com/5457010/nancy-pelosi-speaker-fight-gender/.

72   **"Thirty million dollars on veterans"** Jon Soltz (VoteVets.org chair),
     interview with the author, June 21, 2019.

74   **"A wrecking ball"** Rep. Veronica Escobar, interview with the author,
     November 27, 2018.

74   **"Future of our children"** "Nancy Pelosi Elected Speaker as Democrats
     Take Control of House," *New York Times*, January 3, 2019, https://www
     .nytimes.com/2019/01/03/us/politics/nancy-pelosi-speaker-116th-congress
     .html.

75   **"Unexpected for me"** Rep. Rashida Tlaib, telephone interview, Nov 29,
     2018.

76   **"A totally different political background"** Rep. Debbie Dingell, interview
     with the author, July 9, 2019.

77   **"The dysfunction in our own caucus"** Underwood, interview, January 30,
     2019.

79   **"A lot of antiabortion protesters"** Underwood, interview with the author,
     February 20, 2019.

81   **"What's been a big surprise"** Hill, interview with the author, January 30,
     2019.

82   **"Resting bitch face"** Katie Hill Is a New Kind of California Democrat.
     Can She Help Flip the House? *New Yorker*, June 12, 2018, https://www
     .newyorker.com/news/news-desk/katie-hill-is-a-new-kind-of-california-
     democrat-can-she-help-flip-the-house.

83   **"You, my colleagues"** "House Passes Bill to Ban Discrimination Based
     On Sexual Orientation and Gender Identity," *Washington Post*, May 17,
     2019, https://www.washingtonpost.com/politics/house-passes-bill-to-ban-
     discrimination-based-on-sexual-orientation-and-gender-identity/2019/
     05/17/aed18a16-78a3-11e9-b3f5-5673edf2d127_story.html.

85   **"Prove you belong here"** Hayes, interview.

86   **"If I waited my turn"** Hayes, interview.

89   **"'I hear you have two children'"** Pat Schroeder (former congresswoman),
     phone interview with the author, April 29, 2019.

90   **"Having two moms"** Porter, interview.

90   **"I didn't leave Congress because I did not enjoy it"** Interview
     with Yvonne Burke, National Visionary Leadership Project,
     February 19, 2004, https://awpc.cattcenter.iastate.edu/2017/03/09/
     excerpts-from-the-national-visionary-leadership-project-feb-19-2004/.

91   **"Just a mom in tennis shoes"** "Another Win By a Woman, This One
     'Mom,'" *New York Times*, September 17, 1992, https://www.nytimes.
     com/1992/09/17/us/another-win-by-a-woman-this-one-mom.html.

91   **"Bring her baby on the floor"** Murray, interview.

94   **"The dysfunction has to change"** Press conference, January 15, 2019.

96　**The video meme "Where's Mitch?"** "'Where's Mitch?' Dems Look to Deliver Letter," Associated Press, January 16, 2019, YouTube video, https://www.youtube.com/watch?v=fYRrnThq6Es.

96　**A 'public relations event'"** U.S. Congresswoman Elaine Luria, "Congresswoman Elaine Luria Statement on Congressional Delegation to Afghanistan," news release, January 17, 2019, https://luria.house.gov/media/press-releases/congresswoman-elaine-luria-statement-congressional-delegation-afghanistan.

Chapter Four: Whose Party Is It, Anyway?

98　**"Um, Larry who?"** "Gov.-Elect Larry Hogan, a Republican, Stands Tall in Democratic Maryland," *New York Times*, November 13, 2014, https://www.nytimes.com/2014/11/14/us/politics/republican-governor-elect-larry-hogan-stands-tall-in-democratic-maryland.html.

99　**"The defining image of today's Democratic Party"** "What Republicans Need to Know as We Move Toward the 2020 Election," Public Opinion Strategies, June 2019, https://pos.org/wp-content/uploads/2019/06/Republicans-and-the-2020-Election-June-2019.pdf.

100　**"Let's not get yourself carried away"** Clip of Minority Leader Nancy Pelosi news conference, C-SPAN, June 27, 2018, https://www.c-span.org/video/?c4749510/nancy-pelosi-downplays-alexandria-ocasio-victory-they-made-choice-district.

100　**A January 2019 Gallup poll** "U.S. Still Leans Conservative, but Liberals Keep Recent Gains," January 8, 2019, Gallup, https://news.gallup.com/poll/245813/leans-conservative-liberals-keep-recent-gains.aspx.

102　**"Galvanized the college-educated gentrifiers"** "The Democrats' Culture Divide," *Politico Magazine*, November/December 2018, https://www.politico.com/magazine/story/2018/10/30/democratic-party-culture-divide-wars-working-class-blue-collar-221913.

102　**"The Bernie Bros"** "The Democrats' Culture Divide," *Politico Magazine*.

102　**"You're supposed to be perfect"** Alexandria Ocasio-Cortez (@ocasio2018), "Pep Talk," Instagram video, October 2018, https://www.instagram.com/stories/highlights/17961047563098936/.

103　**"A very headstrong group of freshmen"** Hill, interview, June 5, 2019.

103　*Politico* **popped a story** "Ocasio-Cortez Weighs a New Primary Target: Hakeem Jeffries," *Politico*, December 18, 2018, https://www.politico.com/story/2018/12/18/ocasio-cortez-hakeem-jeffries-2020-primary-1067107.

105　**"People love Hakeem"** Rep. Josh Gottheimer, interview with the author, February 6, 2019.

107　**"The Green Dream"** "Nancy Pelosi Just Threw Some Serious Shade at Alexandria Ocasio-Cortez's 'Green New Deal,'" CNN Politics, February 8, 2019, https://www.cnn.com/2019/02/07/politics/pelosi-alexandria-ocasio-cortez-green-new-deal/index.html.

107　**"I had made very specific requests"** "Alexandria Ocasio-Cortez on the 2020 Presidential Race and Trump's Crisis at the Border," *New Yorker*, July 10, 2019, https://www.newyorker.com/news/

the-new-yorker-interview/alexandria-ocasio-cortez-on-the-2020-presidential-race-and-trumps-crisis-at-the-border.

108 **"Easy to hijack the narrative"** Interview with Alexandria Ocasio-Cortez, "AOC Unfiltered," *Skullduggery*, Yahoo News, April 14, 2019, https://play.acast.com/s/skullduggery/d929e3d4-4b4f-4ddf-91c6-bd225bb91445.

109 **"I choose to forgive you"** "Michael Dunn Sentenced to Life without Parole for Killing of Florida Teenager," *Guardian*, October 17, 2014, https://www.theguardian.com/us-news/2014/oct/17/michael-dunn-sentenced-life-without-parole-florida.

112 **"The gotcha amendment"** Alexandria Ocasio-Cortez (@AOC), Twitter, March 2, 2019, https://twitter.com/aoc/status/1101834036249530368.

115 **A camo-esque blouse** "Hunt," Xochitl for Congress, October 1, 2018, YouTube video, https://www.youtube.com/watch?v=mHViPTnf3lQ.

115 **"Not coming from districts like mine"** Rep. Xochitl Torres Small, interview with the author, March 14, 2019.

116 **"The dangers they pose"** "User Clip: Rep. Debbie Dingell on Gun Safety," March 1, 2019, C-SPAN, https://www.c-span.org/video/?c4783577/user-clip-rep-debbie-dingell-gun-safety.

116 **"Lucy didn't get her big day"** Craig, interview with the author, April 23, 2019.

117 **"We are not afraid of her"** Underwood, interview, February 20, 2019.

118 **"Required to fill 34,000 beds"** "Alexandria Ocasio-Cortez Misrepresents ICE's Detention Bed Quota," PolitiFact, July 6, 2018, https://www.politifact.com/truth-o-meter/statements/2018/jul/06/alexandria-ocasio-cortez/alexandria-ocasio-cortez-misrepresents-ices-detent/.

118 **"Massive accounting fraud"** Twitter, December 2, 2018.

119 **"Being precisely, factually, and semantically correct"** "Alexandria Ocasio-Cortez: The Rookie Congresswoman Challenging the Democratic Establishment," 60 Minutes, January 6, 2019, https://www.cbsnews.com/news/alexandria-ocasio-cortez-the-rookie-congresswoman-challenging-the-democratic-establishment-60-minutes-interview-full-transcript-2019-01-06/.

120 **"A completely depraved lifestyle"** "Alexandria Ocasio-Cortez Talks Popcorn, Politics and DIY with Instagram Followers," Guardian News, YouTube video, April 4, 2019, https://www.youtube.com/watch?v=uQd62qQ-Q5w.

122 **"Winning young people by thirty points"** Hill, interview, June 5, 2019.

Chapter Five: Reclaiming Their Time

123 **"Do you know what an REO is?"** "Video: Ben Carson Doesn't Know What An REO Property Is, Thinks He's Being Asked about Oreos," *Newsweek*, May 21, 2019, https://www.newsweek.com/video-ben-carson-oreo-reo-porter-1431982.

125 **"Hats off to Ms. AOC"** "Trump Economic Adviser Larry Kudlow: Hats Off to AOC, She 'Nailed' Her Questions to Fed Chair," Fox News, July 11, 2019, https://www.foxnews.com/politics/

trump-economic-adviser-larry-kudlow-hats-off-to-aoc-she-nailed-
her-questions-to-fed-chair.

125 **"Did the president ever provide inflated assets"** Alexandria Ocasio-
Cortez, Newsweek (@Newsweek), video on Twitter, February 27, 2019,
https://twitter.com/Newsweek/status/1100962545014267904.

125 **"I watched my baby girl die"** "Yazmin Juarez: 'I Watched My Baby
Girl Die Slowly and Painfully,'" C-SPAN, YouTube video, July 10, 2019,
https://www.youtube.com/watch?v=yAevxfrcFyA.

126 **"I've been so deeply haunted"** "'Tinderbox of Violence': Ocasio-Cortez
Tears into Stephen Miller over Family Separation," video on *Politico*,
July 12, 2019, https://www.politico.com/story/2019/07/12/alexandria-
ocasio-cortez-stephen-miller-family-separation-1414008.

126 **"I cannot unsee what I've seen"** "Ayanna Pressley," video clip of House
hearing on migrant children and border security, C-SPAN, July 13, 2019,
https://www.c-span.org/video/?c4807161/ayanna-pressley&start=0.

127 **"'You're out of time, ma'am.'"** "Commerce Secretary Ross on the 2020
Census," video, C-SPAN, March 13, 2019, https://www.c-span.org/
video/?457414-1/commerce-secretary-ross-2020-census&start=92.

127 **"Something about us three"** Tlaib, interview with the author, July 8, 2019.

128 **"Exactly where I'm supposed to be"** Pressley, interview with the author,
August 27, 2019.

128 **Demanded of Alexander Acosta** "Alexandria Ocasio-Cortez Blasts
Labor Secretary Acosta over Women's Contraceptives: 'The Mediocrity
Is Astounding,'" *Newsweek*, May 2, 2019, www.newsweek.com/
alexandria-ocasio-cortez-birth-control-labor-secretary-1412463.

129 **"An appalling accusation"** "Democrats Clash with Homeland Security
Secretary Over Migrant Children Deaths," *All Things Considered*, NPR,
May 22, 2019, https://www.npr.org/2019/05/22/725845379/democrats-
clash-with-homeland-security-secretary-over-migrant-children-deaths.

129 **"I'm also a former CIA officer"** "Homeland Security Secretary Kirstjen
Nielsen Testifies on Border Security," C-SPAN, March 7, 2019, https://
archive.org/details/CSPAN_20190307_090200_Homeland_Security_
Secretary_Kirstjen_Nielsen_Testifies_on_Border_Security/start/6420/
end/6480.

130 **"Pictures of babies in cages"** "Nielsen Testifies on Border Security,"
C-SPAN, March 7, 2019, https://archive.org/details/CSPAN_20190307_
090200_Homeland_Security_Secretary_Kirstjen_Nielsen_Testifies_on_
Border_Security/start/6540/end/6600.

130 **"Can you explain to me the disconnect"** "Spanberger Demands
Accountability on U.S. Arms Sales to Saudi-Led Coalition," Rep. Abigail
Spanberger, YouTube video, June 12, 2019, https://www.youtube.com/
watch?v=TofisaoHkPM&=&feature=youtu.be.

132 **"The textbook that I wrote"** "How Freshman Rep. Katie Porter
Puts Wall Street in the Hot Seat," *HuffPost*, April 21, 2019, https://
www.huffpost.com/entry/katie-porter-wall-street-dimon_n_
5cb6470be4b0ffefe3b889db.

132 **"Would you recommend"** "One Exchange during a Congressional Hearing Laid Bare the CEO-Employee Pay Disparity," Analysis, *Washington Post*, April 12, 2019, https://www.washingtonpost.com/politics/2019/04/12/one-exchange-during-congressional-hearing-laid-bare-ceo-employee-pay-disparity/.

132 **"Exposing this kind of information"** "Congresswoman Asks Equifax CEO for His Personal Data as She Hammers Company's Legal Moves," *MarketWatch*, February 26, 2019, https://www.marketwatch.com/story/congresswoman-asks-equifax-ceo-for-his-personal-data-as-she-hammers-companys-legal-moves-2019-02-26.

133 **Pushed her into a wall** "Katie Porter Survived Domestic Abuse, Only to Have It Used against Her in Her Campaign," *HuffPost*, May 11, 2018, https://www.huffpost.com/entry/candidate-survived-domestic-abuse_n_5af47e3ce4b0859d11d15299.

134 **"Mental health issues know no boundaries"** Susan Wild, "'I Do Not Want Anyone Else to Suffer': Pa. Congresswoman Shares Story of Partner's Death by Suicide to Spur Awareness,'" Perspective, *Philadelphia Inquirer*, June 27, 2019, https://www.inquirer.com/opinion/commentary/susan-wild-suicide-speech-mental-health-care-20190627.html.

135 **"Lead with compassion"** Rashida Tlaib (@RashidaTlaib), Twitter, October 15, 2019, https://twitter.com/rashidatlaib/status/1184124950455689216.

135 **Which lawmaker is sniffling** "John Boehner Crying Again? Pictures of the House Republican Getting in Touch with His Feelings over the Years," *International Business Times*, September 25, 2015, https://www.ibtimes.com/john-boehner-crying-again-pictures-house-republican-getting-touch-his-feelings-over-2114734.

136 **"Your mom made her choice"** Rep. Katie Porter (@RepKatiePorter), video on Twitter, June 9, 2019, https://twitter.com/RepKatiePorter/status/1137764920714547201.

136 **"They're Cole Haan"** Porter, interview.

140 **"I have not come to this easily"** "California Democrat in Swing District Calls for Trump Impeachment Inquiry," *Hill*, June 17, 2019, https://thehill.com/homenews/administration/449000-california-democrat-in-swing-district-calls-for-trump-impeachment.

Chapter Six: Crisis at the Border

144 **Captioned simply "Squad"** Alexandria Ocasio-Cortez (@ocasio2018), November 12, 2018, Instagram, www.instagram.com/p/BqGTlEPBXXD/.

144 **"Pit us against each other"** Pressley, interview, March 7, 2019.

145 **"Can get swallowed up"** Tlaib, interview with the author, July 8, 2019.

147 **"Since when did the Problem Solvers Caucus"** "Five Takeaways from the Border Aid Vote," *New York Times*, June 27, 2019, https://www.nytimes.com/2019/06/27/us/politics/border-aid-vote-takeaways.html.

147 **"Certainly seem hell bent** "Top Ocasio-Cortez Aide Becomes a Symbol of Democratic Division, *New York Times*, July 13, 2019, https://www.nytimes.com/2019/07/13/us/politics/alexandria-ocasio-cortez-democrats.html.

147 **"Their public whatever and their Twitter world"** Maureen Dowd, "It's Nancy Pelosi's Parade," Opinion, New York Times, July 6, 2019, https://www.nytimes.com/2019/07/06/opinion/sunday/nancy-pelosi-pride-parade.html.

147 **"Just astounding to me"** Rep. Abigail Spanberger, interview with the author, July 16, 2019.

148 **"To see a toddler with her little arms"** Moment of Silence Honoring Migrants Who Have Died Attempting to Reach the Shores of the United States, *Congressional Record*, vol. 165, no. 109, June 27, 2019, https://www.govinfo.gov/content/pkg/CREC-2019-06-27/html/CREC-2019-06-27-pt1-PgH5243.htm.

151 **"There will be many tests for all of us"** Escobar, interview.

152 **A private Facebook group for Border Patrol agents** "Inside the Secret Border Patrol Facebook Group Where Agents Joke about Migrant Deaths and Post Sexist Memes," ProPublica, July 1, 2019, https://www.propublica.org/article/secret-border-patrol-facebook-group-agents-joke-about-migrant-deaths-post-sexist-memes.

152 **"Racist words and venom"** ABC News Politics (@ABCPolitics), Twitter, July 1, 2019, https://twitter.com/abcpolitics/status/1145795774904537088.

153 **"I will never stop speaking truth to power"** Rep. Rashida Tlaib: Migrants 'Treated like Cattle' in Detention Centers," *Detroit Free Press*, July 8, 2019, https://www.freep.com/story/news/local/michigan/2019/07/08/rashida-tlaib-migrant-detention-border-patrol-camps-texas/1635978001/.

157 **A photo of the two of them in Africa** Ilhan Omar (IlhanMN), photo on Twitter, August 1, 2019, https://twitter.com/ilhanmn/status/1157005661311557633.

Chapter Seven: This Is What Diversity Looks Like

159 **"I myself came here as a refugee"** Speech by Ilhan Omar at the United Way Iowa Refugee Summit, October 6, 2017.

159 **"We will keep fighting"** Omar speech.

160 **"Israel has hypnotized the world"** Bari Weiss, "Ilhan Omar and the Myth of Jewish Hypnosis," Opinion, *New York Times*, January 21, 2019, https://www.nytimes.com/2019/01/21/opinion/ilhan-omar-israel-jews.html.

161 **"I don't know how my comments would be offensive"** "Trump's and Miller's Attacks on 'The Squad,'" FactCheck.org, Annenberg Public Policy Center, July 23, 2019, https://www.factcheck.org/2019/07/trumps-and-millers-attacks-on-the-squad/.

161 **"The anti-semitic trope I unknowingly used"** Ilhan Omar (@IlhanMN), Twitter, January 21, 2019, https://twitter.com/IlhanMN/status/1087580652231446528.

162 **"Very segregated from other people"** Omar speech.

165 **"Like 'rock stars'"** Farhana Khera (Muslim Advocates executive director), interview with the author, July 10, 2019.

166 **"A voice for the many Muslim Americans"** Rep. André Carson, interview with the author, July 8, 2019.

166 **"Tweet was 'unfortunate and offensive'"** "Jewish Democrats on Foreign Affairs Committee Not Concerned over Ilhan Omar's Membership," *Haaretz*, January 24, 2019, https://www.haaretz.com/us-news/jewish-dems-not-concerned-over-ilhan-omar-s-membership-on-foreign-affairs-committee-1.6870433.

167 **"Having more women in Congress matters"** Rep. Ilhan Omar, interview with the author, January 7, 2019.

168 **Repeated racist and anti-Semitic remarks** "Letter to House Speaker Paul Ryan regarding Rep. Steve King," ADL, November 1, 2018, https://www.adl.org/news/letters/letter-to-house-speaker-paul-ryan-regarding-rep-steve-king.

168 **Trying to buy the election** "House Majority Leader Deletes Tweet Saying Soros, Bloomberg, Steyer Are Trying to 'Buy' Election," CNN Politics, October 28, 2018, https://www.cnn.com/2018/10/28/politics/tom-steyer-mccarthy-tweet/index.html.

168 **Secretly funded by Soros** "Gosar Accuses Soros of Funding White Supremacist Rally in Charlottesville," *Roll Call*, October 6, 2017, https://www.rollcall.com/news/politics/gosar-accuses-soros-funding-white-supremacist-rally-charlottesville.

168 **The term "white supremacist"** "Before Trump, Steve King Set the Agenda for the Wall and Anti-Immigrant Politics," New York Times, January 10, 2019, https://www.nytimes.com/2019/01/10/us/politics/steve-king-trump-immigration-wall.html.

168 **Notorious far-right internet troll** "Why a Florida Congressman Invited a Notorious Alt-Right Troll to SOTU," *Politico*, January 31, 2018, https://www.politico.com/story/2018/01/31/gaetz-florida-right-wing-troll-380577.

168 **"It's all about the Benjamins"** "Chelsea Clinton Slams Rep. Ilhan Omar for Anti-Semitic Tweet' about Israel before Accepting Democratic Congresswoman's Invite to Discuss the Issue, *Daily Mail*, February 11, 2019, https://www.dailymail.co.uk/news/article-6690073/Chelsea-Clinton-slams-Ilhan-Omar-anti-Semitic-tweet-Israel.html.

169 **"Deeply hurtful to Jews"** "Dem Lawmaker: Omar's Statements 'Deeply Hurtful to Jews,'" Hill, February 10, 2019, https://thehill.com/homenews/house/429358-dem-lawmaker-omars-statements-deeply-hurtful-to-jews.

170 **"Omar's use of anti-Semitic tropes"** Democratic Leadership Statement on Anti-Semitic Comments of Congresswoman Ilhan Omar, February 11, 2019, https://www.speaker.gov/newsroom/21119.

170 **"I unequivocally apologize"** Ilhan Omar (@IlhanMN), Twitter, February 11, 2019, https://twitter.com/IlhanMN/status/1095046561254567937/photo/1.

170 **"That caucus can't be chickenshit"** "Dem Rep. Max Rose: GOP 'Can't Be Chickensh*t in the Face of Anti-Semitism Either,'" *Daily Beast*, February 11, 2019, https://www.thedailybeast.com/dem-rep-max-rose-gop-cant-be-chickensht-in-the-face-of-anti-semitism-either.

172 **Festooned with graffiti** "FBI Investigating Graffiti Targeting Rep. Ilhan Omar," Minnesota Public Radio, March 2, 2019, https://www.mprnews.org/story/2019/03/02/fbi-investigating-graffiti-targeting-ilhan-omar.

172 **Someone hung a poster** "An Anti-Muslim Poster of Ilhan Omar
      Led to Chaos in the West Virginia Capitol," March 3, 2019,
      BuzzFeed News, https://www.buzzfeednews.com/article/juliareinstein/
      ilhan-omar-west-virginia-poster.

172 **"Our country rescued Ilhan Omar"** "Tucker Carlson: US Rescued Ilhan
      Omar," Fox News, Opinion, July 10, 2019, https://www.foxnews.com/
      opinion/tucker-carlson-america-rescued-ilhan-omar.

172 **"More clear today than ever before"** Khera, interview.

173 **"What people are afraid of"** "What Did Ilhan Omar Say?" Institute for
      Policy Studies, March 6, 2019, https://ips-dc.org/what-did-ilhan-omar-
      say-heres-the-full-transcript-of-her-response-to-a-question-about-anti-
      semitism/.

174 **"The daughter of Palestinian immigrants"** "House Overwhelmingly
      Condemns Movement to Boycott Israel," *New York Times*, July 23, 2019,
      https://www.nytimes.com/2019/07/23/us/politics/house-israel-boycott-bds
      .html.

175 **"Rashida has always been Rashida"** Dingell, interview.

176 **"It's love-hate, I guess"** Tlaib, interview, July 8, 2019.

176 **"I never heard the term 'anti-Semitism'"** "Can Ilhan Omar Overcome Her
      Prejudice?" Opinion/Commentary, *Wall Street Journal*, July 12, 2019,
      https://www.wsj.com/articles/can-ilhan-omar-overcome-her-prejudice-
      11562970265.

179 **"The same thing when the Mueller Report came out"** Hayes, interview.

180 **"As a black person in this business"** Michael Hardaway (chief aide to
      Rep. Hakeem Jeffries), interview with the author, April 6, 2019.

182 **"The two loudest Muslim women in the country"** "Muslim Members
      of Congress Host Ramadan Feast at the Capitol," *Washington Post*,
      May 20, 2019, https://www.washingtonpost.com/religion/2019/05/21/
      muslim-members-congress-host-ramadan-feast-capitol/.

182 **"Why don't they go back"** Donald J. Trump (@realDonaldTrump),
      Twitter, July 14, 2019, https://twitter.com/realdonaldtrump/status/
      1150381395078000643.

183 **"No excuse for the president's spiteful comments"** Sen. Lisa Murkowski
      (@lisamurkowski), Twitter, July 15, 2019, https://twitter.com/
      lisamurkowski/status/1150824131576905728.

183 **"Despite the occupant of the White House's attempts"** "Freshmen
      Congresswomen Denounce Trump's Attacks as a 'Distraction': 'We Will
      Not Be Silenced,'" CNBC, July 15, 2019, https://www.cnbc.com/2019/07/
      15/freshmen-congresswomen-denounce-trumps-attacks-as-a-distraction
      .html.

Chapter Eight: Lived Experiences

185 **"What's it like to be a role model?"** Davids, Kansas City event, April 25,
      2019.

188 **"Something symbolic"** Christian Grose (political science professor),
      phone interview with the author, August 15, 2019.

189 **"Call every person you've ever met"** Davids, event at the Wing in Washington, DC, March 5, 2019.

189 **"A college student who was in here"** Davids, interview with the author, July 12, 2019.

190 **"The only hairstyle I was ever allowed to have"** Rep. Deb Haaland, interview with the author, July 15, 2019.

192 **"I don't believe Sharice is a racist person"** "Alexandria Ocasio-Cortez's Chief of Staff, Spokesman Leave Her Office," *Politico*, August 2, 2019, https://www.politico.com/story/2019/08/02/aoc-staff-saikat-chakrabarti-climate-1445478.

192 **"Can you believe"** Rep. Deb Haaland, interview with the author, January 2, 2019.

193 **Davids tweeted a photo of the two of them** Rep. Sharice Davids (@RepDavids), photo on Twitter, September 10, 2019, https://twitter.com/RepDavids/status/1171423431000297472.

194 **"Haaland has made a point of saying"** Michele Swers (government professor), interview with the author, August 3, 2019.

195 **"Very effective coalition builders"** Pressley, interview, August 27, 2019.

196 **"Framing Muslims as the enemy"** Khera, interview.

197 **"I love when a Muslim father"** "Rashida Tlaib, Activist, Attorney, and Congresswoman (D-MI)," Makers, November 6, 2018, https://www.makers.com/profiles/5bbdfbf833132d0d110d3b32/5bbd461fc2ec101d534dfdee.

197 **"The presence of new female candidates"** Christina Wolbrecht and David E. Campbell, "Role models Revisited: Youth, Novelty, and the Impact of Female Candidates," *Politics, Groups, and Identities* 5, no. 3 (2017): 418–34, https://doi.org/10.1080/21565503.2016.1268179.

198 **"Madam Chair, before I get started"** "Rep. Deb Haaland Makes History, Gets a Bipartisan Standing Ovation on the House Floor," Daily Kos, March 8, 2019, https://www.dailykos.com/stories/2019/3/8/1840542/-Watch-the-U-S-Congress-give-Rep-Deb-Haaland-a-standing-ovation-in-a-historical-moment

198 **"Very serious, real barriers"** Davids, interview, July 12, 2019.

Chapter Nine: The Lasts

199 **"Exactly one century after Congress passed"** "The Women in White: Praise from Trump, and Chants of 'U.S.A.!'" *New York Times*, February 5, 2019, https://www.nytimes.com/2019/02/05/us/politics/women-in-white-state-of-the-union.html.

199 **"The Republican women's message"** Rep. Cathy McMorris Rodgers, interview with the author, March 1, 2019.

200 **"How did you go bankrupt?"** Ernest Hemingway, *The Sun Also Rises: The Hemingway Library Edition* (New York: Scribner, 2016), 109.

201 **"The suburban woman voter"** Mimi Walters (former congresswoman), phone interview with the author, July 18, 2019.

201 **"So few elected women in the Republican Party"** Laurel Elder (political science professor), email exchange with the author, July 3, 2019.

203 **"The fact that I was a woman"** Rep. Martha Roby, interview with the author, September 25, 2019.

205 **"Nearly identical to the 16-point gender gap"** Lawless and Fox, *Girls Just Wanna Not Run*.

205 **"Stay home with my kids"** Walters, interview.

206 **"Like a lot of Republican women"** Barbara Comstock (former congresswoman), phone interview with the author, July 16, 2019.

206 **"Thirty to forty years ago"** Melanie Gustafson (history professor), email exchange with the author, February 12, 2019.

207 **"Well-funded and well-organized"** Elder, email exchange.

207 **"Pooled their money"** Walters, interview.

208 **"My biggest donors are Republican men"** Rep. Susan Brooks, interview with the author, September 9, 2019.

208 **"The creation of the Women's Caucus"** Oral history interview with Rep. Yvonne Brathwaite Burke, Office of the Historian, US House of Representatives, July 22, 2015, https://history.house.gov/Oral-History/Women/Representative-Burke/.

209 **"A great opportunity for women to come together"** Connie Morella (former congresswoman), phone interview with the author, July 25, 2019.

210 **"The 103rd Congress produced more legislation"** Irwin N. Gertzog, *Women & Power on Capitol Hill: Reconstructing the Congressional Women's Caucus* (Boulder, CO: Lynne Rienner, 2004), 43.

212 **"Perceived to be more liberal"** Michael Luethy (political consultant), phone interview with the author, August 2, 2019.

212 **"A man campaigning with me"** Joan Perry (congressional candidate), phone interview with the author, August 5, 2019.

212 **Virginia politician associated with white nationalists** "White Nationalists Love Corey Stewart. He Keeps Them Close." *New York Times*, August 5, 2018, https://www.nytimes.com/2018/08/05/us/politics/corey-stewart-virginia.html.

213 **"We have got to rid ourselves"** Comstock, interview.

213 **Shak Hill, who associated himself** "It's Not Just Democrats. Rep. Barbara Comstock Also Faces a Challenge from the Right." *Washington Post*, August 6, 2017, https://www.washingtonpost.com/local/virginia-politics/its-not-just-democrats-rep-barbara-comstock-also-faces-a-challenge-from-the-right/2017/08/06/e4cf9274-73dd-11e7-9eac-d56bd5568db8_story.html.

213 **A large photo essay** "Redefining Representation: The Women of the 116th Congress," *New York Times*, January 14, 2019, https://www.nytimes.com/interactive/2019/01/14/us/politics/women-of-the-116th-congress.html.

214 **"If that's what Elise wants to do"** "After Big Losses, a N.Y. House Republican Clashes with Her Party," *New York Times*, December 20, 2018, https://www.nytimes.com/2018/12/20/nyregion/elise-stefanik-republican-women.html.

214 **"NEWSFLASH"** Elise Stefanik (@EliseStefanik), Twitter, December 4, 2018, https://twitter.com/EliseStefanik/status/1069950316483874816.

Chapter Ten: To Impeach or Not to Impeach

215   "Trying to take in this information in every way possible" Spanberger, interview, July 16, 2019.

216   "A grave moment" Spanberger, interview with the author, September 26, 2019.

216   "'This can't be true" Rep. Elaine Luria, interview with the author, September 26, 2019.

220   "An impeachable offense" "Seven Freshman Democrats: These Allegations Are a Threat to All We Have Sworn to Protect," Opinions, *Washington Post*, September 23, 2019, https://www.washingtonpost.com/ opinions/2019/09/24/seven-freshman-democrats-these-allegations-are-threat-all-we-have-sworn-protect/.

221   "I believe the next step is" "Mueller Report, Health Care Underscore Angie Craig Town Hall," RiverTowns.net, April 25, 2019, https://www .rivertowns.net/niews/4604201-mueller-report-health-care-underscore-angie-craig-town-hall.

222   "If this were a Democratic president" "Nancy Pelosi's Long Road to Impeachment," *Politico*, September 26, 2019, https://www.politico.eu/ article/us-speaker-of-the-house-nancy-pelosi-long-road-to-impeachment-president-donald-trump/.

222   "A sense of extreme credibility" Rep. Cedric Richmond, interview with the author, September 25, 2019.

223   "This president is undermining our national security" "At This Hour," Transcripts, CNN, September 25, 2019, http://edition.cnn.com/ TRANSCRIPTS/1909/25/ath.01.html.

223   "This is a different set of circumstances" Rep. Abigail Spanberger, TV interview, September 25, 2019.

223   "Not why we ran for Congress" Rep. Mikie Sherrill, interview with the author, September 26, 2019.

224   "A really solid and grave responsibility" Houlahan, interview with the author, September 26, 2019.

Chapter Eleven: Paving the Way

227   "With a broken heart" Katie Hill (@KatieHill4CA), Twitter, October 28, 2019, https://twitter.com/KatieHill4CA/status/1188869986116227076.

228   "We must ensure a climate of integrity" "Pelosi Statement on Resignation of Congresswoman Katie Hill," Nancy Pelosi, Speaker of the House, October 29, 2019, https://www.speaker.gov/newsroom/102719-2.

228   "I wanted to show young people" "See Katie Hill Give Her Resignation Speech on House Floor," CNN, YouTube video, https://www.youtube. com/watch?v=KEUUxk9Wg3U.

232   "Since we launched our Black Maternal Health Caucus" Underwood, interview with the author, May 16, 2019.

Index